5,000 NIGHTS AT THE OPERA

Sir Rudolf Bing

5000 Nights
at the
Opera

1972
Doubleday & Company, Inc.
Garden City, New York

PICTURE CREDITS

Author's Private Collection: 1, 2, 3, 4, 5, 7, 8, 9, 16
Reprinted by the Permission of the Editor of the Glyndebourne Festival Music
Book: 6
Anthony Re-Jones: 10
Picture Features, Ltd., Reprinted by the Permission of the Editor of the
Glyndebourne Festival Music Book: 11
Erich Auerbach, FRPS: 12
Copyright ©, Vivienne London: 15
Frederick Ramage, Keystone Press Agency, Ltd.: 13, 14
Times Newspaper, Ltd.: 17
Paul Shillabeer, FRPS, Edinburgh Festival Society: 18, 20
Sedge Le Blang, Metropolitan Opera Archives: 21, 22, 26, 27, 28, 29, 31, 36,
38, 39, 42
Louis Melancon, Metropolitan Opera: 23, 24, 35, 37, 44, 46, 49, 53, 54, 56,
57, 58, 59, 60, 66, 69, 70
Theodore Karr, Editor-Executive Director of Art Projects, Shorewood Publish-
ers, Inc.: 25
United Press International: 30, 41, 48, 51, 55, 63, 72
Photo by Adrian Siegel: 32
Wide World Photos: 33
Harry G. Schumer, Metropolitan Opera Chief Librarian, 1937–1968: 34
Eugene Cook: 40, 61, 67
Associated Newspaper Group, Ltd.: 43
Santi Visalli, Photos Reporters, Inc.: 45
Lotte Meitner-Graf: 50
New York Times: 47, 62
Michael Rougier, Life Magazine © 1966, Time, Inc.: 52
Eli Aaron from Alix B. Williamson: 64
Erika Davidson, New York: 65
Vernon L. Smith, Scope Associates, Inc.: 68
E. Fred Sher, Metropolitan Opera: 71

The publisher and Sir Rudolf Bing would like to gratefully acknowledge the
help of Opera News in obtaining the following photographs: 10, 13, 19,
28, 31, 34, 40, 42, 46, 49, 61, 62, 64, 67, 68

DESIGNED BY EARL TIDWELL
ISBN: 0-385-09259-8
Library of Congress Catalog Card Number 72–76124
Copyright © 1972 by Rudolf Bing

# FOREWORD

There are close to a thousand people working at the Metropolitan Opera; in the following pages I have only mentioned a handful of them—yet every one of them plays his or her part in the huge machinery that makes up the Opera. Every one of them is important and the clock needs the small wheels as well as the large ones to function.

I am referring not only to solo singers, but also to members of the orchestra, the chorus, the ballet; the invaluable stage crew; the wardrobe, the wig, the make-up artists; the large front-of-the-house staff—they all contribute to the daily miracle that at 8 P.M. everyone is at the appointed place and the curtain goes up.

I have come to know nearly all of them—some of them became friends—and to all of them goes my deep gratitude and admiration for hard work admirably done.

Very special thanks to Martin Mayer, without whom I could never have written this book. His knowledge of the subject, his sense of humor, and his sheer ability as a professional writer have immeasurably helped me in writing and organizing these pages and if this book should have any success it is in large measure his.

R.B.

# 1

I first saw the inside of the old Metropolitan Opera House, its grand, glowing auditorium, in January 1939; and of course I had not the slightest notion that it would ever become the focus of my life. I was then general manager of the summer opera festival at Glyndebourne, in England, and I had come to New York with Carl Ebert, the producer of that festival, to discuss a proposal that we bring our performances to the New York World's Fair. Naturally, Ebert and I went to the opera. It must have been a Monday night, because I remember an extremely elegant audience, many of the men in white tie. I remember even more clearly the sight of Lauritz Melchior as Tannhäuser, looking like a moving couch covered in red plush (though he sounded fine). The next night we went to the opera again, to *Fidelio,* and I nearly fell from my chair when I heard recitatives played where Beethoven had left dialogue. The recitatives had been written, I learned, by Artur Bodanzky, the conductor of that evening's performance, in the hope of improving on Beethoven. Then I knew I was in another country.

The artistic adviser of the World's Fair was Olin Downes, who was the senior music critic of the New York *Times* then and many years later, when I was manager of the Metropolitan. Though I think we always respected each other, I must admit we got along much better in 1939. But for some reason I now forget or may never have known—it was probably associated with the rapid approach of the war—Glyndebourne did not come to the Fair.

When I returned to New York ten years later, in March 1949, I was alone but on a very similar mission. Britain's poverty in the aftermath of the war had made it impossible to reconstitute a Glyndebourne season. Indeed, what was keeping Glyndebourne going was the Edinburgh Festival, which had been my own original idea for just this purpose. I was artistic director in Edinburgh as well as general manager at Glyndebourne. An American journalist had suggested to Glyndebourne's proprietor that the reopening of his lovely theater could be financed again if the company repeated each year at some site in the United States the operas it prepared for performance in England. He was, he said, the president of an arts foundation that could sponsor an annual visit by Glyndebourne to Princeton, New Jersey. Things had got to the point where stories had been published in the newspapers, announcing that Glyndebourne would present a season in Princeton in the fall of 1949.

I had never believed a word of it, especially after I learned that Glyndebourne rather than the American foundation was to pay my steamship fare, with the Americans taking care of my expenses only after I arrived in New York. I soon learned that the foundation was even less important and less rich than I had expected. They arranged a room for me in Bryan's Hotel, a seedy theatrical establishment off Broadway just north of Times Square. In the European manner, I left my shoes in the corridor at night to have them polished, and the next morning they were gone. I inquired, and slowly came to understand that the shoes had been stolen. At the meeting of the board of the foundation, summoned to hear me, I was asked to explain the philosophy of Glyndebourne. I said, "I am not here to talk about the philosophy of Glyndebourne, but to ascertain the size and location of your bank account." I never did get this information, and without any formal announcement we quietly dropped the "plans" to visit Princeton in the fall.

The general manager of the Metropolitan Opera then was Edward Johnson, a charming Canadian who had been a prominent tenor in his earlier years. Johnson had visited Glyndebourne, and I thought that while in New York it would be polite to return his call. In the course of conversation in his office, a smallish square room just below street level in a corner of the opera house—my office for so many years—he very suddenly said to me, "How would you like to be my successor?" That night I went to the opera in Johnson's box, where I met, among others, George A. Sloan, chairman of the Metropolitan's board, a courteous, rather stiff man with a southern American accent, who had raised the money to pull the house through a difficult time in the later years of the Depression and was still very concerned about its financial condition.

Though I had no way of knowing it, my visit had coincided with a political crisis at the opera house. Johnson's impending retirement had been announced several times before, but this time he meant it, and there were a number of candidates supported by different factions within the company and within the board. (Supporters of Lawrence Tibbett, I was told later, had actually established a campaign headquarters with a desk and a telephone in an office.) I suppose the first thing that recommended me to Johnson and Sloan was that I had no connection whatever with any of the factions. In fact, apart from Fritz

Stiedry and Max Rudolf, conductors with whom I had worked in Germany many years before, nobody at the Metropolitan knew much about me.

The next day, Sloan arranged an appointment for me with Charles M. Spofford, president of the opera board, at his Wall Street law office. A matter-of-fact, wholly trustworthy man whom I liked at sight, Spofford said he was seeing me "because Mr. Johnson mentioned you," but in conversation it developed that he knew about both Glyndebourne and Edinburgh. He asked me what I would need from his board to take the general manager's job at the Metropolitan Opera.

I told him that assuming I could give up Glyndebourne and Edinburgh—my Glyndebourne contract was expiring, but there was a year or two left on my Edinburgh contract—the first thing I would need from the Metropolitan was a three-year contract. I could probably have stayed for life at Glyndebourne, and at Edinburgh, too, and I did not wish to give up that security for a job that might last only one season. Then, I said, within a budget frame set by the board of directors, I would have to be left free to make *all* decisions related to the house—if I spent less on singers, I would have more for new productions, and so forth. I would need a free hand to engage and fire people, and complete artistic authority.

Spofford was interested, perhaps because I had asked so much, and passed me on to General David Sarnoff, chairman of the board of RCA, who was then active on the board of the Metropolitan. I remember going into his immense office in Rockefeller Center and being amazed first by the absolutely empty, beautifully polished desk, nothing on it at all, then by a little black boy who came trotting in and knelt down and shined his shoes. It was a brand-new thing for me. I thought the little black boy probably had his eardrums pierced, so he could not hear business secrets. But I cannot remember what General Sarnoff and I discussed.

When I went back to London, my relations with the Metropolitan were on a don't-call-us-we'll-call-you basis, and I thought it unlikely that anything would come of my interviews. Nevertheless, I told my wife what had happened. We had moved so often in our lives, she was concerned; she hated the idea of going to New York. But when a call came from Spofford, about a month later, she encouraged me to go.

This time I flew on a Pan Am Clipper, at my hosts' expense; and I was put up at the Hotel Pierre, which was a great improvement on where I had been before. And I was really handed around among the members of the board. I saw a great number of them, including Mrs. Eleanor Belmont, a great lady of New York society who had been a leading actress on Broadway around the turn of the century. After meeting me, Mrs. Belmont flew off to London to inquire there among her friends what my reputation might be. Fortunately, one of her friends was Lady Violet Bonham-Carter, who shortly after the war had offered me the directorship of Sadler's Wells in London, and I got good reviews.

That weekend I was a guest at George Sloan's elegant country house, where I was surrounded by members of the board, including the former international soprano Lucrezia Bori, the only singer on the board. I must have passed this test, too, holding my knife and fork the right way, because the following Monday Spofford and I began talking specific contract terms. The salary offered was $30,000, which was more than I had been receiving in my two jobs together in England (and as real income considerably more than it would be today). Later, when it was discovered that the American immigration laws would not allow the Metropolitan to offer me a three-year contract, the board to make up for this unavoidable breach raised my starting salary to $35,000. I was not to assume the responsibilities of the job until June 1950, but I would spend the 1949–50 season in New York, learning about the Metropolitan, hiring (and firing) people for 1950–51, and planning the new productions for the season when I would become the boss. In those days, unlike today, it was entirely possible to hire singers and conductors at twelve months' or even nine months' notice.

Among those who knew I was in New York was the violinist Erica Morini, for whom I had arranged concert engagements in the 1920s, when I was a young agent in Vienna. She invited me to a party at her apartment, where one of the guests was Bruno Walter, whom I had known in Vienna and in Germany, and whose first reunion with the postwar Vienna Philharmonic I had arranged as the great event of the first Edinburgh Festival. I called Walter aside at the party, and I said to him, "Professor Walter, I have this morning been offered the general managership of the Metropolitan Opera." I had hoped to start a conversation that might lead to some promise that he would return to the house, where he had not conducted since 1946. Instead, Walter broke in on me immediately to say, "My dear Bing, don't *touch* it," and went on to enlarge on why it would be impossible to do a good job at the Metropolitan.

Nevertheless, I proceeded to do whatever else was necessary. I met with the board *en masse,* and one of its members asked me what I would wish to do with the Metropolitan as its general manager. I replied, "I haven't the slightest idea," which was quite true, because I knew nothing of the company or its resources. There was a need for a portrait photograph to accompany a press release announcing my engagement, and I went to a photographer's, where an appointment had been made for me under an assumed name. When my hour struck, the name was called—and I failed to respond to it, because I'd forgotten. But the picture was taken.

On my way to the photographer's, I met on the street one of the few people I knew in New York, whom I had seen on my previous voyage, and who knew that the proposal to bring Glyndebourne to Princeton had foundered. He was amazed:

"Rudi! What are *you* doing back here so soon?" I said, "I forgot my pajamas."

Because I was needed in England to complete the work on the 1949 Glyndebourne and Edinburgh seasons, this conclusive trip to New York took only six days. When I left, it was understood that Spofford would seek to get Edinburgh to release me from my contract. Two weeks later, I received a cable from him informing me that Edinburgh had agreed, and my appointment could be announced. The announcement was made on June 2, 1949.

It had been the best-kept secret since the atom bomb. Only a few weeks before, with the company on tour in Atlanta, Johnson had told a reporter, "I've got lots of successors—John Brownlee, Lauritz Melchior, Jan Peerce, Charlie Kullman . . ." And the story had been printed, perfectly seriously, all around the country. When my name was announced, Emily Coleman, then music editor of *Newsweek*, was in Vienna. Margaret Carson, the press representative of the Metropolitan, sent her a cable to give her the news before she read it in the newspapers: "NEW GENERAL MANAGER RUDOLF BING." Miss Coleman thought conductor Max Rudolf had been named, and the "Bing" was a way of writing an exclamation point in a cable.

In England, I gave an interview to a reporter from the New York *Times*, and what appeared in the paper as my statement about my appointment was the following: "For fifteen years I have known that someday I would reach that goal. I did not know exactly how—but I have always had my eye on it." Considering the totally accidental nature of my introduction to the possibility of the job, the statement was nonsense, and I had never said anything of the sort. But I let it stand, because half of it was true. All my life up to 1949 could be seen as the proper preparation for being manager of the Metropolitan.

# 2

My family was no more musical than many other well-to-do Viennese families at the turn of the century. Ernst Bing, my father, was head of the Austro-Hungarian Steel and Iron Trust; my mother Stefanie sang beautifully in an amateur way and in general cultivated an interest in the artistic aspects of life. We had a box at the opera, but when I began to go, which I did not do very often, I bought my own tickets up in the Fourth Gallery. We all went to concerts occasionally, and a few times a year there would be chamber music evenings at our house. One of my earliest musical memories is of such an evening, when the Rothschild Quartet came to play a very contemporary work by Egon Wellesz. Our chairs were too low for them, and they took the volumes of Schubert chamber music that were in the shelf to raise the seats. I thought to myself, I wish they would sit on Wellesz and play Schubert.

I was the youngest of four children, my sister Ilka being the oldest, followed by Robert and Ernst, both of whom became businessmen. In the convulsions of our time, we have been a lucky family. Though my father's company collapsed with the Monarchy, he and my mother were never at any time what the world would call poor. They both lived to a good age; they retired to Nice in the 1930s, and during the war they were with me in England, where we all benefited from the fact that they had always hired English governesses for their children, and we had spoken with the governesses in English.

As a boy, I was moody—indeed, I am still a rather melancholy person, often wanting to be where I am not, for reasons I cannot explain and do not believe to be explicable. I hated school and was bad at it. As I remember, I disapproved on principle of all discipline, an opinion I later changed. I think I feared school, and the atmosphere of school.

My only game was tennis, at which I became quite good, winning some tournaments for my age group; but in Vienna in the 1910s one played tennis only eight weeks a year, and I did not enjoy playing football with the other boys. Our family took summer vacations in the Dolomite Alps, not far from where I spend my summers now, and I would walk a great deal in the woods, alone. Once as a very young boy, I remember, I met Gustav Mahler thrashing through the woods, singing, looking almost demented; and I fled.

Somehow I felt, and my mother felt in me, an artistic temperament. At first, we looked to drawing and painting. I went to studios after school, and for a while it was thought I had a serious talent, but it was never an individual talent, and I grew tired of it myself. When my voice changed, however, I developed a small but very attractive lyric baritone, which my mother and I agreed merited professional training. I had a strong feeling and nearly perfect memory for the songs of Schubert, Schumann, Brahms, and Wolf, and I still believe that if I had stayed with it I might have become a lieder singer of real distinction.

My first teacher was Franz Steiner, then Vienna's leading lieder singer, who was a frequent visitor at our house. He took me as a pupil less because of my voice than because of the feeling with which I sang the songs. Because he was himself something of a sentimentalist, Steiner was probably the worst teacher I could have had at the age of sixteen, but fortunately I soon came under the tutelage of Helge Lindberg, a great Finnish bass-baritone who had no use for "expressiveness". His taste ran first of all to Bach and Handel. A giant of a man, he had been a boxer in his youth, and he had immense lung capacity: he would take one breath, and then sing a Handel aria for what seemed like ten minutes. He would tell me that when I sang Schubert I should just sing the notes: Schubert had already put into the song all the "feeling" it required.

Much as I hated school, I had always understood that I was to finish the Gymnasium program—something more than a modern American high school—and at least prepare to enter university. Under the old Austro-Hungarian Empire, students were drafted into the Army for only one year, while non-students were made to serve three years. Moreover, students could become officers, as both my brothers did during World War I. But the war ended when I was only sixteen, and I felt that was enough of school. I was clearly not a good enough painter or singer to make a living that way, but I was a big reader, and my father and I decided that perhaps I could get along in publishing. He agreed to let me drop out of the usual school program on condition that I accept a year's private tutoring in literature and the history of art.

My tutor was Frau Dr. Schwarzwald, a Polish educator who had started a girls' school in Vienna and also took some private pupils. There were concerts at the school in the evening, and among those I would meet at the concerts was Rudolf Serkin. Sometimes Frau Dr. Schwarzwald would invite me over for a soiree at her house, which was the closest thing in Vienna to a French salon. I would go and sit and listen to the leaders of the avant-garde in Vienna, to men like the architect Adolf Loos, the poet Peter Altenberg, the painter Oskar Kokoschka, the explorer Fridtjof Nansen, the playwright Arthur Schnitzler. Richard Strauss was sometimes a guest at Frau Dr. Schwarzwald's, as was Hugo von Hofmannsthal, who was a friend of my family—I remember how I read his *Death and the Fool* when I was only fourteen, and cried over it, moved by its very sentimental thoughts and beautiful language. To me the early Hofmannsthal is still the most beautiful German since Goethe and Schiller. These were great evenings for a serious young man. There is a book to be written comparing the Vienna of the late 1910s with Paris in La Belle Époque.

For a seventeen-year-old to make a start in publishing, the logical beginning was bookselling. I got a job with Gilhofer & Ranschburg, an old established Viennese bookshop and *Antiquariat*. The first task I was to master was the use of the *Achter Spritzer*, a watering can with a hole in the bottom—by judicious motions of the arm and of the finger that blocked the hole, one could lay the dust on the floor with a series of perfect figure-eight patterns. My immediate boss was a young man scarcely older than myself, named Prachner, who stayed in the book business and today has a very successful bookstore in the Kärntnerstrasse in Vienna; I went to visit him there, not long ago.

Soon I was promoted to the higher art of window dressing, which would prove oddly useful to me in England twenty-odd years later, and then I was allowed to sell books to the customers. Bookselling is a very interesting art that brings its practitioners into contact with people in a strange, almost intimate way. A clever bookseller soon knows how a customer's mind works, assuming the customer has a mind. There is the mother who wants a book for her little boy, age eight—"but he is intelligent enough to be twelve." Or there is the young man who wants a book that has the reputation of being sexy, but he doesn't dare to ask for it . . .

After only a year, now eighteen, I moved on to the Bookstore Hugo Heller, which was an even more interesting place. Heller had come from the poorest of poor backgrounds, and had risen through ability, energy, and political activity. He had run a Workers' Bookshop sponsored by a radical party, until he persuaded some rich man to lend him enough money to start his own business. A sick man with a violent temper, always threatening people, he had a reputation as someone with whom nobody could ever get along, but I found I had a gift for getting on with him. I admired him: he was a terrific worker, and clever as daylight. In return, he advanced me rapidly in his business.

Heller's was more than just a bookstore. Schnitzler had written a play, *Professor Bernhardi*, about a girl who is dying and not aware of it. The nurses call a priest, and Bernhardi, who is a Jew, prevents the priest from entering the girl's room, so she need not know she is dying. The play had been forbidden in Vienna, as offensive to the Church. Heller hired a company, rehearsed the play, and presented it in a theater in Pressburg, across the Czechoslovakian border one hour from Vienna, which set him up as an impresario.

On the basis of that first theatrical presentation, Heller started a concert agency, which soon became one of the most important in Vienna. Among those whose concert careers he handled were Bruno Walter, Adolf Busch, Lotte Lehmann, Elisabeth Schumann, Richard Mayr, the Rosé Quartet . . . I became more and more interested in the concert management end of Heller's business, and because I had become close to him I was able to move over to that work in 1921, when I was nineteen years old. It was a small operation. The entrance to the bookstore was on the Bauernmarkt; one would walk the length of the shop, past tables stacked with books, into an art gallery in the rear, and the concert management office was just off the art gallery—Heller, his charming wife, two secretaries, and myself, plus a girl in a box office. Frau Rosé, who was Gustav Mahler's sister, was in the office very often. I became friendly with her son and her daughter Alma—I still think of Alma, who was with us in England just before World War II, and went across to Holland to be with some Austrian boy she loved, and the Gestapo got her. Through Frau Rosé and her children, I came to know Bruno Walter, who was very close to them.

Most of the work—and the invaluable part of it, the part that was the best experience for my future—involved holding someone's hand, giving what I now call "Otis Elevator Service" to the artists Heller managed. I would go to recitals, go backstage and tell the artist how wonderful it was, guard the door to the dressing room during intermission. But I was also involved in planning the season. Every fall I had to book the halls for our artists. You knew Mayr wanted to have a recital early in November, not on a holiday; and Rosé would want to give six concerts in the Musikvereinssaal, the medium sized hall, during the course of the season. One had to be on friendly terms with the house inspectors of these halls. I came to live in the concert life of the city, much of which in those days went through the Heller office.

Sometimes there were moments of great agitation, when an assistant would be sent out to take care of some unexpected demand by an artist—I remember best one frantic afternoon when it was discovered that Maria Jeritza, freshly returned from an American tour, was insisting that the lighting in the concert hall had to be changed to match her dress. I learned that artists always see the posters for their rivals, but never see their own— so that I am never surprised when the Metropolitan goes on tour to Cleveland, and the hotel puts up in the lobby pictures of every solo singer in the company, and I receive angry telephone calls from artists who *insist* that their picture is not there. Occasionally, with a new artist, I would be in complete charge of staging a recital: thus, I organized the first appearance in Vienna of a young refugee violinist from Hungary named Eugene Ormandy—an acquaintance that was very useful to me thirty years later, when I suddenly needed a "name" conductor for the first night of *Fledermaus* at the Metropolitan.

In 1923 Heller expanded his operations by hiring Karl Lion to begin an operatic and theatrical agency. Lion had been artistic administrator of the Vienna State Opera—the sort of job I was later to hold under Ebert. He had got into some sort of quarrel with Franz Schalk, the Intendant, or general manager, and was available to Heller. The offices behind the bookstore were much too small for what Lion was going to do, and we moved to new quarters in the Herrengasse, with big rooms. One of them was an audition room, where Lion, who had been a conductor in his youth and was still a very good pianist, would audition singers, playing the accompaniment for them. I began to sit in on the meetings where decisions were made about the prowess and potential of voices as voices and artists as artists, and I drank in Lion's stories of life backstage at an opera house. One of my father's closest friends (though many years younger) was Dr. Paul Eger, who was Generalintendant of the Hessian State Theater in Darmstadt, near Frankfurt, and as a boy I had listened eagerly to all the funny stories he told about what happened in his theater. From Eger and Lion I learned that one could play a useful and important role in the arts without being an active artist oneself. Because Lion was worldwide agent for a number of international singers, I began to travel, visiting German theaters, to negotiate contracts for people under our management.

My first venture into the theater, however, was not happy. Not long after Lion's arrival, Hugo Heller died, which lessened my obligations to the agency; and I learned that Eugen Robert, who was running two or three Viennese theaters, needed a "managing secretary" for one of them, The Neue Wiener Bühne. I applied, and got the job; and came home and told my parents that now I would have a chance to take part in policy decisions in a theater—I would have a voice in repertory, casting, choosing designers, and so forth. But in fact Robert had no intention of listening to a twenty-one-year-old on such matters. My job, it turned out, was to see to it that the dressing rooms and the auditorium were cleaned for each performance, and that the artists arrived punctually for rehearsals and performances—and were paid, perhaps not quite as punctually. I enjoyed the atmosphere of the theater, with its nightly deadline; only journalism and the theater give you this daily excitement, and it is a poison far more habit-forming than coffee or nicotine. But obviously this was not the job I wanted, and after three months I asked Lion, who had not filled my previous position, whether I would be welcome back; and I returned to the agency.

Among the trips I took for Lion that year was one to London, to manage two concerts at the Albert Hall by Alfred Piccaver, who was then the leading tenor of the Vienna Opera. We took a suite at the Piccadilly Hotel, my first hotel suite, which impressed me a great deal—but not so much as London itself. London was the first *huge* city I had ever seen; compared to it, Vienna was a provincial town. Piccaver did not need my services except for a few business meetings, one of them with Harold Holt, who had the largest concert agency in England and some twelve years later would turn down a very good opportunity to give me a job (any job) in his organization.

Most of our week there, I wandered around London. I find a peculiar fascination in wandering around a strange city, and imagining all the happiness and tragedy, hopes and disappointments, loves and hates that abide behind all these windows. Of course, some cities lend themselves better than others to such romantic roamings: Philadelphia and Cleveland, for example, have never inspired such romanticism in me. But London does, and so does Amsterdam; perhaps it is the water. I do not find Vienna romantic: I am always happy to spend a week there, but no more than that. The famous Viennese charm does not impress me—I lived on it myself for too many years.

One English custom made a lot of trouble for me. The Heller firm had recently received some payments from London in the form of checks, and rather than change the pounds to Austrian schillings and back to pounds Lion gave me the checks to cash in London for our expenses. But these were "crossed" checks, with two lines drawn across the face to indicate, in the English manner, that they were to be deposited to the account of the payee and under no circumstances to be cashed. In Vienna we made almost no use of checks. The whole practice seemed to me clearly fraudulent, and even after I had lived in England for some years I found it hard to accept the custom that one was paid one's salary, and in turn paid one's bills, by check rather than by cash.

In the evenings in London I went to the theater—alone, of course (Piccaver had his own sources of amusement in London). Because so much English had been spoken at home when I was a boy, I was able to get along in London. Of the theaters I saw, I am afraid I remember best a music hall, with a wonderful revue, and especially a lovely girl named June. The only concerts I heard were our own, which occurred, much to my surprise, in the afternoon. One of them was with Luisa Tettrazini, and among my duties was giving her a small bouquet of violets, which she pinned on her enormous bosom. Spoiled by the beauty of the Musikvereinssaal in Vienna, I thought the Albert Hall much too big, and totally hideous. But I would have loved to stay in London for many weeks more.

My life in Vienna during those years with Heller was very much controlled by my work. There were important things happening in the political world; I read the newspapers and knew about them, and acquired Social Democratic political preferences that I have never lost (though it was a Conservative Prime Minister who recommended me to the Queen for my knighthood). But politics was not part of my life. Three or four nights a week I was expected to attend concerts, be nice to the artists, and be available as the management representative if anything untoward should happen. I acquired the habit of accepting responsibility for and to the artists of the evening; years later, I would go backstage almost every evening (at the Metropolitan) to wish everyone good luck. It was greatly appreciated until people got used to it.

Twice for brief periods I moved out of my parents' house to be alone, but the fact is that I did not like it. I was very attached to my mother, and as the youngest I would be the last to leave home. I took many of my vacations with my parents in the Salzkammergut (we did not go to the Dolomites so often after the war, when that area was ceded to Italy). Sundays I would go for long walks in the woods near Vienna with a small group of friends, most of them from my Gymnasium days. During my last years in Vienna, I fell in love—as did everyone else in the city—with a dancer of the Ellen Tels Ballet; her name was Nina Schelemskaya-Schelesnaya. But I was more fortunate than all the others, for when I left Vienna, in January 1927, a few days before my twenty-fifth birthday, Nina promised to follow me to Berlin, where I had just been appointed to what seemed a most exciting new job. She did, and presently we shortened her name appreciably, to Nina Bing.

# 3

The job in Berlin came to me through my father's friend Paul
Eger, who was then director of the Deutsches Schauspielhaus
in Hamburg, and active in the Deutsche Bühnenverein, the
organization of managers of theaters. Together with the various
talent unions, the Bühnenverein ran a booking agency that was
supposed to bring together artists who needed an engagement
for a season and companies that needed just the abilities these
artists could offer. The agency was called Paritätischer Stellen-
nachweis, the name meaning that the two parties behind it were
equal and that its purpose was to find and fill jobs. There were
four separate divisions in the agency—opera, operetta, drama,
and ballet. The vacancy was at the head of the opera division.
Eger knew of the work I had been doing for Lion, and recommended me; and it seemed to me a wonderful chance to get to
a situation where I would be the boss, not someone's assistant.

I was wrong: I hated the job with a vengeance. It was a great
disappointment. The problem was, simply, the low level of talent with which the agency had to deal. In Vienna I had been

with a very high-class operation, working with superstars like Jeritza and Slezak, artists who would not dream of appearing for less than a thousand marks a performance. In Berlin I would be asked to find sopranos who would be willing to sing Isolde and God knows what else at a fee of three hundred marks a *month*—and I would then have to choose among some eighty screaming wretches. The little theaters that would come to my agency for service had seasons of perhaps six or seven months, which seems long in the United States; but in Germany it had to be compared with the standard season of ten months in the larger theaters. Nobody who could hope for an engagement in one of the more important theaters wanted the jobs I had to offer.

Among those who have never worked in them, the provincial German theaters—and there were more than eighty of them in my time—have a surprisingly good reputation. They are supposed to be excellent training grounds for the young, and Americans are pitied for not having comparable second-rank (really fourth-rank) theaters in their own country. But except for conductors (who can make use of any experience) these theaters are the worst places to be trained. Training takes time, and such companies never even have the time to do routine rehearsal. They have to throw a *Tristan und Isolde* on stage unprepared. What they need for that is a soprano who has done Isolde at least fifty times before, so nothing can surprise her.

Most theaters that called on my services wrote for what they needed in terms of categories, not roles—a heldentenor for the big Wagner roles, a young heldentenor for roles from Siegmund to Radames to Don José, and a lyric tenor for Mozart and the lighter Italian roles. (Everything, of course, was sung in German.) I would reply with several names and their associated repertories, and the house might then call the young man to do an audition or even a *Gastspiel*—a guest appearance—to see if he met the need. Or the manager might take a trip to wherever this particular artist was now singing to hear him at home. Or, in some houses, he might just sign the man without hearing him, on a recommendation.

That was the management side, and bad enough. But the union side—and the union was an equal partner in the agency —could be even worse. When it was learned that a new man had come to head the opera division of Der Nachweis, as it was called, I was deluged with singers who wished to be auditioned. Obviously, they were all singers who were not good enough to have their own, private management. We had an audition room with bare walls and a wooden floor, and I would spend hours there listening to these poor people who were being robbed of their money by irresponsible singing teachers. I thought it no more than right to tell them my opinion and advise them to seek some other kind of work; but this, of course, was not what they wanted to hear. Some of them complained to the union, and I was told in no uncertain terms that my job was to find positions for union members, not to give them advice.

Once I had auditioned a singer, he or she somehow had the right to come visit me in my office at any time. They would come knocking on my door, and enter with the words, "Any news?"—meaning, did I have a job for them yet. And I would say, "Sorry, nothing yet"—knowing full well that there never would be anything, and in many cases never should be. The problem of these incessant visits was made much worse by the European custom of shaking hands on entering or leaving a room, so that I was shaking hands hundreds of times a day. In the summer, all these sweaty hands became unbearable, and I put up a sign on my door: "During the summer months it would be appreciated if you refrained from handshaking." But the union told me that this attitude was undemocratic, and I had to take down the notice and shake everyone's hand, even on the hottest days.

Really, the union objected to my exercising any judgment at all. What the union wanted was that I act as a kind of post office, recommending to any opera house that requested a kind of singer all those on our list who could possibly be considered appropriate for such roles. Most of my time was spent recommending theaters with a bad reputation to singers with a bad reputation, and vice versa. It should be no surprise that our agency had a bad reputation.

At first, my living arrangements were almost equally unsatisfactory. During my first weeks, I stayed at a hotel which was much too expensive for my salary; so I moved to the Pension am Steinplatz, which was even more expensive than the hotel. I was very lonely: it was my first time "away from home," I knew no one, and I did not know how to make friends. Then Nina came, and we found a room with kitchen privileges in the old house of a very old couple, in Lietzenburgerstrasse. After that my private life became much more cheerful, though we did not get to know many people in Berlin at that period.

One of my duties was to travel around and visit the opera houses with which the agency did business, and during the eighteen months that I was head of the opera division I visited sixty of them. Today when anyone mentions the name of a German city—Breslau or Kiel or Dortmund or Düsseldorf—I can say I was there. The really good theaters frowned on my agency because they knew we had to recommend all the trash —if they asked for help they would get not one or two names but twelve. The best theaters dealt with Mr. Mertens, father of the André Mertens who later came to the United States and was so prominent an agent in the Columbia Artists Management group. Nelly Walter, who also came to New York and Columbia, was at the Mertens Agency in Berlin in my time, and I met her there. It is frightening to think that Nelly Walter and I did business together for forty-five years.

My first duty when I arrived in a city was to call on the

Intendant at his theater, and hear his requirements for the next year. I would promise to send him names when I returned to Berlin. Then I would hear a performance or two, and I would audition singers who had hopes of moving on to better houses than this one. Most of what I heard was awful screaming, though it was true then as it is today that on a lucky night even in a small house one might hear an extraordinary voice. In 1962, for example, you could have walked into the little house in Bremen and heard Montserrat Caballé, not just a promising young talent but already one of the great voices of the time. Because the theaters were so close to each other, they often borrowed each other's singers, and I had considerable opportunity to hear the same artists in different houses, which is invaluable experience for judging voices.

Sometimes I would also sit in on the *Gastspiel auf Engagement,* the tryout performance of some singer who was hoping for a job. There was a story I liked about a *Gastspiel* in Bremen, of a tenor from Chemnitz. He was terrible, but the Intendant, sitting in his box, was amazed to hear the audience calling, "Wonderful! Stay here! Stay here!" He investigated, and found that a good part of his audience had traveled to this performance from Chemnitz.

I was a miserable head of the division. Often I would say to an Intendant, "I don't know a soul to recommend to you"— because the artists on my roster were simply not good enough for *any* professional theater, by my standards. Nevertheless, I learned a lot. I heard and saw an enormous operatic repertory performed on all sorts of levels. I talked to hundreds of singers and learned their problems. I talked to the operatic managers of large and small houses, saw how they were operated, and learned to compare the way different personalities handled similar difficulties.

The great man I met while in this job was Heinz Tietjen,

who was when I came the head of the Städtische Oper—the City Opera, known as the Charlottenburg—in Berlin. Soon after my arrival, however, he was promoted to be Generalintendant of all the Prussian state theaters. The list included not only the Oper unter den Linden (with Erich Kleiber as its musical director) and the Kroll Oper (under Otto Klemperer), but also the Staatsschauspiel, or State Playhouse, and the other Prussian theaters in Kassel and Wiesbaden. Tietjen was my idol, but it was not easy to meet him. He was never seen by a living soul; he lived like the Queen of the Night. His assistants handled singers, and only if there was great trouble would he appear, three hours late for his appointment, and make some Delphic decision.

Tietjen ultimately became a kind of emperor of German opera, dominating all the theaters from Hindenburg through Hitler to Stalin (there may have been a short period right after the war when he was in bad odor and out of power, but I can't remember it). In the Hitler regime he became artistic director of Bayreuth, not because he was a Nazi—nobody has ever said he was—but because he had made himself very friendly with Winifred Wagner, who shielded him with Hitler. After the war he was once again Intendant at the Städtische Oper in Berlin, under four-power control—a place where the lights were on in the midst of the monstrous heaps of rubble—and then he went west to be head of the Opera in Hamburg. He had begun as a conductor, and toward the end of his life he returned to conducting. I remember someone telling me that at the age of eighty he conducted Strauss's *Ariadne auf Naxos* in Hamburg.

I did not see Tietjen often, of course—few mortals ever met him at all—but when I did he seemed to like me, and I admired boundlessly his mixture of charm, wit, and noncommittal diplomacy. I had no hope of imitating his level of high intrigue, supreme control through attrition by indecision, mixed with charm. But I studied his performance. Years later, when I was running the Edinburgh Festival, I saw Tietjen once again, on a visit to Berlin. I was far beyond his reach then, and we had a very amusing dinner together, recalling his days in the Berlin I knew and his invisibility all those years.

In the spring of 1928 I began to find my job impossible, though I continued to do it. What took me out of it was an unexpected visit from Carl Ebert, known to me, as to everyone else in Berlin, as the leading man of the Staatsschauspiel, the State Playhouse. He was a true matinee idol—tall, handsome, flashing eyes—but also very intelligent and ambitious. He had decided that the time had come for him to move from acting to directing. Ebert had been given the appointment as Generalintendant of the Hessian State Theater in Darmstadt, where Paul Eger had been many years before. This would involve him with an opera house as well as a theater. Being new to the management game he probably did not know how bad an agency I ran, and he came to visit me.

First he told me of his needs for singers. I forget now whether what he wanted was a tenor or a bass or a soprano, or all of them at once. What I remember is a kind of aside at the end: "As I am quite new as Intendant and also wish to spend a good deal of my time directing," he said, "I will also need an assistant, some sort of head of the artistic administration, a man with great experience to whom I can delegate much of the work."

I reached for my chance unhesitatingly, really without thinking about it. "I have just the man for you," I said. "Take me."

Ebert was surprised, and asked me what my actual experience in a theater had been. "None," I said—and got the job.

# 4

I think I may have been as happy at Darmstadt as I have ever been. I was at the heart of a theater, where I had always wanted to be, and working with artists whose quality I respected. I was to a surprising extent my own boss; Ebert did not go over the job with me in detail because in fact he did not know it in detail. I remember the childish thrill I received when I was given my first passkey, which enabled me to enter the dark auditorium at any time, even during performances.

Darmstadt was a charming town of well-kept houses, about 100,000 people in all. Nina and I took a furnished apartment in a little old villa about twenty minutes' walk from the theater. There were separate sitting and dining rooms, all with sloping ceilings and dormer windows. The forest was two minutes away, and full of songbirds. Through it, from Darmstadt to Heidelberg, ran the Bergstrasse, one of the sights of Germany, a road lined with fruit trees in bloom. On spring and summer evenings in the garden of our house the air was full of fireflies.

There were three conductors at the opera house—the Generalmusikdirektor, Karl Böhm; a second conductor, Max Rudolf; and a third conductor, Carl Bamberger. Many years later, Rudolf would become my first artistic administrator at the Metropolitan; later he moved to Cincinnati to be conductor of the symphony orchestra there, and then went to Philadelphia to begin an opera program at the Curtis Institute of Music. Böhm would later be a leading light of the Metropolitan Opera conducting staff, following his time as music director in Vienna; he was the conductor for the spring 1972 production of Verdi's *Otello*, the last new production to be mounted at the Metropolitan Opera under my direction. Bamberger too worked in New York during my time, as a conductor at the New York City Opera and a teacher of conducting (on which he wrote and edited important books) at the Mannes College of Music in Manhattan.

We had two theaters, on opposite corners of a red sandstone city square. One was the old Hoftheater, renamed the Landestheater when the Grand Duke was removed from power and the costs of subsidy were transferred from the ducal family to the *land* of Hesse and the city. It was a rather beautiful old-fashioned theater with classical columns on the façade facing the square, and seats for about 1,400 people. The Kleines Haus ("Little House") was for plays and operettas, and could seat just under 600 people. Also on the square was an attractive old coffeehouse where opera and theater people sat—outside, in good weather—and drank innumerable cups of coffee and discussed everything in the world. Behind the opera house there was a lovely park with tall old trees.

When I came in July 1928, I found an established repertory company for both theaters (most of its members away on their summer vacation), plus an already agreed-upon list of operas, operettas, and plays to be performed for the 1928–29 season— *plus* subscription contracts already purchased for a ten-month season by the good burghers of Darmstadt. But there was no schedule of any kind.

I was given a shabby little office with a washbasin and pitcher in case I wished to wash up, and a little window onto a corner of the square. I had a desk and a chair, and a large book of blank pages. In that book I was to write the performances for each evening in both theaters, with the names of the artists who would be needed; and the rehearsals to be held morning and afternoon in the rehearsal rooms and onstage. Only one mercy was vouchsafed me: I knew that all the members of all the companies would be available throughout the season. They were ensembles, dedicated to Darmstadt, not running off to do guest appearances in Frankfurt or London or New York. Even some of the stage directors and the designers were permanently employed by the theater; one had to worry about overworking them, but not about whether they would be in Darmstadt when they were needed.

I decided that the only thing I could do was to work backward from fixed points. The obvious fixed point was Christmas. The repertory included a new *Lohengrin*; I penciled that in for Christmas in the large theater. For the smaller theater in the Christmas season we would want a comedy and Lortzing's *Waffenschmied*. Well and good. How many rehearsals would each of these productions need? (Keeping in mind that the number of rehearsals had to be dictated not only by the difficulty of the piece but by the people working on it: Ebert and Böhm, as Intendant and Generalmusikdirektor, would have to be given more rehearsal time than lesser men on the staff.) Rehearsals were penciled in. Following the *Lohengrin*, perhaps, *Carmen* . . .

After a while I began to find it very difficult to keep track of the sequence of rehearsals by turning the pages in the large book, so I tore the pages out and set them on the floor, allowing me to overlook six or eight weeks at once. But more weeks had to be planned, and more, and soon I was crawling about on the floor, adjusting schedules several weeks apart. I would get a whole month settled, and then suddenly see that I had planned important opera and operetta rehearsals for the same afternoon, though the chorus could not possibly be in two places at the same time. I would adjust that schedule, and then find with a start that in doing so I had eliminated an absolutely necessary lighting rehearsal in the large theater.

After several weeks of this sort of terribly worrisome planning, with no one to help me—really, I was doing by myself everything that my whole staff did when I was at the Metropolitan—I was sure that I had at least the opera schedule completely established. Then I noticed that the one and only work that would fit in the schedule for New Year's Eve was *Tristan und Isolde* . . . I felt ill, and took to my bed for two weeks with a severe case of jaundice brought on by worry.

For quite a while, unfortunate collisions resulting from faulty planning made everyone's life a little harder in Darmstadt. Either it was a singer who had to rehearse the afternoon following a performance, or a subscription series that got *Traviata* two weeks running, or an opera that had not been done in four years that had not been given a stage rehearsal. But I learned, and the techniques of organizing and remembering I acquired in Darmstadt stood me in good stead all my life. My younger colleagues at the Metropolitan used to be horrified when they would bring me a worked-out schedule for the coming season, and just by looking at the planning chart, not even studying it, I would be able to pick out mistakes.

Although I had been around theaters for some years, I had never realized how much work and foresight—quite apart from talent—must be devoted to any theatrical production. I still marvel at how little the public, including a good number of the critics, understand about the infinite variety of considerations, the millions of decisions that come even before the beginning of rehearsals. Then there are the sweat and tears of the rehearsals themselves, weeks of them, for individuals and then for small groups together and finally for the entire company. At the end of all, the curtain rises on a first night, the audience comes late and the critics leave early, and neither really appreciate that they have witnessed the miracle of a birth.

Those weeks of planning, and then the first weeks of rehearsing at Darmstadt, made me understand for the first time why I had been so strongly drawn to a life in the theater, though I never was and never wanted to be active as an artist. Here was a microcosm complete in itself. Controlling such a world gave me the feeling of real power, without the evil that political power so often entails. A thousand aspects of life are involved in theater management. There is no artistic decision that is not at the same time an economic one, no financial decision that does not have bearing on artistic standards—and every decision involves human elements.

Dealing with artists is not like dealing with people in any other profession. Bank officials and law clerks no doubt have their ambitions, but they do not have to put their lives on the line, to fight for their existence every night at eight o'clock. And these are nervous, irritable, sensitive, talented people. These are things that one must not laugh at. We had, for example, an old comedian who was completely bald and had three wigs. He would change from the short wig to the longer wig and then to the longest wig, and one day he would say, "I must go to the barber now"—and that evening he would appear again in his short wig. We all had to pretend to admire his haircut.

Planning is just the beginning of the job of management. Every day there are a million problems someone has to handle, relations between people, accidents, illnesses. Ebert not only spent a great deal of time directing, he also acted in some of his own productions. And he wanted to be—and was—perfectly charming to everyone in the house. I had therefore complete charge of the daily running of the artistic department. The tension under which I worked would, I suppose, be death to those who cannot take it—but it is an inspiration to some of us. I adored it; I thrived on it. The more pressure was on me, the more severe the crisis seemed to be around me, the more calm I felt. It was my task to be the stabilizing influence, and I was.

Ebert was an extremely progressive director, both artistically and politically, and our little theater in Darmstadt in the late 1920s was a focus for agitation in the town. As a publicly subsidized body, we were of course a regular subject of discussion in meetings of the city government. Ebert would engage controversial directors and designers to do productions at our theater as guests, and some of the repertory was controversial, too.

I remember we did a French revolutionary opera by Auber, *The Silent Woman of Portici* (the leading woman was to be played by a dancer, and really was silent). The director was Carl Maria Rabenalt, young and very talented, married, rather unsuitably, to Bruno Walter's daughter Lotte—they had been working on annual contracts at a little theater in Würzburg, she as a soprano, and in these little towns one has nothing else to do, so they were married. Soon they were divorced. The designer was Wilhelm Reinking, who built a whole town on stage for this production. You could hardly have a performance the night before because it took so long to build the set. This was very expensive, of course, not only in original construction but in overtime for the stagehands, and Ebert was fiercely attacked for wasting the city's money—especially by those in the city who did not like revolutionary subjects, French or otherwise.

Our most important controversy was musical: we were the first opera house outside Berlin, where it had received its premiere, to perform Alban Berg's *Wozzeck*—Böhm, of course, conducting, as he did for me years later at the Metropolitan. This was a scandal in the town, and again the excuse was the expense, of the orchestra rehearsals. It has been interesting to see over the decades how much easier *Wozzeck* has become for the opera orchestras, whether or not they have played Berg before. Then it was nearly impossible; now it is a matter of a few more rehearsals.

In some theaters, weeks go by with the regular clicking off of the days, in calm routine. We had little routine in Darmstadt. Ebert and Böhm, as co-directors of the operatic enterprise, were often in conflict—it was from watching them, I think, that I decided that an opera house must have one head, that a general manager must never give away any of his ultimate authority to a musical director. With all this pressure, amid all these crises, with artists losing their nerves and their heads several times a day, a young man who kept his nerve and his head could make a real contribution.

Yet Darmstadt was a small town, and by the end of my second year, for all the delights and excitements of my job, I was beginning to feel I knew it too well. I remember one evening attending a comedy with my wife, and saying to her, "When you can sit in the dark theater and you know who is laughing, it's time to quit."

In 1930 I heard from Raimund von Hofmannsthal, son of the great poet and playwright, whom I had known from my childhood in Vienna. An American film producer named Curtis Melnitz had come to Berlin to exploit the new possibilities of the talking film. He had hired Max Reinhardt to produce and direct the films, and Reinhardt had hired von Hofmannsthal and wanted to hire me. It was a dazzling thought—Hollywood and Max Reinhardt and talking pictures—and I went to Ebert and said I could not resist the offer. He understood completely.

The problem was that between the date of my resignation from the Hessian State Theater and the date of my arrival in Berlin Reinhardt and von Hofmannsthal had a hell of a row with Melnitz, and walked out on him. I reported for work to find nobody I knew; I was left in enemy territory with nothing to do. Nina and I had rented an apartment with a very large sitting room—one of those immense Berlin apartments that could be split, as this one was, between two tenants. There was a built-in maid, employed by the lady who owned the apartment and had moved God knows where. I could not afford to walk out, and for some weeks I sat in the office the film company had given me, watching an unpleasant Hungarian at the other desk trying to improve Dostoevski.

One film was made by this company while I was in its employ —*L'Homme Qui Assassine*, with Conrad Veidt. And these six months were a very unhappy period, which did not increase my admiration for the movie industry. But I did learn some very simple technicalities of preparing movies, how to organize scenes and to time shots. This rudimentary knowledge of film production has not been professionally valuable to me as an opera manager, though it has meant that whenever people come around with schemes to make movies of operas—as they do every so often—I know what they are really talking about and can make some judgment about whether *they* do.

Like anyone else in so insecure and uncertain a position, I was looking around for a possible other job. Fortunately for me, the Charlottenburg Opera, abandoned first by its Intendant Tietjen and then by its musical director Bruno Walter, had fallen upon hard times, and someone who knew I was in Berlin told the new Intendant I could be useful to him. Though I had no political pull at all with the city government, which ran the Charlottenburg, I was asked to take over there the job I had held in Darmstadt. Luckily, my film employers fired me at about the same time. This enabled me to take the job I wanted and get a full measure of revenge by suing them for the remainder of my contract, a case I won in the Berlin courts.

# 5

The Intendant of the Charlottenburg Opera, who had hired me, was a very distinguished . . . gynecologist. Like many German doctors, Dr. Singer was also a keen musician, and he was married to an opera singer, Margherita Pfahl. And, of course, he had friends at City Hall, which is how he came to be Intendant at the opera house. But all these things together did not give him the slightest notion of how a theater should be run.

The Städtische Oper was not supposed to be the very best in Berlin. The Staatsoper unter den Linden, where Erich Kleiber was the musical director, had the highest reputation, both locally and internationally, and the Kroll Oper under Otto Klemperer was at any time ponderable competition. Both of these were Prussian state theaters under the control of Tietjen. But we had a good subsidy from the city government, enough to employ some of the world's great singers. For me, it was my first time in the big leagues. I was working with singers like Sigrid Onegin (a very difficult woman but a uniquely beautiful mezzo-soprano voice), Ivar Andresen, who was a justly famous bass, Hans Reinmar, Maria Ivogün, and others.

Though my title and apparent duties were the same in Berlin as they had been in Darmstadt, the job was very different. In Darmstadt, as in all German provincial theaters, there had been a permanent ensemble, and there was no question about who was to sing what: all lyric tenor roles were sung by *the* lyric tenor, all dramatic soprano roles were sung by *the* dramatic soprano. If one of the singers in the ensemble was indisposed, we would call neighboring opera houses and borrow a baritone or a soprano as a housewife might borrow a cup of sugar.

In Berlin I encountered the star system, and the need to build performances around the appearance of famous guests who were not available for the entire season—they went off on concert tours or even to fulfill guest engagements at the Metropolitan Opera in New York. Their work had to be meshed with that of our regular ensemble, and vice versa. Most important roles had to be cast with more than one singer, so someone could take over when the guest departed or if the guest were indisposed: in Berlin I learned something about keeping a "cover" cast, which was later to be one of the banes of my existence at the Metropolitan.

Of course, the star system as practiced in Berlin was not the kind of problem it became twenty years later. In 1931 singers still had moral and artistic integrity. Their prime concern was the mastery of their craft, the preservation of their vocal ability, and—believe it or not—their duty to their public and to their theater. (We did, however, have in Berlin one episode with a star singer worse than anything I ever experienced later— when the husband of one of our best sopranos, Gertrud Binder-nagel, shot her dead onstage during a performance, I believe for some reason of jealousy.) But even when the star system ran properly, with recognition of obligations on both sides, it was a much more complicated way to run a theater than any-thing I had encountered at Darmstadt.

And in fact the system at the Städtische Oper was very near breaking down when I arrived in January 1931. New produc-tions were not ready on schedule; singers were not notified long enough in advance to be ready for rehearsals (or, sometimes, performances); the musical side had not recovered from the departure of Bruno Walter, who had been the musical director a year before; and Dr. Singer was trying to stage operas him-self, something for which he had not the slightest training or, indeed, talent. Questions were being asked in the city govern-ment, and not long after I arrived it became apparent to every-one that the house could not go through another season under amateur leadership. A committee of the city council searched for a successor, and it became known that there were three candidates being taken seriously. One of them was Carl Ebert. When he was chosen, the Berlin gossip columnists wrote that I was behind it, that I had "engineered" the downfall of Dr. Singer to get the job for "my friend" Ebert. But Dr. Singer had surely needed no assistance in falling down, and at the age of twenty-nine, knowing few people in Berlin, I was scarcely in a position to pull strings at the city council. Ebert, after all, had been a very popular actor in Berlin for some years, and a successful Intendant in Darmstadt.

But I did not try to hide my pleasure at Ebert's arrival. I knew he trusted me and would increase the responsibilities of my job, if only to save himself time for directing. In those days one could still plan in the spring for the season beginning the next fall. Ebert decided to open his first season with Verdi's *Macbeth*, which had not been done, to the best of our knowl-edge, since the nineteenth century. He would stage the work himself; his designer would be Caspar Neher, whom Fritz Busch once delightfully described as having "a combination of innocence and craftiness." The conductor for opening night, Ebert decided, would be Fritz Stiedry, who since the departure of Walter had been the leading musical figure in the house.

Stiedry, unfortunately, had taken offense at something or other—he was a wonderful fellow, but as long as I knew him, including many years when he was a cherished conductor for me at the Metropolitan Opera, he was always taking offense at something or other—and he turned down the invitation to conduct the opening-night *Macbeth*. Ebert then turned to Paul Breisach, a fine younger conductor at the house, and offered it to him. As soon as Stiedry learned that Breisach had accepted *Macbeth,* he changed his mind and said he would do it after all. Ebert had to think first of his performance; Stiedry had been his first choice, and if Stiedry now was willing, he felt it should go to Stiedry rather than to Breisach. But he did not wish to upset Paul Breisach either. Breisach was a cousin of mine, and we had known each other from childhood, so Ebert asked me to draft a letter to Breisach for his signature, letting Paul down gently enough to make sure he would not be hurt. When Breisach received the letter he came to my office, and asked me, because I was a friend of Ebert's, to draft a letter to Ebert for *his* signature, pointing out that he had been offered *Macbeth* and still wanted to do it. For some time I was engaged in a delicate correspondence with myself! Ultimately, Stiedry did the *Macbeth* and Breisach was not too upset.

I was too busy to spend much time at the *Macbeth* rehearsals, but one could sense the mounting excitement in the house. I had a very strange experience in connection with the dress rehearsal. Mrs. Ebert always came to her husband's rehearsals, but today she was late. I was in my office, and received a call that she had been in an automobile accident, and was rather seriously injured. I ran down to the auditorium, where Ebert was seated with his technical staff, studying every detail of the action on the stage. I came up to him and began speaking, and he turned on me in a fury, hissing an order to leave him alone. So I left, but I had to come back. Now he was in a complete rage, but when I broke through it to tell him my message, he immediately turned and ran from the hall to be with his wife. They were extremely close—I believe she came to every rehearsal of his, other than this one, all the time we were in Berlin and Glyndebourne. The accident turned out to be not as serious as first reported, and the rehearsal proceeded to a successful conclusion without Ebert.

That opening night was one of my great evenings in a theater, and the next day all Berlin was talking about *Macbeth*. Among the reasons it was such a great hit was a startling performance of Lady Macbeth by Sigrid Onegin. Hers was one of the most individual and beautiful voices I have ever heard, and temperamentally the character of Lady Macbeth came naturally to her. Later in the 1930s Ebert and I revived this production of *Macbeth*, with very similar sets by Neher, at Glyndebourne, Fritz Busch conducting, and again it was an immense hit. But when I brought it to the Metropolitan Opera in 1959, yet again with Ebert and Neher, the production was, I fear, a flop. I had lost my originally announced Lady Macbeth (as I recall it, a lady named Miss Callas), and though Leonie Rysanek filled in quite wonderfully, people had of course been looking forward to Miss Callas. I had also lost my conductor (Dimitri Mitropoulos had suffered a heart attack a few days before rehearsals were to begin); Erich Leinsdorf rallied round magnificently, but again it could not be the same—he had to pick up the score for the first time too near the date of the performance. But the reason *Macbeth* did not work for us at the Metropolitan was less these pieces of bad luck than the passage of a generation: a conception that had been brilliant and convincing in 1931 was no longer effective in 1959.

Another Ebert production of that season, while it made much less of a splash in Berlin than the *Macbeth,* was destined to have a greater influence on all our lives because it led to one of the great operatic collaborations of the century. It was Mozart's *Die Entführung aus dem Serail,* conceived more dramatically and less as a period charm piece than was the German tradition. Among those who came to see it was Fritz Busch, then music director of the opera in Dresden. Busch had been invited to conduct an *Entführung* in Salzburg at the Festival the next summer, and after observing our production he invited Ebert to come to Salzburg with him. Ebert in return invited Busch to become musical director in Berlin, an invitation Busch did not feel he could accept. But Busch did agree to come to Berlin the next season as a guest, and to work with Ebert and Neher on a new production of Verdi's *Un Ballo in Maschera* (*Ein Maskenball* to all of us, of course), now generally recognized as one of Verdi's masterworks but then relatively little known.

"For once," Busch wrote in his autobiography, "I was able to build up an opera production in the smallest detail and with free imagination and complete respect for the work, by the help of two men of the theater of superior talent. These weeks of intensive preparation I reckon among the happiest experiences of my career . . . Certainly differences of opinion between us were not lacking, when my impression was that Carl Ebert did violence to the music, whereas, to alter a pronouncement of Mozart's, 'production should be the obedient daughter of music.' But as we both understood how to subordinate personality to the matter in hand we always came to a good understanding again."

Busch quotes from the review of this performance that appeared in the *Frankfurter Zeitung:*

The audience applauded as if in a frenzy. There was no trace of theater weariness in this unusual night. There is still life in the drama if it is genuine, sappy, daemonic drama. The daemon presided over Professor Ebert's opera in Charlottenburg. They acted, mimed, played and sang as if possessed . . . Not an arm was stuck out in an operatic pose. The masks were faces. After unveiling herself the heartbroken Nemeth stands helpless, like no other despairing opera heroine . . . A servant puts a light on the table at the right moment and fills up an interval in the action while the orchestra is playing. When the Signori are going away servants run up and bring their cloaks, thus accelerating the end of the act. After the assasination in the masked ball all the masks, which have become unnecessary, are raised. This is drama! . . . The guests in front stand petrified. But quite at the back unearthly figures, shrouded in gray, go on with the dance . . . until they too become aware that murder has been done. Then at last all movement stops. And Richard sings a swan song of pardon. A tragic scene! In Charlottenburg men of intellect are reduced to tears.

In those days reviews were worth reading.

Fritz Busch was not only a great conductor and a courageous man, who stood up to the Nazis in conditions of great personal danger in Dresden (which was Nazi country in a way that Berlin was not); he was also a warmhearted, straightforward, kind, and helpful human being. I was proud and happy that he liked me and that we became friends. Because I had to make the plans for his rehearsals, we saw something of each other in Berlin, and there as at Glyndebourne, as I remember it, we would take walks together.

In 1971, with that nastiness and disregard for truth which I found so common in the New York critics, one of the lesser members of that fraternity wrote that Busch did not conduct in my time at the Metropolitan because he had on some occasion found me so inefficient that he vowed never to work with me again. A few weeks later, the same paper printed a letter from Hans Busch, Fritz's son and an operatic director of distinction, denouncing that lie and stating that his father had always liked me. I do not remember today why Busch did not conduct in my first season at the Metropolitan; he may have been ill or busy, or with Stiedry, Reiner, and Walter on my roster I may have felt that the operas he would want to do were already covered. But we were in correspondence about what he should do for me in future seasons when, tragically and much too soon, at the age of sixty-one, he died.

One other production stands out with special strength in my memory of those two years at Charlottenburg: the premier of Kurt Weill's *Die Bürgschaft* (The Pledge), for which Caspar Neher wrote the libretto as well as designing the sets. Ebert directed, Stiedry conducted, and it was Weill's first hit in an opera house (his collaboration with Bertolt Brecht had already produced several hits in the Berlin equivalent of Broadway). But Neher was as left as could be, and Weill was as Jewish as could be, and the production became the center of a great fuss in the city council.

What most distinguished the Charlottenburg Opera under Ebert's management was, I think, the quality of the theatrical direction. In addition to Ebert himself, I remember particularly Jürgen Fehling and Gustav Gründgens, who gave us an Offenbach operetta that sparkled with unforgettably exquisite comic timing. (In later years, at the Metropolitan, I was astonished to find that critics in New York believed Offenbach and Johann Strauss were somehow below the dignity of a great opera house, for we had staged them with delight in Berlin.) Ebert was always on the lookout for other directors who might work at Charlottenburg. When Walter Felsenstein of the East Berlin Komische Oper was in New York not long ago, he reminded me (I had forgotten) that the first time we met was during those years

[ 46 ]

when I was working in Berlin: Ebert had sent me to Basel, where Felsenstein was directing, to see if I could interest him in staging *La Bohème* for us.

The Städtische Oper was a much more modern opera house than the one in Darmstadt, and my office had better lighting, better heat—and a real washroom down the hall instead of a pitcher and a bowl. There was also an efficient secretarial staff, including a Miss Luise Bernhard and a Mrs. Hilde Lorenz who were still at their posts twenty years later and helped arrange auditions for me when I returned to Berlin as general manager of the world's greatest opera house.

My wife and I kept the furnished apartment we had rented when I came to Berlin to work for the movie company. I would come home for "lunch" and a late-afternoon break at four, and then return to the theater. Someone gave us a ping-pong table to use in our enormous sitting room, and we became fanatics for the game. For some months we had friends from the Vienna days over to the apartment almost every night after the opera, and we would play ferocious ping-pong until two or three in the morning.

I would take the tram to work in the morning, not too early: Ebert never came in early either. In fact, Ebert was late for all meetings, almost in the style of Tietjen. In those days at an opera house, the Intendant was known to his underlings as "Der Chef." In the last act of *Tristan*, Kurvenal looks out to sea and gives his lord the sorrowful news, *"Noch ist kein Schiff zu seh'n"* ("There is still no ship to be seen"). We would assemble for a meeting with Ebert, who would not be there, and someone would say, *"Noch ist kein Chef zu seh'n."* But like Isolde's ship, Ebert would eventually turn up.

My years in Berlin were those Christopher Isherwood later described in his *Berlin Stories*, when the brown pest descended on Germany and the city. I had strong political views: like

Ebert, I was a Social Democrat (though being an Austrian citizen I did not vote or take any other political action). I sailed beyond politics—one saw, but one just did not believe. Not long before the election that brought Hitler to power, my wife and I gave up our apartment and went to live in a pension near the Kurfürstendamm. We could hear and see what was happening on the streets; we turned away from it and went to the opera house. One day very soon after the change in government I was in Ebert's office. There was a knock on the door, and one of our uniformed flunkies opened it and said, "Herr Professor, the S.A."—and the S.A. simply marched in, in their uniforms, and told us we had been dismissed from our duties at the Städtische Oper.

Ebert left almost immediately for Italy, where he had an invitation to direct at the Maggio Musicale in Florence. I sent my wife to Paris, but I stubbornly remained in Berlin: I had a contract, and if I was to be dismissed from my job I wanted my contract honored. I had an idiot belief that I could successfully press a claim for money that was due to me. The administrative director—the business manager—of the opera had long been a good Nazi, and he had remained. I saw him several times, and on the last of these visits it dawned on me that he was afraid to have me in his office. I was a friend of Ebert, Ebert was a "notorious" Social Democrat, it was dangerous to be seen with such people. Suddenly I got an inkling of what I was dealing with, and I realized that not only would I never conceivably get any satisfaction on my contract, I would be lucky if I stayed out of jail. The S.A. was rounding up people on the streets and loading them onto trucks, to go God knows where. I packed my bags and went to Vienna.

1. Rudolf Bing's mother on her wedding day in Vienna

2. Rudolf Bing,
Vienna, 1924

3. With Christiana
von Hofmannsthal,
Austria, 1921

4. Rudolf Bing, Austria, 1921

5. Nina Schelemskaya-Schelesnaya, who later married
Rudolf Bing, Austria

6. Left to right:
Rudolf Bing, Dr. Fritz
Busch, Carl Ebert,
Glyndebourne, 1935

7. With John Christie,
1936

8. Nina Bing with Pip I,
Glyndebourne

9. Glyndebourne

10. Glyndebourne

# 6

Our first problem in Vienna was that we had no money; but fortunately my sister and her husband, a successful industrialist, came immediately to our assistance. The next problem was that I had nothing to do. Plans to start concert agencies in Austria or take over Viennese theaters rattled around and came to nothing. This spring of 1933 was not cheerful anywhere. Then an old friend, Gerhard Scherler, came to the door with a theater in his hands, needing help.

Scherler had been Dramaturg for the theater in Leipzig. There is no equivalent position in an Anglo-Saxon theater. The Dramaturg in Germany is responsible in general for the literary qualities associated with the house. He reads the new plays, and recommends those he likes to the Intendant. He edits the little magazine—the *Blätter*—which every German theater publishes to inform its patrons of the views and plans of the management. To the extent that there is a press that needs handling, he handles the press.

Quite to his own surprise, Scherler had been approached by

representatives of the Nazi Propaganda Ministry. They were interested in maintaining German culture in the Sudeten area of Czechoslovakia, and one town largely inhabited by German-speaking Czechs—the town of Teplitz-Schönau—had a Stadt-theater that was used only occasionally by traveling companies. If Scherler would undertake to run a seven-month repertory season at that theater (as at Darmstadt, it was two theaters, one large and one small), the German government would be prepared to subsidize him up to a certain maximum figure. There were no strings attached. Scherler felt he could handle the planning of plays and comedies well enough, but he needed someone to manage his opera for him. Would I come with him to Teplitz to look over the theater and participate in the nego-tiations with the local city government, which owned it?

Teplitz was on the northern side of the Czech bulge, well beyond Prague. I stopped off at Prague to consult yet again with Dr. Paul Eger, who had been pushed out of his job in Hamburg and had become director of the German Theater (i.e., classical theater and opera) in Prague. Eger was encour-aging; thanks to the Nazi purges, it was possible to engage high-quality German talent on budgets much smaller than those that would have been necessary a few years earlier. But after I had talked with the men from the city government and looked at the theaters—which were perfectly decent nineteenth-century provincial theaters, reasonably well equipped—I told Scherler that his subsidy from Germany would not come anywhere near meeting the deficits a theater-operetta-opera season would incur in Teplitz. The arrangements we were making with the local authorities called for us to begin rehearsals in September and start performances in October. I predicted that we would be bankrupt by New Year's Day, but if Scherler was willing to go bankrupt I was willing to help him. As it turned out, we were bankrupt by Christmas, which I consider pretty accurate budgeting.

I think it was July before Scherler was formally appointed director of the Stadttheater of Teplitz, and appointed me his co-director. We had six weeks to assemble companies for opera, operetta, and theater. Though it was Goebbels' money, there were absolutely no restrictions on us, which we proved immediately by hiring as our musical director Hans Oppenheim, a fine, rock-solid experienced conductor who was no longer working in Germany because he was Jewish. While Scherler auditioned actors, Oppenheim and I spent endless hours listening to singers and investigating their repertories. We also had to arrange to have drops painted and props made (there was, of course, nowhere near enough money to make solid scenery), and to have costumes designed and sewn.

For our first night we would do *Midsummer Night's Dream* with Mendelssohn's music, using the entire resources of the company; then the opera season would open with Offenbach's *Tales of Hoffmann* and Mozart's *Marriage of Figaro*. To save the cost of costumes, and also because somebody thought it was a good idea (I fear it was my idea), we determined to do *Figaro* in modern dress. This was the worst flop I have ever had to witness, and I have since considered myself lucky that I got that sort of stupidity out of my system so early in the game, and so far away.

All this planning and auditioning and commissioning was done in Vienna, where we could most easily find the people we might wish to hire. It took just under twenty-four hours a day. In September everyone moved to Teplitz, my wife and I finding a room in a pleasant little hotel, and Oppenheim began to rehearse a local orchestra—we were of course committed, for every imaginable reason, to use Teplitz people wherever possible. Among our local employees was an aging lady music teacher who served at the beginning of the season as our prompter. She read a score easily and always knew what everybody should be doing. Unfortunately, whenever there was trouble she lost her head—she would close her eyes in agony and hold up both hands and cry, *"Falsch! Falsch!"* ("Wrong! Wrong!").

Though we had an excellent comedian—a Jewish actor who had been evicted from Breslau—what drew the audience for us in Teplitz was operetta. This must have been a strong operation, though I remember little about it, except that our number-two operetta conductor was a vigorous young man named Leopold Ludwig, later to be Generalmusikdirektor in Hamburg and to give me at the Metropolitan a beautiful *Parsifal* in fall 1970 and a much less beautiful *Der Freischütz* the next year.

As the season progressed it became more and more obvious that we were not going to survive our financial condition. The city was unprepared to subsidize, the box office could not come near meeting the costs and was not that well patronized anyway, and given the number of Jews and Social Democrats we had hired the German Propaganda Ministry was, to say the least, in no mood to increase our subvention. In mid-December we had to notify our company that we would have to close the house; by New Year's in 1934 my wife and I were back in Vienna.

The next couple of months were the darkest I knew. The year before, Hitler had seemed an aberration, and there were all sorts of schemes brewing in the musical and theatrical life. Now, there was revolution in Vienna itself. From our Pension my wife and I could hear, and sometimes see, shooting in the Ringstrasse. Thanks to help from my family, we were far from starving, but I did not know where to turn. Then there arrived in the mailbox, unheralded, an astonishing letter from Fritz Busch with a most remarkable commission.

There was, it seemed, a very rich Englishman named John Christie who had a country estate in a place called Glyndebourne, about sixty miles from London, and who had built an opera house there for the purpose of staging a Mozart festival. Christie had gone to Amsterdam to meet Busch, who was there as a guest conductor (his regular job then was with the Danish State Radio), and had asked him to undertake the direction of a two-week festival that May—only a few months off. The scene was later reconstructed for me by the third person who had been present: the sitting room of a hotel suite, Christie's huge bulk stuffed into a delicate Empire chair, Busch with mounting enthusiasm and deteriorating English elaborating a series of plans for a Mozart festival, until he noticed that Christie had fallen asleep . . .

Busch had visited Glyndebourne and inspected the theater, which he considered adequate. He imposed one condition on Christie—that Carl Ebert (with whom he had worked again the previous summer at the Teatro Colón in Buenos Aires) be retained as artistic director. Ebert said, "But this must be nonsense, Fritz," and Busch replied, "You might as well go and see, you know. It's not as if we have so much else to do." The operas scheduled for the first festival season were *Marriage of Figaro* and *Così Fan Tutte*, both in Italian (it would be a principle of Glyndebourne that everything should be done in the original language, which was uncommon in those days). Either in England or from their experience at the Teatro Colón, Busch and Ebert had engaged a few of the principal singers—the tenor Heddle Nash, the baritone Roy Henderson, the soprano Ina Souez, and the Italian basso buffo Italo Tajo. The soprano for Susanna came with the house, so to speak, for Christie was married to the Canadian singer Audrey Mildmay, who had been part of the Carl Rosa company. It was 80 per cent in her honor, I later learned, that the project had been started.

Neither Busch nor Ebert had the time or the knowledge of who might be available that would be needed to find and employ singers for a Mozart season. I knew what voices and personalities were needed for *Marriage of Figaro* and *Così Fan Tutte;* would I undertake to acquire the services of an ensemble for five weeks in May and early June, to rehearse and perform these two Mozart operas? Glyndebourne would pay my expenses, plus a fee.

An absolutely mad period followed. Everything about this enterprise seemed crazy. When I wrote to Glyndebourne for information about what to put in the contracts I was to offer, I received in return cheerful letters with no information from someone who signed herself Frances and did not seem to hold any official position with the organization. Artists wanted to know where they would live while at Glyndebourne—there was no such place on any map, and even after I had ascertained that the nearest town was a place called Lewes it was hard to find a map which showed *that* location. I was rather airily (and wrongly) informed that the artists would live "at the castle," which became a selling point for me. Later, when the wife of the baritone Willi Domgraf-Fassbänder found herself living at a hotel in Lewes (a very lovely hotel, by the way), she complained bitterly that the only reason she had encouraged her husband to accept this engagement was her understanding that she would live in a castle. I could not tell the singers I approached anything about the resources of the place or of the theater, because I did not know and could not find out.

Worst of all, I had to invent a contract form, in a language not my own, that would be acceptable in a country with a legal system I had always been told was very different from ours in Central Europe. Nobody at Glyndebourne had thought about this problem, or was prepared to start thinking about it now. History is full of tales of performing artists being stranded in far places by impresarios; I had just returned from such a failure myself (though Scherler and I had in fact retained enough money to pay everyone his fare back home). I managed to interest some excellent artists in the Glyndebourne project, largely, of course, because it involved working with Busch and Ebert. Domgraf-Fassbänder and Luise Helletsgruber, who agreed to go to England, were leading singers at the Vienna State Opera; Irene Eisinger, a charming soubrette who had left Germany, had a number of other engagements she could accept. The Finnish soprano Aulikki Rautawaara also agreed to sing at the Festival. Oppenheim was more than happy to take a post as Busch's assistant in preparing the performances. But all of them very properly insisted on the security of a contract properly notarized in England.

Finally, I simply drew up a contract form myself and sent it to Glyndebourne. Now, apparently, they seemed to have put a lawyer to work on the problem, because what returned to me was somewhat different from what I had sent. It was also printed, which greatly encouraged the artists; and it was signed by a Mr. Nightingale, identified as the general manager of the Glyndebourne Opera.

As the season neared, it seemed to me more and more important that I get a look at what Glyndebourne was. Vienna was depressing, Germany was hopeless. If Glyndebourne did become an annual event—and it was impossible to imagine a man so crazy he would build an opera house to use only once—I might very well be asked to assume again the sort of duties I had just fulfilled, and the second time I would have no excuse for not knowing about the place. The suggestion that I should visit was very well received at Glyndebourne, but nobody said anything about paying my expenses—I learned later that Christie, while lavish about some things, was remarkably cheap about others (he would spend £30,000 on an opera production, but travel in third-class carriages and carry his own luggage so as not to have to tip a porter). Finally I decided I would have to go on my own.

In May 1934 my wife and I left Vienna; we would never live there again. Nina stayed in Paris with her family there while I crossed the Channel to reconnoiter Glyndebourne. The boat arrived at Newhaven, where, following instructions, I took a train for Lewes, not entirely certain what if anything I would find. But waiting at the station for me in an incredibly dirty old Lancia was the motherly figure of Frances Dakyns, the lady who had been at the other end of my correspondence; and presently we were at that beautiful house in that most beautiful of peaceful countrysides, which was to be the focus of my life for the next fifteen years.

# 7

Glyndebourne was an English manor house and had been such from a time tracing back to antiquity. It had been in the Christie family for about a hundred years before I saw it, and the manor included 10,000 acres of land. John Christie had completely remodeled the house in 1919, taking it back to a more Georgian appearance, and had added an immense "organ room" with an elaborate Tudor ceiling, housing a very large organ that occupied one entire wall of the room. Having found the organ makers' approach to the building of that instrument both inefficient and inflexible, he had bought the organ works and made it and himself a prime factor in the organ trade in England. During the silent-movie days, his Christie Unit Organ had sold all over England, Australia, and New Zealand. Near Glyndebourne he also owned and more or less operated the largest construction firm in the Sussex Downs (a very useful place to have when building sets for operatic productions) and the largest automobile dealership and garage in the area. In addition, he owned an immense estate including a large resort hotel in Devon, a hundred miles or so to the southwest. He was rich enough to support a little opera house, if that was what he wanted to do.

To say that I had never known anyone like John Christie would understate his uniqueness: nobody has ever known anyone like John Christie. He was very short, about five foot four, stocky, and almost bald. In 1934 he was fifty-one years old, and unbelievably strong; he could and did pick up and move large pieces of furniture all by himself. He had been an infantry captain in the war, and had taught physics at Eton for sixteen years, providing much of the laboratory equipment out of his own pocket. He had been a married man, however, for only three years. His wife, Audrey Mildmay, twenty years younger, was a Canadian-English soprano (from a family good enough so that her father, an eccentric clergyman who later settled near Glyndebourne, ultimately inherited a baronetcy). She was slight and delicate, a graceful and intelligent artist who had been singing with the touring Carl Rosa Opera. Cast as Susanna in Mozart's *Figaro* at Glyndebourne, she was both colleague and hostess for the other artists in the casts, and in those prewar years it was her pleasure and charm in both these functions that, more than any other single factor, established the delightful feeling of Glyndebourne.

Audrey had met Christie through music. Except for a few lessons on the piano as a boy and on the cello at Cambridge, Christie was musically without training, but he had become a passionate Wagnerite before the first war. In the later 1920s he made pilgrimages to Bayreuth and spent much of the summer in the Bavarian Alps, from which he would descend to hear performances at the old Residenztheater in Munich; he had also visited Salzburg. The year before he opened his own opera house at Glyndebourne he had become so Bavarian in his tastes that he requested guests at Glyndebourne to wear lederhosen and dirndls, and wore lederhosen himself when he

[ 58 ]

went out to dine with friends in Sussex. This obsession with things German did not, of course, include any ability to speak the language. At his most international, Christie was the insular Englishman of legend: the pound never fell, the franc rose; when the Channel was foggy, he would say the Continent was isolated. Though he was himself without patents of nobility, his mother had been the daughter of the Earl of Portsmouth. Her nephew, Christie's cousin, once wrote about this family that it could boast "one hundred and forty-nine direct (not collateral) ancestors who were Knights of the Garter, eleven who were canonised saints, and sixty-nine who were executed by their rulers, probably rightly."

During the 1920s Christie had taken over and run a theater in Tunbridge Wells, where he sponsored popular plays and films, talked about staging opera, and put on Sunday concerts which occasionally included staged excerpts from Wagner. At Glyndebourne, in those years, he put on operatic excerpts in the organ room, with a mixture of amateur and professional singers (once he himself played Beckmesser in Act II of *Die Meistersinger*). It was through hiring her to sing Blonde in an excerpt from Mozart's *Die Entführung* (for five guineas) that he first met Audrey Mildmay.

In 1931, when Christie projected the theater for his own estate—it was in fact built right onto the manor house, as an addition; the organ room served as its foyer—people referred to it alternately as an English Bayreuth or an English Salzburg, and he did not object to either. He had pretty much designed the theater himself, with help from Hamish Wilson, an English stage designer who remained to do the sets for Glyndebourne productions in its early years; the structure was built, of course, by Christie's own Ringmer Building Works. There was a worldwide economic depression, but it did not affect Christie, and in a sense one could say that he did not know it was happening.

Very plain on the outside, with walls of crushed local sandstone quarried from old buildings to be suitably aged in appearance, the theater was quietly intimate and charming within, holding seats for only three hundred people. There were a few technical problems, most seriously the lack of a fly gallery, which meant that one could not use painted drops to help set the stage, and the absence of storage space for the self-standing scenery that would have to be used. In that first season, as I heard quickly from the artists when I arrived, there were also no proper dressing rooms.

The English had first learned of the existence of this unexpected new opera house during the summer before, when Christie had given an airy interview to the press, saying that he "had asked Sir Thomas Beecham and his orchestra to come down here but that is not settled yet." The theater would open with either *Don Giovanni* or *Die Walküre;* in subsequent years, he said, there would be productions of the entire *Ring,* and probably *Parsifal* at Easter. It was Audrey, who knew that both the theater and her own talents were unsuitable for Wagner, who pushed Christie toward a Mozart rather than a Wagner festival. He was cheerful about it, for he was a Mozartean, too. As he came to know the operas better and better, he became a wholly dedicated Mozartean. He could not bear contemporary music. Late in his life, Glyndebourne produced Henze's *Elegy for Young Lovers,* with a libretto by W. H. Auden and Chester Kallman (who were also the librettists for Stravinsky's *The Rake's Progress*). During a performance, a patron wandering outside found old Christie standing in the garden near the theater, looking out through the twilight across the valley to the distant hills. Christie said, "Do you see those cows off in the distance? Yes? Well, when we do Mozart, they are always right here."

Busch came to Glyndebourne, according to Christie's biographer Wilfrid Blunt, by "the merest chance." In January

1934 Adolf Busch, the conductor's brother, had been stranded nearby after a violin recital, because the roads were dangerously foggy, and the next morning his hostess had mentioned to him and to his unpaid manager and general factotum Frances Dakyns the curiosity of the new opera house just completed at Glyndebourne. There was to be a Mozart festival there in the spring, but as yet neither a conductor nor a stage director had been found for it. Miss Dakyns immediately thought of Adolf's brother Fritz. A visit to Glyndebourne that morning produced an invitation from Christie to Miss Dakyns to make contact with Fritz Busch—and that was for me the beginning of the story.

At first, Frances and Christie planned to perform the Mozart operas accompanied by the Busch Quartet, the organ filling in the wind parts, but Busch persuaded them that an orchestra was a necessity. Then the musicians' union in England vetoed the proposal that the four members of the Busch Quartet should be the leaders of the string sections of the orchestra, and members of the London Symphony were engaged. Frances, who was like Kundry to all the Busches, thus had only one of them at Glyndebourne, and this concentrated her devotion. If Fritz so much as uttered a wish, Frances would bother everybody with her insistence that it *had* to be done just that way; in later years, I would sometimes have to go to Busch himself to get rid of her. Not a musician herself, she had a high standard of taste and a real feeling for quality; she was a wonderful person and an infernal nuisance, God rest her soul. Because I had come to Glyndebourne under the aegis of Busch, and had been of service to him, she wanted to see to it that I was well taken care of, and she appointed herself the person to meet my train.

The winding road from Lewes to Glyndebourne was to become so familiar to me that I can hardly believe there was a first time for seeing it, in Frances's Lancia, which never changed (and was never washed) during the fifteen years I was there.

[ 61 ]

It is still beautiful country, farmland, dotted with the lovely woods in which I used to walk. The house itself was very grand, and I was warmly greeted by Audrey Christie. Her husband was quite pleasant to me. (He called me "Rudi" on the second day I was there. First names being uncommon as a form of address in Europe, I briefly believed I was being made the universal heir; in fact, there were so many strangers around his house he barely knew who I was or what I was doing there.) I was reunited with Busch and Ebert, and with Hans Oppenheim, who turned out to be only one of three musical assistants working on the preparation of the singers. (The others were Alberto Erede, whom Busch had brought to Glyndebourne from a conducting job in Holland and who later conducted for me at the Metropolitan; and Jani Strasser, a Hungarian vocal coach who had been Audrey Christie's singing teacher in Vienna.) And I met for the first time several other people who were to be quite important in my life.

One of them was W. E. Edwards, a self-taught, conservative English businessman who had started with Christie as an accountant in 1920 and was throughout my time at Glyndebourne the chief administrator of all Christie's varied enterprises. Whenever in later years anything would seem completely incomprehensible, it was necessary only to mention it to Edwards, who would either explain it or take care of it. What made Glyndebourne possible was Christie's resources; but what made Christie's resources possible was the organization supplied by Edwards. Always forthright, honorable, and capable, Edwards came to symbolize for me all I most admired in England.

Another stalwart was Jock Gough, a professional backstage boss whom Christie had found at Tunbridge Wells. For years, Gough kept his own kind of absolute order in the physical aspects of Glyndebourne productions, and during the off-season did everything from plumbing to paving for Christie. He was a strong-minded and totally independent fellow. Once when he disapproved of the designs for *Don Giovanni,* he told Christie, "If you're going to do *Don Giovanni* that way, I'm off," and he simply left the theater. It took personal visits from Busch, Ebert, and Christie to his cottage in Ringmer before he could be persuaded to come back to work.

Perhaps the most remarkable of all was Childs, Christie's perfect butler—P. G. Wodehouse could have modeled Jeeves after him. Once in later years when I needed Christie for something and could not find him, I asked Childs where he was, and Childs told me; it was some entirely unexpected, out-of-the-way place. "Childs," I said, "how do you know he is *there?* Did you ask him before he left?" Childs said, "A good butler never asks his master where he is going, but he always knows." On one of the first occasions that I was an overnight guest at Glyndebourne, Childs woke me with that abominable English custom, the early-morning tea, and said, "Breakfast at eight-thirty, sir." I said, "Good morning, Childs. What time is it now?" "Nine o'clock, sir," he said. Among his other services to the household, Childs ran the local boy scout troop. For the opera company, he once acted the role of the deaf-mute in *Die Ent-führung,* and very successfully, too; he explained that he had once worked for a master who was deaf, and had studied all his reactions.

All that, of course, was for the future. On this first evening I dressed for dinner—everyone always dressed for dinner at Glyndebourne—and was seated at a beautiful mahogany table without a tablecloth. Childs served. The food was excellent, and the wine delicious; and it was a happy evening. But there was no room for me in the manor house, and after dinner I walked across the fields to Ringmer, to a charming inn, The Green Man, where I shared a room with Peter Ebert, Carl Ebert's adolescent son.

The next day I went back to Glyndebourne to watch the rehearsals, which were coming along in a rather disorganized fashion. When Edwards had realized that Christie had been serious about this foolishness of a professional opera season, he had decided that some professional theatrical guidance was absolutely necessary, to keep Frances Dakyns and this man Bing far away from making too many outrageous commitments in Christie's name. But the professional he found to give that guidance was Alfred Nightingale, who had been house manager, which meant booking agent, for a Liverpool music hall that happened to be called an opera house. Poor Nightingale was bewildered by all these people. He had never heard of Mozart, let alone *Figaro,* and he had not the vaguest notion of how one organized the preparation of an opera: there were no rehearsal schedules, and everything was being put together *ad hoc.* Fortunately, there was enough time before the opening night: singers had been engaged to report May 1 for an opening night on May 28. In addition to all the coaching sessions individually, the cast of *Figaro* had no fewer than twenty-four three-hour stage rehearsals with Ebert.

It soon became clear that there was nothing for me to do at Glyndebourne. I had come to England looking for work, and work could be found only in London. I took the train there and found a little furnished room at Granville Place, near Selfridges, behind Oxford Street; and I called the people to whom I had an introduction. One was Harold Holt, whom I had met on my previous visit with Piccaver a decade before; he was very friendly, certainly, if any opportunity should offer itself . . . but none did. Another was the Austrian ambassador, Baron George Franckenstein (later to become an English citizen, and Sir George Franckenstein). His brother had been Intendant in Munich, and he knew something about theatrical management. He arranged for me a number of useless introductions, and invited me to lovely parties at the old Embassy in Belgrave Square. Between appointments, I would sit in Hyde Park, reading *The Times* with a dictionary, improving my English. Every few days, to see how things were going and to cheer myself up, I would take the two-hour trip back to Lewes and Frances would drive me to the opera house to watch rehearsals.

Christie had not been able to announce his dates and casts until April, and many people in London scarcely believed that the Festival was real. Everyone was to wear at least black tie, and evening gowns. There would be a special train in midafternoon from Victoria Station for Lewes, where ticket holders would be met by buses. There was a restaurant at the theater—Christie had built it himself—where a meal, with wine, would be served during an intermission, or patrons could dine on the collation they had brought with them, served by their own butler, if they had brought *him*. The gardens of the manor would be open for strolling; the brochure especially recommended "a chain of woodland pools following the course of a Downland stream, leading to coppices carpeted with wild flowers." Tickets were outrageously expensive by the standards of the time—£2, then $10, with a value today of perhaps $30.

That any of this would actually happen never seemed really likely. Yet when the day came the elegant London first-nighters did go to Victoria, dressed as requested (to the amazement of the others in the station), and rode through the countryside to the Sussex Downs; and thanks to Edwards and Frances the buses were there to pick them up, and they saw a wonderful performance of *Figaro*, in Italian (which was then rare), staged with handsome artists all of whom knew precisely what they were to do on the stage at every moment (which is still rare), played under the direction of a great conductor (which is perhaps the most rare of all). Returning to their dressing tables at the end of the performance, the artists found a chilled half bottle of champagne for each, from Mrs. Christie, to allow celebrations to begin immediately. And for once the press was responsive: several of the London papers said that the performances of *Figaro* and especially, the next night, of *Così Fan Tutte* had outpaced Salzburg itself. HMV called and made arrangements to record *Figaro* before the company dispersed; and this recording, now almost forty years old, is still on sale today.

Thanks to the reviews and to the fact that everyone in London society was talking about Glyndebourne, ticket sales for subsequent performances improved, but they had been almost non-existent before: there were only seven passengers on the Glyndebourne special for the first *Così*. That first two-week season averaged less than two hundred seats sold for each of the twelve performances, but the audience grew larger toward the end of the run. Christie's loss was worked out by Edwards at $35,000, which says something about the costs of producing opera to international standards in the 1930s. What was more important to Christie was that he had had a wonderful time, his wife had made a triumph as Susanna, and all the critics had been impressed. Busch and Ebert were asked to return the next year for a four-week season that would add *Die Zauberflöte* and *Die Entführung* to the two Italian operas. Hans Oppenheim was asked to return to work on the musical preparation, and I was re-engaged to be the talent scout to fill all the roles. That job, of course, could not come near supporting us in England, but I liked England—and it was more work than was waiting for me anywhere else. I wrote my wife to come join me. When she arrived, the two of us with Hans Oppenheim and his wife took a summer cottage at a place called Gerrard's Cross, about an hour out from London, and we all relaxed.

# 8

During that rather carefree summer of 1934 we and the Oppen-heims took English lessons from a local girl, and my wife and Hans's wife kept house. We wrote letters busily to possible English employers—I tried publishing houses and bookshops and theatrical agencies—and every so often went up to London for interviews. But it was summer, and nobody expects anything to happen in the summer.

When summer ended my wife and I found a one-room apart-ment in St. John's Wood, modern, with a little kitchenette and bath and central heating—all my time in England I never got used to heating by fireplace, which leaves most of the room cold and damp, and makes those who approach the fire simultaneously hot in front and freezing in back. We had about £250 (then $1,250), and agreed we would stay in England until it was gone. The little apartment was an extravagance: modern and in a good neighborhood, it cost us three guineas ($15.75) a week. My wife fed us both—three meals a day—on about a pound a week, and we never went hungry.

But there was no work. For a while I paid calls on all the West End musical producers on behalf of the delightful Irene Eisinger, who was also more or less stranded in England and did not wish to return to Central Europe; and I did in fact find her a place in a rather short-lived revue staged by the King of Impresarios, Charles B. Cochran. During the run of the show she paid me a small weekly fee, which made a difference. In early 1935 there was also one large fee, a strange story in itself.

Among those who visited us in London that fall was Gottfried Reinhardt, Max Reinhardt's son, who was on his way to Hollywood, where one of his brothers was already working. As he was leaving, at about two in the morning, he asked by the bye if I knew a soprano named Miliza Korjus, whom his brother had mentioned in a recent letter. I said I did; she was a good-looking girl and a singer of quality; and Gottfried went off.

A few weeks later my telephone rang, and the operator said it was a Mr. Thalberg from Hollywood. I said I was Mr. Bing but it had to be some mistake. She assured me it was not a mistake and presently I was talking across the ocean and the continent to the head of M-G-M, the greatest film studio in the world. Mr. Thalberg said he was interested in the services of Miss Korjus for a picture, with options for subsequent pictures, and Mr. Reinhardt had said I knew her. He asked me to approach her with a fantastic offer—I have forgotten the figures, but they were staggering for the 1930s—on the understanding that if she signed I would have acted as her agent and would be entitled to commissions. I said I could not operate that way in this matter, but that if he were prepared to employ me as *his* agent I would be delighted to try to make a deal with the girl—but I didn't understand why he was offering so much money, as I was sure Miss Korjus would never expect nearly so much. He was surprised; reasonable figures did not occur to the Hollywood great in those days. We came to an agreement

[ 68 ]

on what my fee should be, and he added that if I were able to sign Miss Korjus for less than the figures he had mentioned my fee would be higher. The conversation occupied thirty minutes of telephone time across the Atlantic, and I was very impressed.

The next morning I received from Thalberg a cable many pages long, and the London Post Office was impressed—the girl who read it to me suggested that if I was going to do much business on this basis the LPO would be delighted to install a direct line from the cable office to mine. I called Miss Korjus in Berlin and spoke with her husband, identifying myself as representing M-G-M. Her husband sensed an opportunity, and told me that he didn't know whether he could possibly do business with me, because he was in negotiations with UFA, which was the biggest German film studio. I made him repeat the name and pretended never to have heard it before, which shook him.

During the next few weeks, there were several telephone calls back and forth to Berlin, and we reached an agreement—as I remember it, at a figure only slightly more than half of what Thalberg had originally expected to pay. I cabled Thalberg the news and requested contracts for Miss Korjus to sign. They came; I forwarded them to her; she signed them; and Thalberg by cable instructed me to take them to M-G-M's London office. This was a large establishment, with several hundred employees, none of whom had heard a word about the negotiations I was conducting on behalf of their boss. They were dumfounded when I walked in the door, someone they had never seen before, carrying contracts signed by Irving Thalberg and involving a lot of money for a woman in Germany none of them had ever heard of before.

A little more than a year later the film was played in London. It was called *The Great Waltz*, and it was supposed to be about

Johann Strauss and Vienna. Of all the idiotic pictures ever made in Hollywood this must surely have been the most idiotic. It showed sheep and shepherds in the Vienna Woods, where in all history no sheep has ever set foot. There was a scene with Johann Strauss driving through the Woods in a carriage, listening to the birds singing and noting their melodies on his cuff. Finally the carriage arrived at a little inn, the sort of place where one might sometimes find a broken-down piano and an ancient fiddler, but Strauss found a sixty-piece ladies' orchestra which proceeded to play (apparently from his cuffs) the *Tales from the Vienna Woods* . . .

Anyway, it was my first business contact with the United States. The fee was very useful, but my wife and I decided it was luxury money: I bought her a fur coat and myself a car, and we continued to live in our one-room apartment. Miss Korjus stayed in America, by the way, and through most of my time at the Metropolitan there was a small ad every issue in *Opera News,* the publication of the Metropolitan Opera Guild, by which Miss Korjus sold recordings of her own singing. But we never had any further personal contact.

During the early part of 1935 I was in touch with various European talent agencies on behalf of Glyndebourne, and in the course of my letter writing I mentioned to some of the agents I knew best that I might wish to return to Austria if there was a decent job for me there. One of those letters bore fruit, and it was understood that if I returned to Austria the next fall I could count on a responsible if not very attractive position in a concert firm.

Meanwhile, I thought that for this second Glyndebourne season I should try to be closer to the company than I had been the year before. I wrote and offered my services as a stage manager, and I was engaged as assistant producer. Then I discovered that the second season was running into quite serious trouble. A little of it touched me in my work as the talent scout for European singers. Miss Rautawaara, for example, I had signed for Pamina in *The Magic Flute* as well as for the Countess in *Marriage of Figaro*—Mrs. Christie, who had rather thought she would like to sing Pamina, had decided that with a child expected around the first of the year (George Christie, now chairman of the Glyndebourne Trust), she could not make herself ready for what is a pretty demanding role by May 27, which was opening night. But her delivery had been easy and her recovery rapid, and now she wanted Miss Rautawaara to give back Pamina, which our Finnish star would not do. Rather than lose her services as the Countess, the Christies finally decided to keep Miss Rautawaara as Pamina.

Most of the roadblocks that had suddenly risen in the way to the second Glyndebourne season, however, concerned the singers who had originally been hired in England. Some were fighting about salary—the locally recruited members of the cast had been paid considerably less than the artists I signed in Central Europe, and for a second season they wanted substantial increases. But many of the problems were simply matters of delay and inefficiency at Glyndebourne. Neither Nightingale nor Edwards had any notion that if one did not sign singers and musicians some months before their services were needed, they would simply go and sign up elsewhere. It had never occurred to Christie that an artist or player who saw a chance that he might be tapped for Glyndebourne would not hold himself eternally available for that great honor.

The most damaging loss was that of Ina Souez, who was next to irreplaceable as Fiordiligi in *Così Fan Tutte*. Busch, in fact, thought she was completely irreplaceable, and when he learned that she had signed to sing Micaela in *Carmen* at Covent Garden during the weeks when Glyndebourne was to do *Così Fan Tutte*, he wrote to Christie canceling his own participation in the season. Unfortunately, one of Christie's favorite parlor sports was the denunciation of Covent Garden, and Sir Thomas Beecham knew it; no one at Glyndebourne felt safe in approaching him for a favor. Soon after I signed on as stage manager for the coming season, I was asked if I could somehow manage the Souez difficulty for Christie, and it was in this context that I first met Beecham, an impossibly charming and impossibly difficult man, with whom I would later spend many hours, trying to persuade him to link his work with Glyndebourne's. He knew even better than I did, of course, that Fiordiligis were harder to come by than Micaelas, and he agreed, in a very gracious gesture unfortunately regarded at Glyndebourne as nothing more than proper, that when there were schedule conflicts between his *Carmen* and Glyndebourne's *Così* he would permit Miss Souez to give Glyndebourne priority.

Rehearsals began again around May 1 for a season to start May 27, and again the organization was a terrible mess. I remember that on the morning after Busch's arrival he asked Nightingale when he had scheduled the first rehearsal for the ensemble of the Three Ladies, which is the first concerted number in *The Magic Flute,* and the poor general manager did not have the vaguest idea what the conductor was talking about. Though I was really only a stage manager, which is a fairly lowly job—keeping track of props, sequences, entrances and exits, and such—I was increasingly pressed into service to get the days organized and minimize the waste of time.

To be fair to Nightingale, one of his problems was that he had great difficulty understanding Busch's English, which even years later was hard to follow for those who did not know him well. During the rehearsals for *The Magic Flute* there was an amusing blowup—except that it did not seem very amusing while it was happening—that resulted directly from the deficiencies of Busch's English.

Ebert and Hans Oppenheim had been working with the chorus and lesser members of the English cast for some days before Busch arrived, and Ebert in coaching the lesser priests had put special stress on the need to stand absolutely still. For some reason it is much harder for English and American choristers to stand still than it is for Continental choristers, but Ebert had finally drilled the lesson into the head of an unfortunate English bass. Then Busch came, and for some reason felt in a rehearsal that the man involved was not giving his best efforts to his singing. "Work!" he shouted to the bass from his place beside the rehearsal piano. But what came out when he said "Work!" was "Vaurk!"

The poor singer looked at Busch, looked toward the back of the theater where Ebert sat glowering in one of the rear seats, and continued as before. "Vaurk!" Busch shouted again, now genuinely angry, and the bass began to stroll about the stage: Busch was nearer to him than Ebert was, and probably more important, and if Busch wanted him to walk he would walk. Ebert came tearing down the aisle, screaming at the unfortunate singer in English scarcely better than Busch's, and it took almost an hour to calm everybody down so work could resume.

To talk about trouble at Glyndebourne, however, seriously misstates the nature of the experience, which was one of joyous, productive—if incessant—work. Busch himself, who was never weary, set the tone. There were no unions. Often at dinner something would come up relating to that day's rehearsals, and as the port came round, an old bottle with spider webs clinging to it, the ruby liquid poured to the glass through a filter, Busch would say to some of the singers, "Come, let's do it again!" The lights in the theater would be turned back on, and at nine o'clock everyone would return to work. (If there was no work, Busch as likely as not would play four-hand piano duets with one of the other conductors, just to have music.) Everyone was committed, spiritually and physically—there was no earthly reason to be at Glyndebourne unless one wanted to be part of the best operatic production that could be mounted. As Busch put it to the assembled *Magic Flute* company after opening night, Glyndebourne had the advantage that "even work is more attractive than the night life of Lewes."

Always there were the Christies, John sitting in the hall for almost every rehearsal, Audrey onstage or backstage. Between the first and second seasons, Christie had built twenty-four decent dressing rooms and storage areas for the scenery, a greenroom, a second dining room for patrons of the theater with an enlarged kitchen to serve both restaurants, and (the authentic Glyndebourne touch) a special room for the chauffeurs of those who arrived in limousines. One would step outside with Christie during a break in rehearsals, and he would bend down—not easy for him—to pick up some minuscule scrap of weed out of the Glyndebourne lawn. An American visitor once asked him how one could get so perfect a lawn, and he said, "It's easy: just mow it for two hundred years." That sense of quality, the aristocrat's preference for perfection, surrounded all of us at Glyndebourne—that, plus Christie's genius that had started organ businesses and garages and building works, planting something to see how it grows.

The artists were staying in cottages on the estate or at Shelley's Hotel in Lewes, a lovely hotel, extremely comfortable. One thing Nightingale had arranged efficiently was a fleet of cars and chauffeurs to pick up artists and take them to and from Glyndebourne. After a day or two on the spot, even the coldest-hearted singer was thoroughly charmed by the place, and by Audrey Christie. For Nina and myself, this was the first year of close contact with the family: as assistant producer, I was entitled to a room at the manor house, and we spent the two months of rehearsal and season at that beautiful place in the spring.

At Glyndebourne everybody did anything that had to be done, and the job of stage manager turned out to encompass a number of little chores. For *The Magic Flute*, for example, I operated one of the three dragons Ebert had chasing Tamino (instead of the usual one dragon: with three, there was a dragon for each of the Queen's ladies to kill). Mine was the third to be killed, and I thought I made it die rather touchingly, but then as later the press took no notice of my efforts. I had occasion to be grateful for this neglect, however, when *Così Fan Tutte* was revived, and I served as a backstage dresser. In this opera the dresser has one big moment, when he must work fast. The sound of the military chorus is heard, announcing the return of the lovers from the war; and the two men, who have been disguised as Albanians, must dart offstage, peel off their mustaches, and put on new jackets to return as their old selves in about forty seconds. I was to dress Fassbänder, and I did, pulling off his old jacket and slipping the new one over his arms. Unfortunately, I forgot to get the clothes hanger out before putting the jacket on him, so he went staggering back onstage with a new kind of brace across his shoulders, which somewhat damaged my relations with our leading baritone.

The hit of the season was *Die Entführung*, with Irene Eisinger a delightful Blonde and Ivar Andresen, with whom we had worked in Berlin, a most satisfactory Osmin. (Ebert himself played the non-singing role of Bassa Selim.) Altogether, there were twenty-five performances, more than twice as many as the first season, plus Sunday concerts, at one of which Rudolf Serkin played a Mozart concerto. Christie's losses rose from $35,000 to $50,000—but that was a reduction on the loss per performance, and he had no doubts at all about continuing his Festival. Nina and I stayed after the end of the season to help with the closing-up work and the preliminary plans for the next year. During the course of this season, however, Edwards had decided that he needed a general manager much more experienced than Nightingale in solving problems of opera—and the problems of Busch and Ebert. Without my realizing it, he had been watching me as I helped organize the rehearsals. A few days after the end of the season, he and Christie asked me whether I would accept the post of general manager of the Glyndebourne Festival, with a permanent office in London and year-round employment.

I remember that Christie offered me £700 a year ($3,500), and I asked for £750. We compromised on £720—how odd it is to think today that £20, $100, made such a difference then. I have the contract, dated August 7, 1935, in which it is agreed that I should serve John Christie Limited as "General Manager of Glyndebourne Festival Opera House near Lewes in the County of Sussex for the term of ONE YEAR from the First day of September One thousand nine hundred and thirty-five." It was a tough contract—I could be fired at any time by resolution of the board of directors "without any previous notice or payment in lieu of notice." But there was no reason to worry: professional management would do Glyndebourne more good than Christie or Edwards could imagine.

Since moving to St. John's Wood, my wife and I had passed every day a handsome new block of flats called Florence Court, looking rather wistfully at it and wondering whether we would ever live in any place so grand. Shortly after signing the Glyndebourne contract I took a lease on an apartment in Florence Court, giving us a sitting room as well as a bedroom, and a full-sized kitchen. I notified the agency in Vienna that I was no longer interested in returning to Austria. Edwards found an office for lease in Trafalgar Square; and Glyndebourne and I were in business.

# 9

There was plenty to do to put Glyndebourne on a proper footing, especially in the areas of financial planning and publicity. I will take some of the credit for the fact that although our season lengthened to as many as thirty-eight performances, the deficit never again touched $50,000, and for one year, 1937, we even showed a profit. I must admit, though, that the major source of our profit was the sale of wines in the restaurant. A refugee wine merchant, a Dr. Loeb, persuaded Christie that Mozart deserved the very best in German wines, and that the audience for Mozart would be willing to pay for them. Sales often exceeded 100 bottles in an evening, though Glyndebourne at its largest never held more than 450 seats. Christie had to build a new cellar to hold the supply. He became an official adviser to the King on German wines as a result of Glyndebourne's reputation in this area, and during the war he sold the cellar at auction—feeling that postwar patrons would not be able to afford such luxuries—for almost $100,000. My own palate was both educated and spoiled by Christie's German wines: to this day, I can drink nothing but the best, which is far too expensive for a mere general manager of an opera house, let alone a retired general manager of an opera house.

In addition to the budget, I felt it necessary to organize Glyndebourne's publicity and selling efforts. Despite excellent notices and constant appearance in society pages and the like, Glyndebourne was not selling out. It was, of course, an expensive evening, and the reception of anyone who came dressed in something other than evening clothes was decidedly chilly. But people were more used to wearing evening clothes before the war (especially in England) than they are today; rental firms abounded in London. It was not necessary to patronize the restaurants; indeed, some of society's leading figures packed picnic baskets and ate in the parking lot. We established a continuing effort to convince London concertgoers and opera patrons that Glyndebourne was for them, too, not just for the snobs. I remember hiring sandwich men to parade in front of Queen's Hall, advertising the availability of tickets to Glyndebourne. We organized a subscription series, which Glyndebourne had not offered before, and sent out mailings. Starting in 1936, we also permitted the BBC to broadcast one act of several of our productions, setting the music in a description of Glyndebourne, complete with country sounds, that made a visit seem most attractive. In the 1936 season there were in fact many fewer open seats at Glyndebourne than there had been before. With sales up, Christie took the further gamble of enlarging the house to 450 seats for the 1937 season; of course, he loved any excuse for building.

For the 1936 season, my first as general manager, we added *Don Giovanni* to the four Mozart operas of the previous season, and there were many changes of cast. Miss Eisinger was again singing for Charles Cochran in an Adelphi review, and Fassbänder was ill. Busch engaged the Australian John Brownlee, who had been singing in Paris, as our Don Giovanni; Mariano Stabile came from Italy to sing a Figaro of grace and elegance; and the Englishman Roy Henderson sang Guglielmo in *Così Fan Tutte*. Our outstanding additions, however, were in the lower voices—Alexander Kipnis as a startlingly resonant Sarastro in *The Magic Flute*, and Salvatore Baccaloni as Leporello in *Don Giovanni*.

Baccaloni was unquestionably the hit of this and the succeeding seasons. Fat, jovial, and I think intelligent—I had no way to know: there was no language in which we could communicate— he brought to Glyndebourne the blessing of absolutely perfect comic timing, and a plummy voice of incomparable richness. He could be a trouble to directors, conductors, and general managers. For four seasons a regular feature of my life at Glyndebourne was the arrival of a furious Baccaloni in my office, sputtering streams of rapid Italian despite his knowledge that I did not understand a word of the language, furious about something that had just happened. I would listen until he seemed to have completed what he had to say, then reach into the desk and give him a five-pound note. That always seemed to be the right reply, and he would go away content.

In 1936, however, he was cast not only as Leporello but also as Osmin in *Die Entführung*. It proved impossible for him to memorize a role in German, and we had to take emergency measures to keep him going. The cuffs of his costume, changed when he came offstage, were made into a mass of cues and lines for him to sing, and we stationed prompters in both wings and behind the scenery to supplement the efforts of the prompter in the box. What we needed, it now seems clear, was the Tele-prompter device that arrived with television to help politicians recite *their* lines; then every time Baccaloni rolled his eyes he could have read what he was to sing next. Unfortunately, this invention was still in the future, and what we had to work with was insufficient to our problem. We did not ask Baccaloni to sing a German role again.

Among the events of the 1936 season was a pair of performances—the only ones before the war—conducted by someone other than Busch, who loved to conduct, never got tired, and felt (not unreasonably) that the audience came expecting him. But this year Hans Oppenheim took over two evenings of *The Magic Flute.* They were not very well received, and the situation was rather awkward, because no such opportunity was given to Alberto Erede, whose position as a coach and assistant conductor was equal to Oppenheim's on our organization chart. Erede, who later conducted for me at the Metropolitan, never accused me of influencing anyone to help Oppenheim, which was generous of him, because he knew Oppenheim and I were good friends—not only had we shared the house at Gerrard's Cross after the first Glyndebourne season, but we had known each other in Darmstadt, Berlin, and Teplitz, and had even lived in the same pension in Vienna during the hard times between jobs. The task of keeping Erede reasonably happy was to some extent mine, and I have always been pleased to think I succeeded in it.

Erede's difficulties were complicated by the general and not unreasonable feeling that Glyndebourne was very German. Christie himself was immensely Germanophile, and because he and his wife were totally non-political the fact that Germany was now governed by Adolf Hitler did not change his feelings in the least. In the fall of 1936 Audrey sang in Germany, which was not well received by some of us who had left that country on principle. There was even worse trouble in early 1939 when she sang in Hamburg and Berlin despite representations from myself, Busch, and Ebert: Spike Hughes's history of Glyndebourne quotes me as having written to ask whether Audrey realized that "she would not just metaphorically, but literally, be shaking hands with murderers." Her acceptance of an invitation to sing in post-Anschluss Salzburg in 1939, however, was withdrawn after Christie consulted the British Foreign Office and learned—much to his surprise—that his friends in the government felt such an appearance by Audrey would be damaging to the future of Glyndebourne.

The feeling that Glyndebourne was very German surfaced a little unpleasantly in 1937, which was a coronation year. Christie in public speeches had invited British composers to submit operas to his staff and learn whether any of them was up to Glyndebourne's standards, but there were no takers, and much grumbling about the fact that Glyndebourne's standards appeared to be German rather than English standards. Busch thought that for the coronation year perhaps Verdi's *Falstaff* should be added to the five Mozart operas, but I could not see how we could do it with the resources at our command. If we were to expand from Mozart, Christie liked the idea of doing Donizetti's *Don Pasquale*, which had a grand part for his wife and a starring role for Baccaloni—and which had been a considerable hit at Salzburg under the direction of Bruno Walter. When the decision was made to repeat the five Mozart operas for the 1937 season, Christie proposed that in honor of the coronation a greatly increased number of British singers should be employed, but Busch and Ebert refused the names proposed to them. It was Christie's opera house and Christie's money, but he had signed away ultimate control in artistic matters to his producer and conductor, and in the end he had to yield. Then Audrey suffered some sort of throat infection and could not sing in that season, which was a sad one for Christie—somewhat redeemed by the fact that, having no new productions and a larger house, we made money. At the end of the 1937 season I was re-engaged at a considerable increase in salary—£1,200, or $6,000 a year.

For the 1938 season Christie won his fight to do *Don Pasquale,* but Busch demanded in return some other non-Mozartean work of greater specific gravity. The choice fell on Verdi's *Macbeth,* never before performed in England, which appealed to Christie in part because the Queen had been born in Glamis, Macbeth's castle, and could perhaps be lured to Glyndebourne for the opera. (In fact, she agreed to come, but her mother died a few days before the performance, depriving us of royal patronage.) Ebert arranged to have Caspar Neher come to Glyndebourne to duplicate on a smaller scale the sets he had designed for Berlin. Casting *Macbeth* gave Busch terrible problems, not entirely unlike the problems I would have later in New York. His first two choices for Lady Macbeth canceled out despite signed contracts, and only ten days before opening night I had to scour the world by cable and telephone to find a soprano. Vera Schwarz, a Yugoslavian soprano who later settled in New York (where she became Risë Stevens' teacher), volunteered, learned the work en route to England, and made a great success—though she could not reach the D-flat in the sleepwalking scene, and the note had to be supplied from the wings by a chorister.

Before that opening night, I went through a rather different part of the experience of being Germanic in the 1930s. The Czech government was sponsoring some sort of international arts conference—the details are not important now and I do not believe they were important then—and thanks again to the intervention of Paul Eger, who was still in Prague, invitations were sent to Christie and myself to represent Glyndebourne. Christie, of course, was not interested; but the occasion, in March 1938, offered me an almost free trip to Vienna to see my family—the Czech government was flying me to Prague and the only part of the expense I would have to bear myself was the round trip between Prague and Vienna during a day devoted to ccremonials at the conference.

As I was about to board the bus for the airport at the London terminal, an official of the Czech Embassy saw me and asked me to take a document. Among the guests going to the conference was Sir Hugh Sealy, M.P., and the Czech government had issued him a special *Grenzempfehlung*, a V.I.P. border pass, to make sure he was treated with due respect on his arrival in Czechoslovakia. Apparently Sir Hugh had gone straight to Croydon rather than taking the bus from London, and the embassy official asked me to give the document to him when I saw him at the airport. But Sir Hugh did not turn up at Croydon either —he had decided at the last minute not to make the trip—and I had his border pass.

The day I chose for my trip to Vienna turned out to be the day Hitler's army annexed Austria for the Third Reich. Through a friend in the government, my sister got an hour or two of advance notice of what was to happen, and insisted that I get out at once. I rushed to the railroad station, and got on a train the like of which I had never seen before: people desperate to escape Austria had jammed the carriages so that they were literally hanging out of the windows. I barely pressed myself inside a *wagon-lit*. As we rode through Austria to the Czech border the Nazi flags were hanging from homes and municipal buildings all along the route, and even the railroad officials were already wearing Nazi badges. No doubt there were many Austrians who did not welcome the arrival of Hitler, but my experiences on that day gave me a very cynical view of the later decision to treat Austria as a "liberated" country rescued from Hitler rather than as a deliberate, conscious collaborator with the Nazi menace.

On the train we were told that the Austrians would do nothing to keep people from leaving, but that the Czechs had closed the border on their side. It was true: when we arrived at the Czech border the Czech guards and military men dragged off the train everyone with an Austrian passport. God knows what eventually happened to those victims of barbarous governments. I saw what was going on, hid my Austrian passport, and when the border guards came to me I showed them Sir Hugh's pass. They tried to question me, but I pretended not to speak a word of German—I could not even understand the German word for passport. They consulted with each other and decided that even though the border was sealed they had better not start a fight with a British M.P. Having ridden to the border in a train so crowded people could not move at all in the corridors, I continued to Prague in a sleeping car that was absolutely deserted except for myself. When I returned to England I wrote to Sir Hugh to thank him for his unwitting help, and to apologize for using his documents. Sir Hugh was delighted with the story, and wrote back that the only thing he would ask in return was that whenever he wanted to get in at Glyndebourne he should be allowed to use my name.

Toscanini, who was personally friendly with Busch and of course violently anti-Fascist, had canceled his Salzburg season, and I returned to London to find feverish efforts being made to extend our season and have Toscanini come to conduct the *Don Pasquale* and possibly a new production of Verdi's *Falstaff*. Fortunately, nothing came of these proposals, or of similar proposals that were more seriously discussed the next year, Toscanini in the interim having come to Glyndebourne for a performance of *Macbeth* and having been very pleased with Ebert's staging. For all its wonderful qualities, I doubt that Glyndebourne was big enough to take either Toscanini's personality or his musical conceptions.

The 1939 season duplicated that of 1938—Mozart's three Italian operas, plus *Don Pasquale* and *Macbeth*—preceded by rather scratch performances of *Figaro* and *Don Giovanni* in Antwerp and Brussels using the second-string, "cover" cast of English singers. The 1939 season ran from June 1 through July 15, with thirty-eight performances, and after the final curtain fell on what was to be the last performance of opera in that theater for the next seven years, Christie came before the curtain to utter an idiosyncratic valedictory. There was, he told the audience, "serious news." With rumors of war in all the papers, the audience stirred uneasily. But the news which Christie felt could not wait until Glyndebourne's patrons returned home was news from Lord's, not from Downing Street. For the first time since 1908, the annual Eton-Harrow cricket match had been won by Harrow.

All my year was busy with Glyndebourne—engaging the artists, planning the rehearsals and the season, having the tickets printed, looking after the catering arrangements, organizing the box office, fighting with the railroad about the train arrangements, seeing to the bus service from Lewes to the theater, making sure our artists would have the accommodations they required, on Christie's estate or in Lewes, and so forth. Many of the pleasures came from working with Busch and Ebert in the artistic end, watching them get twelve weeks' worth of work out of the four weeks of rehearsals we actually had. To see Ebert give each member of the chorus his or her own stage personality, to be carried through from scene to scene and reflected in every gesture of the hand, every inflection of the head, was to learn something about the theatrical possibilities of opera that many directors to this day (not to mention critics) have never even begun to understand. To watch Busch work with an orchestra, using his personal blend of firmness and kindly humor, was to learn something about artistic leadership that only a master can teach. One of the favorite stories at Glyndebourne dealt with Busch's very first orchestral rehearsal, when he raised his baton, then dropped his arms to his sides and before anyone had played a note said to the men in mock reproach, and thickly accented English, "Already is too loud."

Yet most of what I remember about Glyndebourne centers around Christie and a way of life never possible anywhere but in England and now, I suppose, quite impossible even there. Artistically, Christie was a total innocent, but never without opinions: even if it had not been his money, he would have felt that his position in life entitled him to opinions. I remember being with him when he first saw the Neher backdrop for the second scene in *Macbeth*, with a staircase leading up into black nothingness. "Rudi," Christie said, "where does that staircase *lead*? It leads to nothing. Where is the bathroom?"

I said, "It doesn't matter."

Christie shook his head. "But it *leads* nowhere," he repeated. And he continued to be concerned about where the painted staircase should lead, long after opening night.

My wife and I spent many weekends at Glyndebourne, at all seasons of the year, drinking in this English country house atmosphere, some of which could have come out of a play. One morning, I remember, some guests and a number of county people, one of them a general, were sitting about at breakfast when Childs, Christie's butler, came in and said, "I'm sorry to disturb you, sir, but the cook is dead." There was a moment's uncomfortable silence, broken by the general, who said, "Under the circumstances, do you think I could have another sausage?"

People were not admitted late to Glyndebourne productions, and only the brave tried to leave early—Christie kept the lights out in the halls until the singers had been given their due at the final curtain. He would sit in his box (the only box in the theater, seating twelve) through every performance all season long, wearing white tie, hugely enjoying himself. He and his wife had frequent fights, most often because he was doing something she regarded as not quite proper—and often she had both custom and logic on her side. One evening it was very hot in the theater, and Christie, having walked over to the house during the first intermission, took scissors out of his pocket when he returned to his seat, and to his wife's horror cut off at the elbow the sleeves of his full dress jacket and his shirt.

He always assumed that normal people must be much like himself, and must know more or less what he knew. During the war we were out for a walk together on his grounds, Christie carrying his pug dog—he always had a pug dog; this one was named Bimperl, after Mozart's dog. We met some soldiers, also idly walking, and Christie greeted them in a most civil manner, then asked them if they knew where they were. The fact was that they didn't; they were in cantonment, part of the force guarding the southern coast of England, and of course they had never heard of Glyndebourne, which was visible on the rise of the nearby hill. Christie graciously undertook to explain: "*That*," he said, pointing to his manor house and theater, "is Mozart's house."

"Ah, yes, sir," said one of the soldiers.

Then Christie pointed to the pug playing at my feet. "And that," he added grandly, "is Mozart's dog."

The soldiers then knew who I was, of course. "Very pleased to meet you, sir," one of them said to me.

It was during the war that Christie and I came to know each other really well. Nina was at Oxford and Audrey had gone to America with the Christie children, and we were living alone in that part of the manor house which had not been turned into a nursery. There was supposed to be a ghost in the house, and Christie did not like to sit up nights alone. He would detail for me his plans to take over and improve British musical life, or talk about his wife and children, very rarely about the past.

He was always unself-conscious, even about his fantastic

physical strength. Once our way along a narrow road was blocked by a baby tank that had tipped into a ditch. Three soldiers were trying to right it again, so it could proceed on its now useless treads. Christie left his car and came up to them to inquire what their problem was. They told him, and he simply stepped into the ditch and *singlehanded* lifted the tank back onto the road.

Perhaps because of his strength, though I sometimes thought the cause was a certain lack of imagination, he was also absolutely fearless. We rode to London together on the train once in a while in those early war years, and he would insist on taking a no-smoking third-class carriage. Once there was a large, rather ugly man smoking in the next seat. Christie in his best Oxford accent asked the man to stop smoking, pointing out that it was a no-smoking compartment, and when the man ignored him Christie took the cigarette from between the man's fingers and ground it out under his foot. I continued to read my newspaper assiduously.

Socially, too, he was fearless. The newspapers noted that occasionally he wore tennis shoes with his white tie. He had injured an eye in a game when a boy, and as a man he had the eye removed surgically and a glass eye substituted. He told everyone about the glass eye, and indeed recommended the removal of an eye to one and all as a way to improve the health of the rest of the body. A mutual friend told me that when the Queen Mother came to visit Glyndebourne Christie took his eye out to show it to her. The closest I ever saw to such a gesture came when he had an attack of lumbago during the war, and rode the train to London with a hot-water bottle tucked in against his side. As we left the train at Victoria, he calmly reached into his clothes, removed the hot-water bottle, and before the startled gaze of our companions in the compartment poured its contents onto the platform.

His fights with everyone else in English musical life are subject for the next chapter, because they did not seriously affect my own work until after the war. But there was a time during the war when I bribed the postmaster at Lewes to deliver to me all the letters Christie wrote to the organization that would later become the Arts Council, and especially to its chairman, Lord Keynes, with whom he had some feud probably dating back to their Eton days. He was tactless and crude, and when his wife was absent he could be megalomaniac. But often he was right, and all his boasting came back to the fact that he had built Glyndebourne and nobody else could have done it; and on that matter he was entirely right.

# 10

Anschluss had made Austrian passports invalid, and instructions had gone out that all holders of such passports should apply to the German Embassy for German passports. I would not do that, of course, and arrangements were made at the Home Office to give me some temporary papers that legitimized my residence in England, though they left me in a condition of virtual statelessness. The fifth anniversary of my arrival occurred in spring 1939, and I immediately applied to become a British subject. Sometime in August, I was granted an interview, and left it with reason to believe that my application for naturalization would be approved; but it was still pending when the war came and the processing of such applications was suspended.

In the meantime, all my family had left Austria. My sister and her son (who later became a captain in the British Army) were living in England, and my two brothers went to France. (Years later, near the end of the war, I would hear on the short-wave radio a call on the Austrians to surrender, broadcast by an anonymous leader of the Maquis—and would with an indescribable start recognize the voice of my brother Robert, from whom we had not heard in four years.) Between us, my sister and I brought my parents to England, and settled them as paying guests in a home atop a hill in Lewes, near enough to Glyndebourne so that I could walk over and see them. They came in time to attend the performances in our 1939 Festival, which delighted them.

The first weeks after the close of that season were occupied with the usual process of preliminary scheduling and budgeting for the next year, in which we planned to add *Carmen* to the repertory—in fact, before the plans for a 1940 season had to be canceled I was in touch with, I believe I had actually signed, Risë Stevens to be both our heroine in *Carmen* and our Cherubino in *Figaro*. Once the 1939 season had been packed away and 1940 sensibly projected, my wife and I took off for a seaside resort in Devon, for our vacation. We were there when the war broke out, and we drove quickly back to Glyndebourne.

During the Munich crisis, Edwards had volunteered Glyndebourne as an evacuation center for London children in the event of war: a manor as large as Christie's, not far from the coast, would otherwise almost certainly be taken over by the military. The day after Nina and I returned to Glyndebourne, the buses arrived from London; and some three hundred children and seventy-two adults from south London—the children ranging in age from upper-nursery-school down to ten days— were dumped on the Glyndebourne lawn. There were not enough rooms for so many, of course—and nowhere near enough bathrooms. I raced to Woolworth's in Lewes, and asked the shop assistant, "Do you keep chambers?" She said the store did have chamber pots available, and I said, "Give me six dozens, please." It made quite a sensation.

In addition to sleeping and feeding and toilet arrangements

for our new arrivals, we had to prepare the house for wartime, which meant blackout curtains on hundreds of windows and skylights painted black. Fortunately, the Christies were at their Devon home, not at Glyndebourne. Edwards made representations in London, and many children were sent on elsewhere, until our population stabilized at one hundred children (all of nursery-school age) and about thirty-five adults to look after them. It was still a full house, but what with the many dressing rooms and theater spaces as well as the manor, the children had place to live and to play.

This was the time of the "phony war"; the fighting was over in Poland and had not begun elsewhere. Perhaps there could be a restricted 1940 season. My wife and I returned to London and to the Glyndebourne office there, and I began sketching out the prospects for a two-week June season offering two Mozart operas. Then our lives were immensely complicated by an unexpected order that all enemy aliens—and we were technically enemy aliens—would be interned, even though most of them were more violently anti-Nazi than any Englishman was. Every morning we telephoned our friends, and sighed with relief when they picked up the phone, proving they were still living at home. Edwards arranged matters so that we were reasonably safe from arrest in London, and also protected my parents, whose situation was more vulnerable. The house they were in was quite prominent, and if so much as a chink of light escaped between the blackout curtains some of the natives of the Sussex Downs were sure these foreigners were giving flashlight signals across the Channel to Hitler personally.

As the prospects for any 1940 season began to vanish, Audrey decided to keep herself and the Glyndebourne spirit busy by means of a tour of *The Beggar's Opera*, a work in which she had starred in America before coming to England. I put this production together, hiring John Gielgud to direct and Michael

Redgrave, who had never sung onstage before, to play opposite Audrey as the bandit Macheath. Roy Henderson, who had sung the Mozart baritone roles for us, undertook Peachum. Frederick Austin conducted, making his own orchestrations of some of the old folk songs and seventeenth- and eighteenth-century art songs. I was given special dispensation to travel with the company, though as an enemy alien I was required to register at the police station wherever we might go. There were theaters to be checked out and booked, hotel accommodations to be reserved, advertising to be placed—Glyndebourne and I were in a new business.

The six-week tour started toward the end of January in Brighton, and wended its way north to Edinburgh, which my wife and I had seen briefly a few years before at the end of a motor tour to the Lake Country. I noted on this trip—and so did Audrey—that the castle on the hill had a Salzburg flavor; and we admired both King's Theatre, where our operetta played, and Usher Hall, where the Scottish Orchestra gave concerts. Even the living conditions were not bad, especially by comparison with Manchester, where our accommodations had been filthy and ill-served.

At the end of the tour we took our production to London, where it played at the Haymarket until almost the end of May; the company also recorded the work for HMV (the recordings were issued in the United States by RCA Victor, and taught many Americans *The Beggar's Opera*). By then Redgrave was acceptable enough as a singer to be recorded in the role, a remarkable accomplishment for an actor.

Now the war became our lives: a week after the last performance of *The Beggar's Opera*, the evacuation of Dunkirk began. Glyndebourne's London office was closed. In July Audrey Christie and the children went off to Canada. I went to Glyndebourne to see what help I could be there, and to be near

[ 93 ]

my parents. My wife went to Oxford and stayed with Gertie von Hofmannsthal, the poet's widow; for some reason we had the belief that there was a deal between England and Germany, by which neither Heidelberg nor Oxford would ever be bombed. But when the bombing really began, in September, we were both back in London, spending our nights in the hallways with the other tenants of Florence Court.

Where one spent time during the bombings was a matter of personal taste. Christie himself, if he was in London, often went up onto roofs or into the streets to observe the spectacle. My wife and I at no time ever entered an air raid shelter—we thought we would be uncomfortable so far underground. On the other hand, ours was a top-floor apartment, and the sound of shrapnel from the anti-aircraft shells hitting on the roof made an uncomfortable obbligato to a night at home. Bombs were unpredictable in their effects. Walking the streets, one could see houses with upper floors entirely destroyed and lower floors unharmed—and also houses with the lower stories blasted and the upper floors apparently untouched. For some reason, we decided to wait out the bombings in the second-floor hallway. Houses around us were destroyed; ours shook a few times from the concussion of a nearby bomb, but was never harmed. For me, the horrors of this time were compounded by unemployment, being an enemy alien, worrying that I or my friends would suddenly be hauled off to an internment camp.

What rescued me from this situation was a telephone call from Tyrone Guthrie, then running the Old Vic, which included the Sadler's Wells Ballet and Opera. (Lilian Baylis had founded all of them and run them all; and it seemed entirely natural then that they should be managed jointly, though nobody would think so today.) Guthrie needed someone to help handle the work, and knew I needed a job. The opera had closed down, perhaps temporarily, but the ballet was in being,

[ 94 ]

touring the southwestern part of the country to keep spirits up, with an administrative base at Dartington Hall in Devonshire. This was not far from the water, and thus a "protected area"; a good deal of string-pulling was necessary to get me a permit to live and work there. But it was done, and my wife and I went off to the southwest, to what turned out to be a dull if necessary job of keeping accounts straight and plans sensible for a group of touring dancers far away. I cannot say I enjoyed the work, but I must admit it was a pleasure to sleep through the night in one's own bed.

Guthrie himself had taken the Old Vic to the north of England, where he set up headquarters in the town of Burnley while the company toured the industrial midlands. One day I got a call from him, asking me to come up to Burnley. He thought it was a simple matter, and I did not disillusion him, but in fact it was quite an undertaking. Police permits were necessary for me to do anything. Train service in that winter when England stood alone was anything but reliable; sections of track were bombed out, and military trains took priority, pushing passenger trains onto sidings for lengthy delays. I had to change trains at Manchester, which meant going from one station to another in the middle of an air raid—I remember running through the streets, holding my little suitcase over my head in hopes that it would block the chunks of metal that were falling all around me.

When I got to Burnley, Tony picked me up and took me to the house he and his wife had rented, where I remember being colder than I had ever been before or have ever been since— the north of England, in the winter, in wartime, in a blackout. There was a tiny little fire glowing in the grate, giving off almost no heat. I remember Mrs. Guthrie going to the fire and putting something on it, and hearing myself say sadly, "That looks pretty final"—as indeed it was, for whatever she had put on the fire put it out entirely, and we could not start it up again. But what Tony had to say to me warmed me almost as much as a central-heating system.

At that low point of the war, with that combination of madness and courage that was Tony Guthrie's genius, he had decided to revive the Sadler's Wells Opera, which was considered the national opera—Covent Garden was for the snobs. The people needed opera, and the company could tour all the cities, playing in music halls or movie theaters or on factory floors, wherever. Guthrie had asked me to come to Burnley to discuss how this project could be accomplished, and to ask me to be its managing director. For two or three days in that cold little house we discussed how a wartime opera company could be managed. I told him from the beginning that I thought the prospects for reviving opera exceedingly dim, and that I simply knew I would not be acceptable as the man to run it—after all, I was an enemy alien. But he brushed all this aside, and as I recall the mad project was still a possibility when I retraced my route through Manchester on the way back to Dartington. Of course, his board of trustees turned down the whole idea: not only was the Opera not to be revived, but the touring ballet was to be shut down. My job at Dartington came to an end; Nina returned to Gertie von Hofmannsthal in Oxford, and I went to Glyndebourne, simply because there was no better place to go.

Christie had been at his family's estates in Devon, with nothing to do and apparently almost nobody to talk to. When he heard I was at Glyndebourne he decided to move there. He was a pathetically lost man, waiting for letters from his wife and reading them aloud to everyone—to Edwards, to me, to the gardener, to the cook. He had nothing to occupy his time—except for *The Times,* he did not read—and he had strings of grievances against the world that he wanted someone to hear. He also, fortunately, had a vision, a National Council of Music that

11. With John Christie in Glyndebourne office, 1937

12. With Carl Ebert at Glyndebourne, 1937

13. With Pip I in London home

14. Nina Bing with Pip I in London

15. Audrey Mildmay
as Zerlina,
Glyndebourne

16. At Glyndebourne
during the war

would take over the production of musical performances in England and raise them from what he considered their intolerably amateurish level (everywhere but at Glyndebourne). Foreseeing that Glyndebourne itself might be beyond his resources to sustain in the postwar world (among his grievances was the intolerable burden of taxes in wartime), he was also trying to start a Glyndebourne Society, which would raise money now, invest it in war bonds, guarantee the future of his theater, and repay the donors of today with tickets tomorrow. He wrote to Rab Butler, then president of the national Board of Education, and actually had a meeting with him, to propose a Society of a million members at £10 each, the Cabinet to lead the way by taking personal subscriptions themselves. He wrote to Anthony Eden, then Foreign Secretary, to solicit his support for an international Glyndebourne, to start off almost immediately in Canada, backed by a National Council of Music with members in America and Canada. "This scheme," he wrote, according to Blunt's biography, "gives Roosevelt and the Federal Government just what they want . . ."

I was to be a participant in all of this, of course. At one point, Christie drew up a detailed plan for a single management of Covent Garden, Sadler's Wells, and Glyndebourne, with myself to run them all. Oddly, his plans in this direction did bear some fruit. Among those he brought into the meetings at which he outlined these visions was the music publishing firm of Boosey & Hawkes, and it was out of Christie's dinners that Boosey & Hawkes developed their own plans, realized shortly after the war, to buy and operate Covent Garden. But the sort of thing Christie had in mind was actually taking form elsewhere, under the leadership of his old enemy Lord Keynes, and while Christie's schemes faded the Arts Council was born.

It was during this period that Christie and I often traveled to London together. There were few trains, and we would leave the house early in the morning, when it was still dark. At first I was not permitted to use my car at all, then special permission was won for me to drive between Glyndebourne and Lewes, and I would feel my way along the familiar roads in the dark. When Christie drove, of course, he never worried about headlights—he would blaze through the strictest blackout. He was not concerned about Glyndebourne being bombed; with that political idiocy that was one of his unshakable characteristics, he once wrote his wife that he was perfectly safe at Glyndebourne because "Hitler respects us." But I had to be ultra-careful never to show a light.

Most of the time in those desperate months of early 1941 I just stayed at Glyndebourne. My wife joined me and helped out in the nursery. In the afternoons we would walk across the downs to Lewes to see my parents; in the evenings we would sit with Christie and some of the more intelligent nurses in the darkened organ room, while Christie played records, especially Glyndebourne's own, with his wife's voice, but also others. I remember once trying to explain the first act of *Rosenkavalier* to this group of rather starched upper-middle-aged English nurses; it was a difficult assignment.

Of course, one was not paid for such assignments. I was making myself as useful as I could be to Christie, but there really was nothing he could pay me for—there was no Glyndebourne Festival for me to be general manager of. Though we had virtually no daily expenses at Glyndebourne, I had to pay for my parents' accommodations and for our flat in London. When I went to London, I would look about for work, but it all seemed hopeless. As the time passed I grew increasingly depressed about the war, my work, our future.

Then quite out of the blue there arrived a letter from Spedan Lewis, chairman of John Lewis Partnership, a huge organization of London and provincial department stores. Mr. and Mrs.

Lewis had been great Glyndebourne patrons before the war, and I had come to know them. He now wrote to say that he assumed I had no work for Glyndebourne at this time; would I consider working for him? Indeed I would consider it; I replied by return mail and soon went up to London to meet with someone on his staff. And very soon thereafter I was, much to my own surprise, in the department store business.

# 11

The store to which I was sent was Peter Jones, an elegant, modern establishment on Sloane Square near Belgravia. It was one of the first buildings in London to have glass curtain walls, the corners rounded in the 1930s style. My job was menial but annoyingly difficult. Clothes rationing had just been introduced in England, and coupons had been issued to everyone. New regulations were sent out by the government every day to tell people how many coupons they would need in addition to money to buy the things they wanted. I was assigned a tiny desk on the ground floor, to which customers could come to ask about the new restrictions—"Yes, madam, stockings are four coupons"; or "No, madam, I'm sorry, but a slip is six coupons"—all day, every day. The regulations were confusing, and it was often hard to find the information. Eventually I devised for my own use a little booklet which categorized all items of clothing in a way that made it much easier to find the answers to customer questions. This booklet became the "standard work" for all branches of the Partnership, and I was taken out of Peter Jones and put to work as assistant to the director of selling for all the John Lewis stores.

The director to whom I was assistant was Sebastian Earl, a highly intelligent and cultured Englishman—and a dominating presence, six and a half feet tall, handsome, always well dressed. He, too, had been a Glyndebourne patron, and we had a strange relationship, both of us ill at ease in our respective roles. There were nearly twenty stores reporting to Seb Earl, from London and the provinces, and he kept on top of all of them, inspecting every department in every store and receiving regular reports from every department manager. It was my job to follow through on these reports, many of which dealt with what seemed to me very trivial matters. There was, for example, a Partnership policy that we would never be "knowingly undersold," but I could not get excited at the terrible tidings that a store in Streatham was charging tuppence ha'penny less than we charged to clean a pair of gloves.

I was very unhappy in this job, and Earl no doubt was often very unhappy with me, but we both stuck it out for almost a year. Then I was reassigned to Peter Jones, this time in a much more important capacity. The store had a general manager, a retired admiral, a figurehead, who knew about retailing as little as I did; and under him there were three divisional managers, one for ladies' fashions, one for housewares, and one for everything else, which was my job. My division covered gifts, modern and antique furniture, men's wear, china and glass, and—of all things—ladies' hairdressing. I rather liked the hairdressing department, where everyone was hysterical, which reminded me of the theater. The hairdressers were difficult and temperamental, and the customers, after a couple of hours under a hair dryer (usually interrupted by an air raid), were not always helpful themselves. Frequently I would be called upon by an irate customer in the salon. Mrs. White, the division manager in charge of ladies' fashions, told me how to handle the problem. I would put a finger through a curl in the customer's hair and say, "But, madam, it springs back beautifully." I never knew what this meant, but it always seemed to work, as Mrs. White had said it would.

As a division manager at Peter Jones I learned things I would never have believed. One could actually guide people to certain departments by arranging carpets and fixtures—people, like ants, will follow patterns devised for them. Moreover, people will buy what they see, not what they need, and if you really want to sell something you need merely put it in the window. My department managers knew that very well, of course, and every week there would be a fight to see which department got the window space allotted to my division. I started a book department, which gave me a lot of pleasure and was the one area where I felt I could confidently give orders to a buyer. I remember I had read Davies' *Mission to Moscow* and was certain that with Russia as an ally English readers would buy the book, even though it was an account by an American ambassador. My book buyer presented me with three copies of it, and I told him, "I cannot sell three copies; but I can sell three hundred." He most reluctantly supplied three hundred copies, I filled a whole window with them, and we had them sold in no time.

One of the worst battles I had was with a buyer who had purchased a consignment of inkpots with covers depicting the heads of Churchill and Roosevelt, complete with cigar and cigarette in holder. One lifted their scalps to find black or red ink (I imagine in those days it was Churchill's head that held the red ink). I simply refused to place these monstrosities on display, and ultimately I was summoned to explain my conduct to the chairman himself. I told him that I thought the customers of Peter Jones lived on a higher standard of taste than the customers of some of the other stores, and should not be confronted with such merchandise; and Lewis agreed.

My wife and I had returned to our London flat not long after I took the job at Peter Jones, but as the bombing continued we took a furnished room in Oxford, near Gertie von Hofmannsthal, who gave my wife company and fed us both home-cooked Viennese dinners. Commuting from Oxford in wartime was very hard, especially in the winter, when I could pass a whole week without being outdoors in daylight. I would have to leave home at six in the morning, walk to the station, and catch the seven o'clock to London. At Paddington I would stand on the bus queue, which was always orderly and polite. During the buzz bomb days, one would wait on line listening to the droning sound of the self-propelled bombs flying overhead, and then the buzzing motor would cut off, indicating that the bomb was coming down. We would all scatter to the wall or fall on the ground, hoping for protection; then we would hear the explosion elsewhere, and re-form the line, everybody always in the same place he had been before the bomb. In the evening I would catch the five-thirty back to Oxford, arriving, if I was lucky, a little after seven at night, usually having stood all the way.

Among the duties of the staff at Peter Jones was nightly fire-watching. Everybody had to take one night a week; as a division manager and a foreigner, I volunteered to take two nights. After the store closed, those who were on night duty, usually a group of about a dozen, would go across the square to a pub where we would have an ale or a stout and talk about the war and business before returning to the store, where some sort of supper was provided. There were beds in the rest rooms for everyone, but we usually stayed up late, hoping that there would be only one raid, that we could do our job, and then get some unbroken hours of sleep. There was a dart game going almost every night, and I became quite expert at the sport.

After a while, I arranged to have an antique couch put in my first-floor office, and I would go there after the dart game and stretch out, reading until the first alarm sounded. Then I would have to feel my way to the roof with the aid of a pinpoint flashlight: with all the glass walls, there was no way to black out Peter Jones. The elevators did not run during air raids, and the solitary walk up the stairway to the sound of the sirens in the dark and empty store (or down the stairway after the all clear) was in some ways more frightening than the bombs; I remember once a moment of terror when I found myself facing a naked lady with upraised arms—one of the mannequins that had been stripped for a change of costume the next morning.

In preparation for possible fire duties, everyone at the store had taken an extensive fire-fighting course. I remember my amazement that one could creep safely through a hut full of dense smoke if one kept one's mouth not higher than an inch or two above the ground. (It was important, though, to tie a long length of string to the doorpost and to one's leg, to make sure of finding one's way back after the explorations in the smoke.) On our roof, we had sandbags for protection and buckets of sand to smother incendiary bombs. Peter Jones was miraculously lucky: a good part of Sloane Square was laid flat, but, miraculously, not a pane of glass was broken on the store building.

One saw terrible sights standing on the Peter Jones roof and watching the fires start all over dear old London. There was one dreadful night when a block of flats near the store took a direct hit. There were hundreds of casualties, and the wardens and ambulance attendants needed help, so I and half the Peter Jones crew went over. Even now, more than a quarter of a century later, I am sometimes haunted at night by the unsought memory of poking in the rubble and uncovering a girl's hand. When I pulled at it, the arm came out of the rubble alone; the rest of the poor girl was elsewhere; she had been blown apart.

My division apparently did well at Peter Jones, and one day Spedan Lewis called me to his office and offered me a considerable increase in salary if I would sign a long-term contract with the Partnership. Department stores were still definitely not what I wanted to do with the rest of my life, but I could not tell Mr. Lewis that. I accepted his offer with the proviso that if Glyndebourne were to start up again he would release me from my contract to rejoin Christie. And when the time came he accepted my departure with good grace. In fact, his relations with Glyndebourne remained so satisfying to him that the deficit on the first full postwar Glyndebourne opera season (in 1950, the year after I went to the Metropolitan) was met mostly by a contribution from the John Lewis Partnership, which put up twice as much money as Christie himself.

Audrey Christie had returned to England with the children in the spring of 1944, and that summer, as the Allied forces swept through France, Edwards and I began what became a long series of discussions about what could be done at Glyndebourne after the war. It was clear that there could not be any early return to the prewar arrangements. The group had broken up. Busch had quarreled at a great distance with Ebert (who was in Turkey) over a production of *Macbeth* Busch had done in a Broadway theater in New York, with his son as stage director; Ebert felt that they had appropriated his ideas without giving him credit. More sadly, Busch had also quarreled with the Christies. John had not been able to send Audrey much money from wartime England, and there had been months during her exile when she was struggling for a living. Busch, in assembling his New Opera Company for Broadway, had hired someone other than Audrey to play Despina in *Così Fan Tutte*, and she was resentful—especially after Beecham engaged her to sing Susanna in *Figaro* for him at the Montreal Festival. The quarrel was triumphantly made up about a year before Busch's death, but at the time Edwards and I were talking there was no desire in the Christie family to reconstitute the Busch-Ebert partnership.

Even if the same personnel could have been acquired, of course, Glyndebourne as we had known it was an impossibility in the dark, gasolineless years immediately after the war. Yet one had to keep the name before the public if there was ever to be a revival. Assuming that it would be impossible to return opera to Glyndebourne for a while, Glyndebourne productions could be mounted in another setting. It seemed to me that the ideal setting would be an international festival in which the other nations of the world could join in paying tribute to Britain's courage and sacrifice in the struggle against Hitler, and that the ideal place for such a festival would be Oxford. With Edwards' encouragement, I explored the idea in meetings with the wardens of the colleges and with the city fathers, but it proved totally impossible to bring town and gown together in a joint venture, and without help from both no festival could be staged.

One of these conversations about the future of Glyndebourne was held over a long, cheerful lunch at the Cadogan Hotel, and at the end of it Edwards asked me to reopen a London office for Glyndebourne. In the autumn of 1944 I left Peter Jones and started work at a provisional Glyndebourne office on Cumberland Place; presently, we acquired permanent housing in Baker Street. The immediate job was the administration of the Children's Theatre, a professional touring company based on Toynbee Hall, a settlement house in the London slums. The Theatre had outgrown the resources of the settlement house, and the Christies had offered both funds and management services.

The first venture of the Children's Theatre under Glyndebourne management was a dramatisation of Dickens' *Great Expectations*. To write the adaptation I engaged Alec Guinness—whom I met still in his naval officer's uniform, not yet demobilized. To direct the play, I hired Anthony Quayle, a young actor with no previous professional directing experience. The resulting production was a great success, playing for twenty weeks in London and the provinces to an audience that totaled more than 200,000 children. (The play also had a major influence in the private life of the Bing family: Nina and I acquired our first dachshund at that time, and named him Pip for the Dickens hero.) Later we would perform James Bridie's *Tobias and the Angel* and Goldsmith's *She Stoops to Conquer*.

In 1945, shortly after the end of the war, there was another theatrical venture, the "Company of Four"—Glyndebourne, H. M. Tennent Ltd., Cambridge Arts Theatre, and Guthrie—which took over the Lyric Theatre in Hammersmith for a season of straight plays to introduce works of serious modern playwrights and to give employment to actors being demobilized from the armed forces. Our first play was *The Shouting Dies*, by Ronda Keane, which opened in October 1945; later we presented plays by Thornton Wilder, William Saroyan, Sean O'Casey, Jean Cocteau, and others. Alec Guinness adapted *The Brothers Karamazov* for us in 1946. With unfamiliar plays and mostly young actors, in a small theater some distance out from the West End, this was inevitably a losing proposition, and it didn't interest Christie much: he rarely came. As the losses mounted, he became increasingly unhappy about the Company of Four, and in early 1947 the venture collapsed.

At about the time the Company of Four opened its first Lyric Hammersmith season, we began to plan seriously for a possible reopening of Glyndebourne on some terms the following summer. The impetus to serious planning was given by Sir Thomas

Beecham, who to his amazement and fury had been locked out of the reopened Covent Garden by its new owners, Boosey & Hawkes, who hired Karl Rankl as their music director. He offered his services without fee for three operas—*Carmen, Figaro,* and *The Magic Flute*—for a season at Glyndebourne in summer 1946. Unfortunately, Christie and Beecham, the last two great eccentrics, were totally unable to work together, especially after Christie, concerned about mounting cost projections and eager not to appear less patriotic than Covent Garden (which had proclaimed a reliance on native talent), suggested the employment of young English singers, whom Beecham and Ebert would bring to perfection through a lengthy rehearsal period. Lady Beecham in a letter to Mrs. Christie which marked the beginning of the end of this collaboration said that her husband "after forty-three years of operatic work carried on in every country of importance in the world . . . is now being asked to be a kind of nurse in a species of musical kindergarten."

But as the prospects for this musical kindergarten receded, a rather different one took form. Benjamin Britten had scored an immense success with *Peter Grimes* that summer at Sadler's Wells; and, as sometimes happens, success had produced frictions. What later became known as the English Opera Group split off from Sadler's Wells. The leading figures were Britten, the director Eric Crozier, the tenor Peter Pears, and the soprano Joan Cross. They were looking for a home for Britten's new opera, *The Rape of Lucretia,* being written for small orchestral forces to a text by the poet Ronald Duncan. I liked the libretto, and found Crozier's financial projections convincing; he had some private sources of funds, and it seemed likely that he, unlike Christie, could secure a grant from the burgeoning Arts Council. Crozier wanted the use of the Lyric Hammersmith, but I urged him and Christie to consider the use of Glyndebourne itself.

Among my reasons for special pleasure with *The Rape of Lucretia* was that its leading role was being written for contralto, which made the opera right for the introduction of a new artist I was especially eager to have Glyndebourne sponsor: Kathleen Ferrier, to whose beautiful voice and outstanding, straightforward personality I had been introduced by Roy Henderson, who had sung many of our baritone roles and was now Miss Ferrier's teacher. The English Opera Group were suitably enthusiastic about the casting of Miss Ferrier, though somewhat resistant to my proposal that Carl Ebert come back from Turkey to be artistic director for their one-opera Glyndebourne season. They did accept this idea pro forma, however, and also my proposal that a conductor of recognized international stature should be acquired.

I made contact with Ernest Ansermet, who was pleased with Britten's opera and with the idea of working at Glyndebourne, and accepted our offer. This began a long-standing friendship with Ansermet, a most distinguished musician and a delightful man with a fine, dry wit. When I brought him to the Metropolitan some years later, to conduct *Pelléas et Mélisande*, he happened to arrive in the middle of a string of performances conducted by our youth movement, who scorned artificial aids in their work. One day Ansermet came to my office and said, "Bing, I am going to make an innovation at the Metropolitan Opera." He stopped. I said, "Yes?" Ansermet said, "I am going to introduce the use of *le bâton*."

*The Rape of Lucretia* had its world premiere at Glyndebourne on July 12, 1946, and then played every night but Sunday for two weeks, alternating two separate casts and the English conductor Reginald Goodall with Ansermet. Though there could be no special train for Lewes, and nobody could drive down from London in the gas-rationed world (it was all I could do to get coupons for the buses), we were able to produce a reasonably festive atmosphere in what was still a beautiful and beautifully kept property, and attendance was not too bad.

Unfortunately, the Glyndebourne debut was part of a package deal for a long season for *The Rape of Lucretia*, and immediately after finishing at Glyndebourne the company packed off for a week in Manchester, followed by a week in Liverpool, a week in Edinburgh, a week in Glasgow, a month in London, a week in Oxford, and a tour of Holland. This was in every way a total and unmitigated disaster, and looking back I can easily see that the tour was stupid: Liverpool and Glasgow certainly could not have been ready to support a week of a contemporary work, and the Dutch had no good reason to be interested in a new English opera. I now learned bitterly the lesson I had started to master when I worked for Hugo Heller— that artists notice signs on hoardings and kiosks for every other attraction in the world, but never see their own, and thus blame their management for failure to give adequate publicity whenever their sales are disappointing. The English Opera Group leadership turned on me as the architect of their disaster, and I had a most uncomfortable summer and early fall from them. Christie found the financial losses "startling."

What made this experience especially frustrating was the fact that it took so much time from something that was much more important both to Glyndebourne and to me. For even before *The Rape of Lucretia* had its premiere I had proposed and carried, at Glyndebourne and in Edinburgh, the idea of an Edinburgh Festival.

# 12

Though the experience at Oxford had been disappointing, I had never entirely abandoned the idea of an international music festival both as a second market for Glyndebourne and as a tribute to Britain's accomplishment in the war. Inevitably, one thought of Salzburg; but England had no cities like Salzburg. The provincial centers were either too big and would swallow up a festival (Manchester, Liverpool, Bristol), or were too poorly supplied with theaters, concert halls, and hotels (York, Lincoln, Chester, etc.). My mind kept returning to the sight of the castle on the cliff in Edinburgh, not really like the castle in Salzburg, but equally memorable. The statistics indicated that the city was really a little big for a festival, but it had beauty and tradition, a native culture, enough theaters, including one that could (just barely) be an opera house, good rail connections, and a number of hotels.

Edinburgh had one other advantage—it was in territory where the British Council, an organization devoted to the spread of English culture to foreign parts, had been authorized to work.

I was already in contact with the new Arts Council for help with our Children's Theatre, and it was discouragingly clear that the Arts Council under the leadership of Lord Keynes was all but adamant against giving money to anything associated with Glyndebourne. I never did find out what lay behind the mutual animosity of Keynes and Christie. Keynes was often in attendance at Glyndebourne (he had a house in Sussex), and his wife and mine, both former Russian ballerinas, got on very well. Keynes was a remote presence at the Arts Council so far as I was concerned—our rejections came from Miss Mary Glasgow, its secretary-general, and from Steuart Wilson, its musical adviser—but Christie saw his influence everywhere.

A festival of the sort I had in mind would obviously need government support. Because Scotland was not England, we might be able to bypass the Arts Council through the good offices of the British Council. I outlined what I had in mind in a two-page memo to Edwards and Christie, suggesting Edinburgh as the place, Glyndebourne opera productions as the festival centerpiece, with several orchestras from the Continent, chamber groups from Europe and America, at least one imported theatrical attraction (after six years of war, the English were starved for imported attractions), and either Sadler's Wells or a European ballet. There were several artists I knew I wanted and was fairly sure I could get—Yehudi Menuhin, the only foreign soloist of major importance who came to London during the bombing to play concerts; Artur Schnabel; and Bruno Walter, whom I had known since Vienna days and whom I hoped to reunite with the Vienna Philharmonic as our most newsworthy attraction. Edwards gave me a green light, and I called Harry Harvey-Wood, head of the Scottish office in the British Council, and asked him to lunch.

Harvey-Wood turned out to be a charming, highly intelligent, extremely cultured Scotsman, an artist and author who knew all about Glyndebourne and Salzburg and was intrigued by the idea of a festival in Edinburgh. He offered to gather a small committee of Edinburgh notables and to set up a meeting at which I could explain the scheme. If this group approved, they would arrange for me to meet Sir John Falconer, Lord Provost of the city, and would put their shoulders to the wheel when the time came to promote the idea of a festival to the various sections of the city government. The committee Harvey-Wood formed was perfect for the purpose. It included the Countess of Rosebery, who was a fine amateur pianist herself and was friendly with the Queen; James Murray-Watson, the editor of *The Scotsman*, Edinburgh's leading paper; Dr. O. H. Mavor (better known as the playwright James Bridie); John Cameron, later Lord Cameron and a distinguished judge; Professor S. T. M. Newman, who taught music at the university, and a few others. Several of them became stalwart friends in later years; all were immensely helpful in the long and difficult negotiations that were to follow.

With this committee, I went to see Sir John, an awfully nice little old man, a lawyer, who had not the foggiest notion of what I was talking about. He had never heard of Glyndebourne, or of the Amsterdam Concertgebouw, or even of Bruno Walter. But he understood perfectly well my central argument, which was that the continental festivals like Salzburg, Bayreuth, and Munich were sure to be out of business for some years, and it would redound greatly to the reputation and perhaps even to the economy of Edinburgh if his city took their place. As I wrote in an obituary tribute in 1954, "He gave the first Edinburgh Festival . . . the security that only confidence inspires and the prestige that derives from dignity." He wanted to know how much it would cost, and I had to say I couldn't tell him—this was a situation where costs would have to be dependent on program, rather than the other way around. If he would invest some city funds in the formation of a Festival Society, however, I would be able to work with a program committee to determine what we could get and what it would cost.

These preliminary meetings occurred in early 1945, before the end of the war. Not long after the surrender of the Germans, the Edinburgh city government began to consider in earnest what a festival might involve. During the summer and early fall of 1945, when not required by the Children's Theatre or the Company of Four, I made frequent trips to Edinburgh, to explain my proposal to the City Treasurer, the City Chamberlain, the Town Clerk, and various "bailies" or town councilors. On one of these visits, incidentally, I had my only ghost experience (so far). I was staying at a beautiful old Adam house some distance out from Edinburgh, and had been given a bed with a canopy, which made me uneasy in itself. I woke up in the middle of the night to see and hear a figure walking through my room with a tray of tinkling glasses. I never slept again that night. On a later visit, I was urged by Lord Haig to stay with him and his family in their "nice spooky little cottage," and I quickly turned down the invitation.

A few months before, I had barely known where Scotland was, and now I plunged into the middle of Scottish town politics. Some individuals were very difficult—there was, for example, a town councilor who was in charge of concerts in the park on summer Sunday afternoons, and he feared a festival might compete with his concerts. I cannot say that I handled everything perfectly, either. I was a long time learning that one did not say "English" when referring to the people who lived in Edinburgh. My worst moment—so bad I sometimes wonder how the idea of a festival survived the *faux pas*—came when I outlined some specific ideas for a committee of the city council, and said more or less in passing that the Festival would open with a

High Mass in the cathedral. Being Catholic, and ignorant of British history, I had no notion of the offense I had committed until Harvey-Wood rather forcefully explained it to me.

The Edinburgh city council did not approve the Festival and establish the Society until November 1945. The formal arrangement was that Glyndebourne would act as "organising centre," supplying managerial skills and experience, but would not under any circumstances be out of pocket for expenses I incurred in setting up the Festival, or for Glyndebourne performances at the Festival, regardless of ticket sale. By the time the contracts were signed, it was far too late to hold a first festival in 1946, and I informed the Edinburgh authorities, to their surprise, that we would have to move fast if we hoped to open the doors in 1947.

Locally, I began negotiations with the Hallé Orchestra, the Liverpool Philharmonic, the Old Vic, and the Sadler's Wells Ballet, and I began making contacts at the embassies of the European countries from which I would be asking for contributions. Meanwhile, Lady Rosebery spoke with the Queen, who was herself Scottish, and received reason to believe (if not yet assurance) that royal patronage would be granted. Under these circumstances, the Arts Council could not remain opposed. In any event, Lord Keynes was gravely ill (he died that spring), and doubtless too busy with the nation's economic crisis to pay much attention to old personal feuds even if he had had the energy to do so. What Glyndebourne might not have been able to do was possible for the Edinburgh Festival Society. While the British Council remained involved—Harvey-Wood was chairman of my program committee—the Arts Council chimed in with a welcome grant.

Initially, my approaches to European organizations were greeted with a puzzled air familiar to me from the days when I was trying to tell European singers about a new theater in

Glyndebourne. I wrote a long letter to Bruno Walter in America, outlining not only the events in which I hoped he would participate but also everything else I was trying to do, and he accepted by mail. After that we were on the map. Whenever anyone asked me what all this was about, I had merely to say that Bruno Walter was coming, and no further questions were asked. I remember that Walter made a trip to London that year—I have forgotten exactly why—and we talked over festival plans at length. I also arranged a late afternoon at the apartment of the publisher Hamish Hamilton, where Walter met Kathleen Ferrier for the first time, auditioned her (playing the piano accompaniments himself), and engaged her to sing *Das Lied von der Erde* at Edinburgh.

Sometime in the spring of 1946, the immensity of the enterprise I had undertaken burst upon me. So many things had to be synchronized with so many other things. We had set the last week of August and the first two weeks in September 1947 as the time for the Festival. The city owned Usher Hall and a smaller concert hall, but the three theaters I would need—King's, for opera; the Lyceum, for drama; and the Empire, an old music hall, for ballet—were in private hands. They had to be rented, if possible with some sort of cancellation clause. We had to be certain that the hotels would hold rooms open for festival patrons. One of the things I found was that several of the hotels still had windows painted black from wartime, and there was no material available from which to make new curtains and drapes; I had to arrange myself with the proper ministries to de-ration curtain and drapery materials for the hotels. That does not sound like what an artistic director does for a festival, but the provision of food and housing for festival visitors was something I did not dare trust to normal procedures in a city where few people even knew there was going to be a festival.

With five theaters to operate six nights a week, there would be no fewer than 180,000 tickets to sell. As the hope and belief was that people would visit Edinburgh to attend the Festival, tickets had to be made available in London and America and on the Continent; I made arrangements with Thos. Cook and American Express to sell Edinburgh Festival tickets worldwide. Before tickets could be sold at all, we had to have a definite schedule of attractions, names, dates, and places, and we had to have an experienced international publicity representative who could let the world know what we were doing. I established a timetable: a date by which the program would be ready, followed by a date for publicity to start, a date for tickets to go on sale, etc.

Everything hinged, of course, on the groups we could attract to Edinburgh, and the terms on which they would come. I had sold the city fathers the idea of the Festival on the theory that European governments would be prepared to subsidize the appearance of their artists; now the theory had to be put to the proof. I flew to Vienna, for the first time since 1938. It was a sad and exciting experience, the drive from the airport through the old and badly damaged streets I knew so well—and a very depressing thought, when I checked into the hotel, that if I needed help in the city of my birth the only place I could go for it would be the British Embassy.

The Vienna Philharmonic was enchanted by the opportunity I offered, to play again with Bruno Walter. In 1972, when the Secretary-General of the United Nations is an Austrian who fought in the German Army in World War II, it is hard to recapture the fragility of Austria's public reputation right after the war, when many remembered the reception the Viennese had given Hitler and scoffed at the decision by the Allies to consider Austria a "liberated" rather than a conquered country. The presence of Bruno Walter on the podium would in itself de-Nazify the Vienna Philharmonic and guarantee against the

[ 117 ]

kind of political demonstration that would have been inevitable if they had appeared abroad under, say, Clemens Krauss. At the same time, however, the Viennese knew very well that I was counting on their presence at the Festival—and the Austrians in those days right after the war really were poor as churchmice. The negotiations were complicated and difficult, and my theory did not prove true: the Austrians would not, probably could not, subsidize the appearance of the Vienna Philharmonic. But it was possible to make a deal Edinburgh could afford.

Elsewhere my embassy met with better results. In Paris, thanks in large part to the support of M. Philippe Erlanger in the cultural affairs division of the Foreign Ministry (who later thanked me for my role in these negotiations by suggesting the award to me of the Légion d'Honneur), we reached agreement that the French government would deliver to Edinburgh at its own expense the Louis Jouvet company with its wonderful Christian Bérard production of Molière's *L'École des Femmes*, and the Orchestre des Concerts Colonne under the direction of Paul Paray. Meanwhile, my correspondence to America had borne fruit: Schnabel would come and would play both solo recitals and a cycle of Brahms, Schubert, and Mendelssohn chamber music with Joseph Szigeti, William Primrose, and Pierre Fournier.

All of this was, obviously, an immense amount of work; and when it became clear that Glyndebourne was to be reopened in 1946 for the Britten opera, I told Edwards that I would need assistants both for Glyndebourne and for Edinburgh. My choice for Glyndebourne was Moran Caplat, a young man who had worked in the London theater before the war and was about to be demobilized with the rank of lieutenant-commander in the Royal Navy. For Edinburgh I picked Ian Hunter, a Scotsman who as a student conductor had worked for Fritz Busch in the last prewar Glyndebourne years—which was invaluable experience for a man with managerial talents. Both were not only extremely able but also extremely nice, with a good sense of humor. Not the least of my pleasures when I left Britain for the Metropolitan was my knowledge that Glyndebourne and Edinburgh, following my recommendations, had appointed my former assistants to take over my jobs. Nearly a quarter of a century later, Caplat is still general manager of Glyndebourne. Hunter after a few years left Edinburgh to become head of Harold Holt, the largest London concert agency.

For that first season, when Edinburgh barely knew me and none of us knew what it meant to run an international festival, almost everything I wanted to do had to be approved by either my program committee or my finance committee in Scotland. Hunter and I had regular arrangements for visiting Scotland. Every week on the same night we would take the sleeper for Edinburgh from King's Cross. The next morning we would breakfast on the train (kippers, which I loved), and have the entire day free for meetings. To say the least, not everyone was a believer; Beecham had been quoted as saying that my supporters "were damned fools to throw away sixty thousand pounds on a festival." Then we would take the sleeper back to London that night. In the end, everything I proposed was in fact approved—even the guarantee to Glyndebourne of about $55,000 against the losses the company might suffer by presenting three weeks of opera at the Festival.

The question of meshing Glyndebourne with Edinburgh was troublesome. Clearly, anything Glyndebourne did in June, only an hour or so from London, would not draw Londoners to Edinburgh in August and September. But the Edinburgh arrangement was less valuable to Glyndebourne if it did not help to cover the costs of rehearsing performances for our own season. These conflicts were never resolved, and were among the reasons why Glyndebourne after my departure did not always participate at Edinburgh.

For this first Edinburgh year, however, Glyndebourne was still to a degree involved with the English Opera Group, with whom we offered a mixed season of twenty-one performances—nine of Britten's new comic opera *Albert Herring*, three of *The Rape of Lucretia*, and nine of Glyndebourne's own production of Gluck's *Orfeo* (in Italian). This opera was chosen to some extent as a showcase for Kathleen Ferrier. Carl Ebert returned to active work at Glyndebourne to produce it, but Busch was still in the bad graces of the Christies, and the conductor was Ebert's old partner from Berlin days, Fritz Stiedry. Caspar Neher did the sets. *Orfeo* presented in perhaps its purest form a problem which has stalked me all my life in opera—the problem of how to get a decent ballet onstage. For a few performances at Glyndebourne, it was totally impossible to prepare even a presentable execution of the ballet *Orfeo* requires. In my annual report to the directors, I wrote that the *Orfeo* was "not too unsuccessful, though the ballet was an outstanding failure." But the losses Christie had to absorb were about $35,000.

What Edinburgh needed from Glyndebourne was not this speculative *Orfeo* but some of the works that had made Glyndebourne's reputation before the war. The two that we decided on were *Macbeth* and *Figaro*. To conduct, I engaged George Szell, whom I had known more or less distantly since the Heller days in Vienna. The Glyndebourne staff took a brief vacation after the close of our own season in July, and then welcomed Szell and the casts of our Edinburgh productions, which were to have all their piano rehearsals at Glyndebourne before moving up to Scotland, where orchestral rehearsals could be undertaken by Szell and the cast while Ebert got the sets and lighting properly arranged at the King's Theatre.

My wife and I tried our best to make Szell comfortable and happy at Glyndebourne, but the task proved beyond our resources; he was a nasty man, God rest his soul. I remember that on his second or third day there we took him for a drive up the downs in our lovely little Hillman, a car of which I was inordinately fond; and as we returned to the car from a walk to some scenic spot I said, "Tell me—what would a car like this cost in America?" Szell replied with cruel scorn, "A car like this doesn't *exist* in America."

Mrs. Christie had hoped to sing Susanna again, but her health did not permit it (in fact, she never again sang in public after the war), and we had imported a young American soprano. Unfortunately, the girl had never played the role before, and she arrived knowing only Susanna's arias and her lines in the concerted numbers. As the recitatives in Susanna's role are almost as long as all the rest put together, she was seriously unprepared. Szell made a terrible scene, announced that he could not possibly work with an artist who didn't know her role, and to our amusement abandoned both productions. I always felt that he had believed he was going to work with a London orchestra of the quality we had engaged for Glyndebourne before the war, and having heard some negative comments about the Scottish Orchestra that would be in the pit in Edinburgh he decided to seize on the soprano's failings as his excuse to quit. He undoubtedly could have taught the girl her recitatives if he had wished to do so. But he did quit; it would not be the last time George Szell walked out on me.

# 13

When the day came, everything went as planned. The hotels were full. Our "Festival Club" fed those the restaurants were unable to handle. Our press office was praised by no less a connoisseur than Claudia Cassidy of the Chicago *Tribune* as the most helpful the musical press had ever enjoyed. ("In my case," she wrote, "the management was courtesy personified and next door to clairvoyant.") Somehow, the tickets had been sold —the great majority of them. Deficits, though not inconsiderable, were lower than I had forecast—instead of $55,000, for example, the Glyndebourne productions at the King's Theatre lost only $37,000. International tourism was still in its postwar infancy—a visit to war-ravaged Europe was not exactly what the American vacationer needed—but in addition to large numbers of English and surprising numbers of visitors from all over Lowland Scotland we did have a sizable foreign contingent. Among the biggest hits was Edinburgh's own contribution, a military tattoo in the courtyard of the castle. We were remarkably lucky in the beautiful weather, with three weeks of bright sunshine, so rare in Edinburgh. And the war was over and everyone was happy.

Our most glamorous night offered Walter and the Vienna Philharmonic, with the Queen in attendance. I told Walter, "The time of the concert is seven-thirty. You come onstage five minutes before that time, accept applause, and wait. I am informed that the Queen will come to the hall at seven twenty-seven, and these things here, you know, are guaranteed by God. When you see a lady enter the Royal Box, you step forward and begin 'God Save the Queen.'" The Queen did appear at seven twenty-seven, I met her outside, and as we were walking through the corridors to her box, suddenly I heard the orchestra begin "God Save the Queen." The Queen was embarrassed, which should *never* happen. She didn't know whether she should stand still where she was or hurry to the box. Eventually she decided just to keep walking at the same pace, and enter the box toward the end of the anthem. Later I asked Walter what had happened, and he explained that he had waited for a lady to come into the box and one had done so—a late arriver, taking a short cut to her own box nearby. But Walter never knew the lady was simply running through the back of the Queen's box, because the moment he saw her he turned to the orchestra and began conducting.

(I must admit in passing that I have never had much luck with this sort of ceremonial. Many years later, Mrs. Lyndon Johnson came to my box for a performance at the Metropolitan Opera, and as she took her place the audience, alerted by the press to expect the distinguished visitor, applauded her. Somebody had stupidly put her armchair in the second row, and as she rose to take a bow I said to her, "I am changing your chair." I had not been able to understand her Texas English, and it now developed that she could not understand my Austrian-English English, for after bowing she sat right down into the empty space where her chair had been. Before four thousand people. She was very gracious about it, but the Secret Service men had apoplexy.)

Among others who came to Edinburgh was the Princess Royal, the King's sister, with her son George Harewood, who had become a friend of mine at Glyndebourne before the war, and had while a POW in Germany learned everything about opera that could be learned from reading books. Later he would succeed Ian Hunter as artistic director of Edinburgh, and later still, having acquired his earldom, he would figure in one of the most surprising pieces of politicking on the Metropolitan Opera board—but we must wait for that till the time comes. Harewood himself was not in the least to blame. There was a reception for the Princess Royal, and my wife was told she must curtsy when introduced, which she did not like at all. Actually, as we soon discovered, the Princess Royal liked it all even less; a very shy woman, she was terrified of official functions, and had to spend her life at them.

All in all, the three weeks of the Festival were for us an unusually social period. At a reception for Princess Margaret, my wife even danced a Scottish reel, partnered by Lord Haig. I watched. As an ordinary matter, I have never gone to parties for artists after a performance. I think it is improper for a manager to appear to be on terms of personal friendship with any of the artists who work for him, since he cannot be personally friendly with all. And unlike the artists, I must be at work at a decent hour the next morning. But in Edinburgh everyone was a visitor, and thus entitled to hospitality—and a man running a festival is rather expected to be on duty twenty-four hours a day. I remember many evenings when Nina and I returned late to the Caledonian Hotel and took Pip out for a necessary late walk, trying to defend the shoes lined up in the long hotel corridor against his natural dachshund curiosity.

I was also, of course, in a very happy frame of mind. Until Edinburgh, I had worked all my life as someone's assistant. This Festival was the first time I had been the author; its triumph was mine, and I enjoyed it. In 1971 the announcement that I was to be knighted in recognition of the twenty-fifth Edinburgh Festival brought from one of the New York critics the "explanation," typical of the accuracy and generosity I found in the New York press, that the Queen had been told of services I had rendered as a kind of glorified office boy to Carl Ebert at Glyndebourne. The critic's description was wrong about my role in Glyndebourne, too; but it was certainly Edinburgh that first gave me that fine sense of freedom which accompanies the assumption of ultimate responsibility.

With that first Festival, Edinburgh obviously had begun a tradition. But soon after the tumult and shouting died, there arose questions about how that tradition was to be handled. Many of the participants in the work of the Edinburgh Festival Society felt that their organization was now bigger than Glyndebourne, and that Glyndebourne's contribution had been among the lesser achievements of the occasion. Glyndebourne's future in its own theater seemed rather uncertain; why should Scotland continue to take instruction from Sussex? But my loyalties were first to Christie, and I made it clear that I was not available to Edinburgh apart from Glyndebourne; and after some short uncomfortable time Glyndebourne was re-engaged as "Artistic Management" for 1948.

The fact was that Christie's resources were no longer great enough to pay for the production of opera in his own theater. His income was very large, but much more than half of it was being taxed away. In Britain, unlike the United States, contributions to charitable and educational institutions must be taken from post-tax, not pre-tax income. Confronted with the rising costs of operatic production in the general inflation (and the impossibility of raising ticket prices much beyond the £2 that had been charged before the war), Christie would have had to sell off his assets to pay Glyndebourne's bills, and with two children to endow he was unwilling to make such quixotic gestures.

In fall 1947 Christie went to the United States for the first time in his life, hoping to establish some sort of American Glyndebourne—or at least to find a place in America where Glyndebourne productions could be given with some profit to the company. After another such visit, in spring 1948, he actually announced a Glyndebourne season in Princeton for fall 1949 (it was to investigate what if any reality lay behind this announcement that I went to New York early that year). But meanwhile there was to be no opera at Glyndebourne itself in 1948. Instead, we invited Sir Thomas Beecham to bring his Royal Philharmonic Orchestra for four late-afternoon concerts from July 14 through July 17, and supplemented the orchestral fare with three afternoon chamber music concerts and a lecture by Sir Thomas himself. All the music performed was by Mozart.

Meanwhile, Glyndebourne assumed the artistic direction of another local festival, the relatively unambitious Bath Assembly, for which we produced Mozart's *Die Entführung aus dem Serail* in English, at something less than Glyndebourne standards. And we once again contracted to fill the King's Theatre throughout the Edinburgh Festival, this year with a new production of *Così Fan Tutte*, with sets by Rolf Gérard, and a revival of our prewar *Don Giovanni*. To conduct *Così*, I brought Vittorio Gui from Italy; to conduct *Don Giovanni*, I brought Rafael Kubelik from Czechoslovakia for what was, I believe, his first appearance outside Central Europe. Carl Ebert was again, of course, the producer and director of the operas. Among the singers engaged for these performances was Ljuba Welitsch (as Donna Anna), a woman of great billowing charm and gaiety as well as a wonderful artist. She quickly became, in the festival atmosphere, one of the relatively few artists with whom I have been on first-name terms. She was en route to her great debut triumph at the Metropolitan, as Salome, and she would be during my first years at the Metropolitan a unique combination of a joy, a disappointment, and a trouble. I remember that some aspect of the schedule I had drawn up for my first season did not please her, and she insisted it be changed. The files reveal a telegram: "Ljuba: I could never resist you so of course you have won again. Details via Mertens. Much hate. Bing."

For this Edinburgh Festival my travels had taken me to Holland, France, and Italy. We opened with the Concertgebouw under the direction of Eduard van Beinum, with Charles Munch conducting alternate concerts. The other foreign orchestra was the Augusteo of Rome, conducted by Wilhelm Furtwängler. Most of the orchestral work, however, was English, and included the Liverpool under Malcolm Sargent, the Scottish, the BBC under Adrian Boult (with Yehudi Menuhin among the soloists), the Hallé under Barbirolli, and the Boyd Neel chamber ensemble. France sent the Renaud-Barrault company to alternate an evening of Marivaux and mime with an evening of Gide's translation of *Hamlet*—a presentation that probably put us on the international map more visibly than anything else in the early years of the Festival, and convinced me that Barrault was one of the towering theatrical figures of our time. We also had a fascinating production of *Medea* with Eileen Herlie under John Gielgud's direction. Among the soloists who gave recitals were Maggie Teyte, Kathleen Ferrier, Alfred Cortot, and Gregor Piatigorsky, another artist who became a friend.

During the planning for this season, the officers of the Edinburgh Festival Society told me that they were not prepared to continue a situation where I could work for them only in a

Glyndebourne context. They had no objection to my continuing as director and general manager of Glyndebourne, but on Edinburgh matters they wished me to act directly as an employee of theirs. That fall, direction of Edinburgh shifted from Glyndebourne as an organization to myself as an individual, and the fact that I was doing two entirely different jobs received legal (and financial) recognition.

Christie had by now been given an advisory position on the Arts Council, from which he kept soliciting a grant for Glyndebourne, but it was not forthcoming. We planned our Edinburgh season—an Ebert production (alas, still without Busch) of Verdi's *Un Ballo in Maschera*, plus more performances of the new *Così Fan Tutte*—but again we could not marshal the resources to restore opera to Glyndebourne. Among the reasons for my willingness to go to New York, despite my strong and correct doubts that the group Christie thought would sponsor us at Princeton was more than a figment of its own imagination, was a feeling akin to despair about the prospects of renewed opera at Glyndebourne without help from some kind of new world. A year after my departure, such help did arrive, first from Spedan Lewis for a 1950 season, then from the Festival of Britain for 1951, finally from a combination of new founts of support—the Arts Council, the formation of a Glyndebourne Trust to operate the property and receive charitable contributions, and the development of a very elaborate souvenir program in which companies would take high-priced advertising pages, charging off their help to Glyndebourne as a business expense. By then, of course, I was at the Metropolitan, and Moran Caplat was capably filling my old chair.

That spring Sir Thomas returned to Glyndebourne with his orchestra for another round of concerts, and he and I put our heads together to seek a new solution to the opera problem. His feeling was, as I wrote to the Christies, that Glyndebourne spent too much money on production and on dramatic rehearsals, and that it could survive only "if it expands its operations and ceases to be a small luxury organization, necessarily too expensive for a wide audience and therefore not in line with present trends, whether we like them or not." Beecham was prepared to revive his old British Opera League to support tours around England by Glyndebourne, if the costs could be controlled. But the Christies could not see Ebert agreeing to such arrangements, and in fact Christie himself was uncomfortable with the slightest suggestion that Glyndebourne should present anything less than his view of "perfection."

All this became a matter of academic and nostalgic interest for me after May 1949, when the Metropolitan secured my release from my Edinburgh contract and I notified Christie that I would not seek renewal of my contract with him. Word that everything was set in New York reached me while I was lunching with the director Peter Brook at The Ivy, a Soho restaurant that serves the London theater world rather as a more dignified Sardi's would serve New York's. I swore Brook to secrecy, told him the contents of the telephone call that had summoned me from our table, and secured a promise from him that he would direct for me at the Metropolitan—which he did, twice, for *Faust* in 1953 and *Eugene Onegin* in 1957, before a combination of demands on his time elsewhere and an ungrateful reception from the New York critics removed him from our roster.

Handling one of the problems raised by that year's Edinburgh Festival gave me invaluable practice for the first crisis of my work at the Metropolitan. The bicentenary of Goethe's birth occurred in 1949, and was celebrated throughout the Western world. We wanted to bring to Edinburgh the Düsseldorf Theater of Gustav Gründgens, and the Germans, already recovering economically, were more than pleased to help pay the

[ 129 ]

bills. But what had Gründgens' political attitudes been during the Nazi regime? Would he be—*should* he be—acceptable in England? He had been in Berlin at the end of the war, and had been incarcerated briefly in a Russian prison. I put both the Foreign Ministry and the British Army of Occupation to work on my problem, and they came back with chapter and verse. Gründgens had passed an honest de-Nazification tribunal; while no one could guarantee against demonstrations, Edinburgh would be safe in inviting him—which I did.

During that London summer prior to my departure for New York, I met two of the people who would be most helpful to me at the Metropolitan. One, Mrs. Nin Ryan, daughter of Otto Kahn (who had been the dominating president of the Opera in the days of Gatti-Casazza), was a friend of my old friend Raimund von Hofmannsthal, who brought us together for dinner. The next summer, Mrs. Ryan would sell a Rembrandt to finance my debut *Don Carlo*.

The other, Mrs. Lewis Douglas, was the wife of the American ambassador to London, and when she and her husband read in the newspapers that I had been appointed general manager of the Metropolitan she invited Nina and myself to a reception at the Embassy. The occasion for the reception was a performance by some American university glee club, which did not quite awe me—but Nina liked these earnest young men, and got down on the floor with them to sing Russian folk songs, which rather upset Ambassador Douglas. Peggy Douglas came onto the Metropolitan board not long thereafter, and was a great source of support for quality—and through her immense number of friends, a great source of funds to pay for quality—through my penultimate season. She also became one of our closest personal friends, a very special person in our lives as well as in my work.

Then Edinburgh was on and over, and Nina and I said

goodbye to everyone, sent most of our luggage to America, and took what little we needed for a vacation into the Swiss Alps. Though I have remained a British subject (a status I finally did acquire right after the war), I had returned to England only once or twice in the early 1950s before I went back in 1971 for the ceremony of knighthood. We arrived in New York on November 3, 1949, and were interviewed before the boat docked. "I am supposed to ask tactless questions," said the ship's reporter for the New York *Herald Tribune*. "Ah, yes," I replied, getting off on the right foot, "and I am supposed to give evasive answers."

George Sloan, chairman of the Metropolitan board, had kindly arranged a suite for us on the thirty-sixth floor of the Essex House on Central Park South, with a grand cityscape view looking south through the skyscrapers of midtown New York to the harbor. We settled in there very cheerfully, and as I write, more than twenty-two years later, we are there still.

# 14

Fortunately, I have always enjoyed tight places and hard decisions that have to be made fast. What I found at the Metropolitan was *much* worse than I had expected, in every way—physical conditions, artistic integrity, sense of professionalism, support from the board were all well below anything I had lived with before. Even the financial status of the house was very discouraging, especially in the richest city in the richest country in the world.

My position for 1949–50 was that of an observer, and most of what I observed was a lesson in how not to organize an opera house. In planning for my own first season, to start one year later, I would obviously have to make many changes and survive a great deal of trouble. Before I left England, Beecham told me a story of hailing a taxi in New York during the war, when he was working at the Met, and asking the driver to take him to the Metropolitan Opera. "I'm sorry, sir," said the driver, "but we have gas rationing now, and the rules are that I'm not allowed to take passengers to a place of entertainment."

Sir Thomas settled into the seat and waved his hand imperiously. "The Metropolitan Opera," he told the driver, "is not a place of entertainment but a place of penance." I soon learned why Beecham had told me the story.

The first blow was in some ways the worst: virtually on the day I arrived, Charles M. Spofford, president of the Metropolitan Opera Association, resigned from his law firm and took leave from the Opera to serve in the American Military Government in Germany. He was the person who had most impressed me on my visits, and he much more than board chairman George Sloan had been the man who hired me. Spofford was replaced by Lowell Wadmond, a very shrewd Wall Street lawyer, but a man who had never even been on the board before and knew nothing of the opera house. Of necessity, he was Sloan's man, and almost from the first day Sloan and I did not get on.

Sloan was a handsome, very elegant Southerner, whose family had textile and department store money in Tennessee. In New York, he ran something called the Nutrition Foundation, which must have had some function in life, though I never found out what. It left him a great deal of free time for his social life, and he considered the Metropolitan Opera part of his social life. My predecessor Edward Johnson also enjoyed parties, and during the opera season he and Sloan saw each other all the time at a constant round of cocktail parties, dinners, and after-theater suppers. It came as a great disappointment to Sloan to learn that I had no intention of "being seen" at the right cocktail parties. He insisted that I "had to join" the Century Club, from which I resigned almost immediately after his death; I believe I am the only living person to have resigned from the Century Club.

Politically, Sloan was a reactionary to a degree almost impossible to find in Europe. He had all the racial prejudices of the Old South—even if everything else had gone well, his discovery that I intended to employ blacks at the Metropolitan would have been enough to make him an enemy for life. And he had no real feeling of responsibility for the people who worked in the Opera. One of my earliest discoveries was that much of the chorus was thoroughly superannuated, far too old to play the roles choristers must assume in a well-prepared opera, often far beyond whatever vocal prime they may have had. They were wretchedly paid—$85 a week, for less than thirty weeks a year, after which they went and sold ties at Macy's to keep alive (the Metropolitan did not even carry unemployment insurance for them)—and it was quite impossible that they had any savings. I went to Sloan and told him we would have to dismiss a number of members of the chorus, and would have to make some sort of pension arrangement for them. "Why should they have a pension?" he said. I said, "Because without one they will probably starve." Sloan shrugged his shoulders: "Too bad," he said; "the Met has no funds for pensions." But I told him I would not sign death warrants, and ultimately I made do with many people I should have dismissed, though others did leave with some minimal benefits from the company.

Worst of all, because Sloan's interest in the Opera was primarily social, he saw little reason why any number of expensive new productions had to be done, or why any great amount of money had to be spent on rehearsals. From 1944 to 1947, thanks to a virtual absence of new productions, a necessary reliance on local rather than on international talent, and a government-enforced wage freeze, the Metropolitan Opera had broken even. Sloan, though willing to help make up deficits as his entry fee to the chairmanship (his family foundation contributed up to $25,000 a year), did not see why opera could not be made to pay its own way. Though it was understood that for my first year I would be entitled to a certain number of new productions, thereafter Sloan was always trying to cut back production

[ 134 ]

costs. Anything new I wanted to do he opposed. He and Wadmond being of a suspicious nature anyway, they believed whenever a deficit went over budget that I was personally running
away with the petty cash. I remember one especially unpleasant
Sunday afternoon spent in Wadmond's Wall Street office after
an ignorant treasurer's report had raised questions to which the
answers were, in fact, rather easy—but nobody had asked me
for them before the report was written. Eventually, Wadmond
learned that I knew what I was doing and we became friends,
but my relations with Sloan were always more or less strained
until ill health forced his retirement in the spring of 1955.

I must point out, of course, that I also had allies on the
board—otherwise I could never have stayed as long as I did.
Perhaps the most important in the first years was Mrs. August
Belmont, then still quite young, only in her seventies; and then
as now, when she is in her nineties, a remarkable combination
of charm, sense, and authority. Mrs. Ryan, a dear friend, was
on the board; and then Mrs. Douglas. Later there were Colonel
Joseph Hartfield, like Sloan a Southerner but of much more
liberal stamp, an extraordinarily small man who was senior
partner of a Wall Street law firm and had a brain like daylight;
and C. D. Jackson, one of the senior men at the Luce publishing empire; and, a close collaborator for eight or nine years,
Anthony A. Bliss, son of a former president of the Association,
who became the leading figure on the board not long after
Sloan's retirement. And, of course, Spofford eventually returned.
But in the first years I was dealing with men of much lesser
vision.

Opening night in 1949 was depressing in the extreme, not
so much the performance (a creditable *Rosenkavalier* conducted
by Fritz Reiner with a cast including Eleanor Steber, Risë
Stevens, Erna Berger, and Emanuel List) as the audience. I
had never seen such antics in an opera house. Johnson explained

to me that although the opening night was part of the regular Monday subscription series, many of those in the audience were people who came to the Opera only this once, every year—cafe society of the lowest order, gossip writers from the gutter press, celebrity-seekers and clowns looking for the publicity the newspapers and now television would give any freakish occurrence or appearance at the Metropolitan's opening night. I decided immediately that if I could not prevent such fun and games I could at least make sure that those who enjoyed them paid the Opera for their pleasures; and from the beginning I removed opening night from the subscription program and sold tickets to it on a separate basis. Openings had been reserved for the Monday night subscribers, who were the most socially prominent, though they paid no more than the subscribers who came on other nights, and George Sloan was furious at the idea that his friends would lose this perquisite of their Monday season tickets.

Then as I looked over the schedule I found that the Metropolitan did not play at all in New York on Tuesday nights: the house was dark while the company went down to Philadelphia to present its productions there. This was a terrible burden. Orchestra players and chorus members who had to take a milk train back at two in the morning were in no condition to perform the next night (let alone rehearse the next day). Sets and costumes took a beating. And for no purpose whatever that I could see, for our performances in Philadelphia played at an enormous loss—just the cost of trucking everything there and back guaranteed a deficit.

When I asked why this strange game was being played, I was referred to Earle Lewis, who ran the Metropolitan box office. In any opera house where some events are completely sold out and important people are always seeking entry at the last moment, the man in charge of the tickets can acquire great political power unless the management watches him very carefully. Johnson had not been watching Lewis, whose status went back to the days of Otto Kahn, and who considered himself only a half step or so below the status of general manager, or perhaps not so low as that. Lewis informed me rather pityingly that New Yorkers would not go to the opera on Tuesday; it was common knowledge. When I asked why, he brushed me aside as an uninformed foreigner. Whether there was something he particularly liked to do on Tuesdays, I never knew.

It seemed to me that if we were to play Philadelphia the proper procedure would be to add it to the list of cities where the Metropolitan toured after the end of its regular season in New York. A week or even two weeks of performances would be less damaging to the health of the company and to the physical productions, and might even make money. But the Biddles and their friends wanted their regular Tuesday night social event, not a week when they would come in every night, and Sloan, who often went down to Philadelphia for performances and had many friends there, was entirely on their side. Nevertheless, I determined to introduce a Tuesday night subscription at the Met and to cut back on if I could not entirely eliminate our one-night stands in Philadelphia.

Year by year I whittled Philadelphia down, until finally, in 1961, more than ten years after I took over, the Metropolitan gave its last Tuesday night performance at the Academy of Music. This was, incidentally, a particularly brilliant occasion, with Birgit Nilsson, Leontyne Price, and Franco Corelli singing our brand-new Cecil Beaton production of *Turandot* (which had received its premiere in New York less than three weeks before), and Leopold Stokowski, Philadelphia's pet, in the pit. At someone's urging, I came out after the cast had taken its bows, to make some expression of the Metropolitan's regrets at being no longer in a position to serve Philadelphia, but I never got a chance to say a word: never in my life have I heard such booing as this very dressed-up audience uttered the moment they saw me.

The more I learned about the technical resources of the Metropolitan, the more alarmed I became. The auditorium was of course one of the glories of the world—that deep Diamond Horseshoe that gave the box holders, who had once owned the house, an opportunity to look at each other unrivaled in any other opera house anywhere. But the depth of the Horseshoe meant an immense number of side seats that had limited views of the stage, and the public areas were seriously inadequate for those who were not members of the Metropolitan Opera Guild or the Metropolitan Opera Club, which had their own exclusive spaces. (The former is a mostly feminine organization Mrs. Belmont had formed during the Depression to help the house, and it did contribute substantially to the company, especially to new productions; the latter is simply another social club for businessmen and lawyers who in my early days sat around in tails and top hats, paying the house a most inadequate rental for their facilities.) Because the public areas were so deficient, with no soundproofing whatever between access halls and auditorium, one had to permit latecomers to enter at any time and climb over people's knees with noisy apologies; the brief noise they made arriving was less disturbing on balance than the continuous noise they would have made on the other side of the doors. Still, it must be said that the auditorium was very beautiful, and somehow immensely theatrical: one could not step into that house without a feeling of excitement.

Behind the proscenium and its golden curtain, however, the theater had nothing at all to recommend it. Everything backstage was cramped and dirty and poor. There were neither side stages nor a rear stage: every change of scene had to be done from scratch on the main stage itself, which meant that if

[ 138 ]

an act had two scenes, the audience had just to sit and wait, wondering what the banging noises behind the curtain might mean. The lighting grid was decades behind European standards, and there was no revolving stage. Cecil Smith, then editor of *Musical America*, gave a concise description of what was wrong backstage not long after my arrival: "It is exceedingly cramped . . . The settings for each opera must be carted to and from the warehouse for each performance. Often they lie for several hours, half covered with tarpaulins and at the mercy of rain or snow, on the sidewalk of Seventh Avenue at the back of the house. One of the pastimes of those who stroll down Seventh Avenue is to look for the stenciled stamp on these pieces of scenery ('Figaro' or 'Forza' or 'Tristan') to see which opera is being exposed to the elements this time. The principal singers complain about their dressing rooms, which amount to a rabbit warren, with worse plumbing than most rabbits are willing to tolerate. Chorus, ballet and orchestra are herded into crowded, poorly ventilated common rooms . . ."

The productions themselves were mostly scandalous—thirty years old, never substantially refurbished, and low-quality to begin with. With few exceptions, they were simply collections of drop curtains and flats, leaving the singers standing on the bare stage with occasional prop pieces for variety. The solid structures and differing elevations that had characterized the best European work for more than a quarter of a century were rarely in evidence. Admittedly, solid structures cost money to make, cost money to set up, cost money to handle, because they had to be built up between the acts. But they make the difference between a provincial house and a great house. When the soprano took a deep breath on the Metropolitan stage the year I came, the whole castle behind her would be seen to tremble. Moreover, the indiscipline of the stage crews was a hazard to everyone. Some men showed up only when they felt like it, assignments were switched around at the last minute, stagehands could be heard talking behind the drops while artists were singing—and some of them even smoked backstage, though the place was a tinderbox and could have been condemned as a firetrap by any conscientious building inspector.

Dressing rooms were inadequate—and had to be used during the day for coaching sessions, because of the lack of rehearsal space. (The chorus rehearsed in the public bar!) A single roof stage had to be used for both orchestral rehearsals and dramatic rehearsals, alternately. Not that there was any overwhelming demand for rehearsal facilities. New productions were scarce (there were only two of them during my observation year, and that was more than the house had seen in most recent seasons), and repeats from last year received few ensemble rehearsals. When casts were changed, which happened very frequently, the newcomers might do their individual scenes with a coach and with such of the holdovers as deigned to attend.

In an ill-run house there is, unfortunately, a kind of competition among artists to see who can get away with the most. Once one artist neglects to come to rehearsals, everyone who *does* come seems to be admitting that he (or she) is not as important as his colleague. The Metropolitan was the fortunate possessor of the finest heldentenor in the world—Lauritz Melchior, distressingly fat and aging and not quite as good as he had been, but still without a rival. (Some would say that nobody since Melchior has been really of his vocal quality.) But Melchior would not come to rehearsals. His publicly expressed position was that if it was felt he had something to learn from one of the *maestri,* the conductor in question could make an appointment to meet with him at his apartment. The evil effects of this unprofessional conduct by its leading tenor could be felt everywhere in the house.

Dramatically, what the artists were asked to do when they

did come to rehearsals was scarcely worth their time. Though the Metropolitan had commanded the talents of able directors—Herbert Graf, whom I knew from Vienna days, had been associated with the house since 1936—it had made little use of what they could offer. Production after production revealed the chorus standing in a semicircle around the singers lined up at the apron of the stage.

In the provincial German houses of the 1920s I had run into the saying that when the basso buffo gets too old to sing, he becomes the *régisseur,* the stage director. At the Metropolitan, the exemplar of this tradition was Désiré Defrère, a baritone who had grown too old to sing. He was, in fact, an orderly and efficient director, with an excellent instinct for performances and what happens at them. I remember once a man clearly laboring to get through a scene, about to run out of voice, and Defrère from the wings supplying the necessary high note just as the man ran completely out of voice; very few in the audience even knew anything out of the ordinary had occurred.

I kept Defrère on the Metropolitan staff until he retired of his own choice, and I valued his contributions, but the fact was that he did not have the foggiest notion of what constituted a dramatically valid operatic presentation. In the succeeding years, whenever news of a financial crisis would run round the house, Defrère would come to me earnestly to urge that I abandon at least some of those time-consuming and expensive stage rehearsals we had whenever we were putting on a new production or mounting an older one for its first appearance of the season. I should just leave it to him, he said; he could get any opera onstage with just one day's rehearsal. No doubt he could, too; and he never understood that the results he would achieve were precisely those I did not want to have in any opera house of which I was general manager.

For an incoming manager, the most startling problem was

the absence of a budget. When I asked for this year's budget, I was shown rudimentary accounts for *last* season: the Metropolitan's business affairs were *ad hoc*. Because there was a cash inflow to worry about, the box office had been well routined, and one knew day by day how much revenue could be credited to a performance. But when I tried to find out how much the chorus had cost us the year before, nobody could give me an answer—there were so-and-so many regular choristers, paid so-and-so much, but of course others had been added for certain productions, and that would have to be looked up separately, and was this information I really had to have? At the end of the year, someone added up how much had come in and how much had gone out, and reported a surplus or a deficit (not always accurately). Figures were assigned to very large categories, and any breakdowns I wanted had to be made separately. I had promised my board that I would give them a budget and live within it, expecting that I could work "incrementally" from existing figures. Instead, I found I would have to make a budget almost from scratch, as though the Metropolitan were an Edinburgh Festival, something new in the world.

Of course, I found assets, too. The orchestra was first-class, and had worked in recent years under conductors of the quality of Fritz Reiner, Fritz Stiedry, Fritz Busch, Bruno Walter, George Szell, and Sir Thomas Beecham (though only the first two on this list were actually working at the Metropolitan during my observation year). Most of the world's greatest singers were under contract to the Metropolitan, though too often they sang only very short seasons in New York. A cadre of healthy, important American voices, many of them new to me, had become a strong backbone for the house during the war years. I was at first concerned about the effects of a union contract which required me to hire American soloists in a ratio of at least two to one as against foreign soloists, but my year of observation removed any fears that this so-called "Chicago convention" would harm the artistic quality of Metropolitan productions. Most important of all, the Metropolitan had a loyal audience who nearly filled the house for most performances, with a waiting list for subscriptions. There was a foundation on which I could build, but there was a lot of building to be done.

I told the administrative staff that I would try to let everyone know by the first of the year (two months after my arrival) whether or not I would be able to renew their contracts for 1950–51. And I let it be known that I hoped to reach contract terms with most singers before February 1 at the latest. That meant, in the case of leading soloists, that I would have to decide within two to three months on the repertory the Metropolitan would be offering the next year. But how luxurious it now seems—looking back from a time when any conductor who can lift a baton is booked three years ahead and every major artist knows exactly what he will be doing 747 days from today —that one could plan an entire season, singers, conductors, directors, designers, less than ten months before that season was to begin. I enjoyed it all. Every morning when I woke up I could hardly wait to get to the problems.

# 15

First I had to choose my immediate staff, and the hardest choice was necessarily of the man who would hold at the Metropolitan the post I had held for Ebert in Berlin. Johnson's artistic administrator was Frank St. Leger, a conductor, knowledgeable about opera and, of course, about this theater. I received a good deal of conflicting advice. Several people with the company told me, very confidentially, that St. Leger was hated, which to me meant no more than that he was doing his job. A good artistic administrator must be disliked, as I was in Berlin and Bob Herman has been in his years with me at the Metropolitan, because the artistic administrator is the man who must keep telling people they can't do what they want to do (like take an engagement to sing in Portland, Oregon, the night before they are scheduled to sing at the Metropolitan) and make them do things they don't want to do (like come to rehearsals). Others, Johnson himself and his friends on and off my board, told me that I would need St. Leger badly during my first years and, really, could not run the house successfully without him.

23. Left to right: Erich Leinsdorf, John Gutman, Robert Herman, Rudolf Bing, Mrs. Gutman, Francis Robinson, Paul Jaretzki

24. Left to right: Julius Burger, prompter; Rudolf Bing; Eleanor Steber as Vanessa; Samuel Barber, composer; Gian Carlo Menotti, director-librettist; Nathaniel Merrill

25. Mr. and Mrs. Rudolf Bing at Sherry's Restaurant in the Old Met

26. Left to right: George Sloan, former Chairman of the Board; Nina Bing; Trygve H. Lie, former UN Secretary-General; Kirsten Flagstad; Rudolf Bing; Lowell Wadmond

27. Picketing *Don Carlo*, 1952

28. Leonard Warren in 1952 wearing *Forza del Destino* costume in which he died onstage

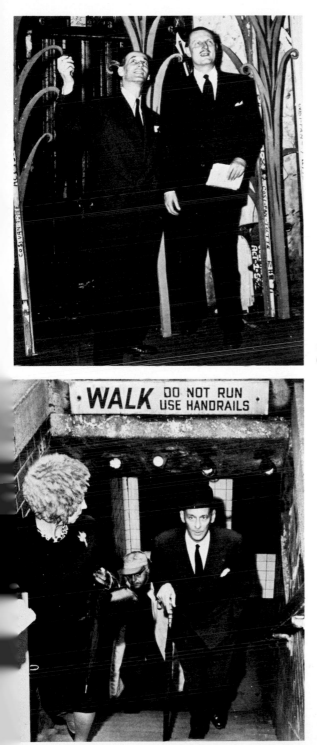

29. With Sir Tyrone Guthrie

30. Exiting from the BMT at Fortieth Street and Broadway

31. Left, Marion Anderson and
Rudolf Bing before her first appearance
at the Met

32. Below, with Bruno Walter discussing
*The Magic Flute* at Old House

33. With President and Mrs. Eisenhower in Washington, D.C.

That was the problem; St. Leger was the symbol of the old regime. To a much greater extent than I would want from an artistic administrator, he rather than the general manager was really running the Metropolitan. He was an older man than I and would expect to tell me what could and could not be done. Under the circumstances, I decided not to retain him.

Fortunately, St. Leger's assistant, very nearly as knowledgeable as himself, was Max Rudolf, whom I had known since Darmstadt days. Rudolf, who eventually left to become conductor of the Cincinnati Symphony, was then committed to management rather than conducting, and was willing to put his full time into the necessary organizing and liaison work of artistic administration. St. Leger at my request resigned, and I appointed Rudolf to the post. Though he had been mostly a kind of musical secretary, he had kept his eyes open: I could ask him how something worked—for example, the system for hiring and training "supers," the spear carriers some operas need—and he could tell me.

My business manager I found already in place: Reginald Allen, a very cultivated American who had been manager of the Philadelphia Orchestra (and a tennis champion in his youth), and who had come to the Metropolitan a year before. He already knew enough to help me, without being committed to the obviously hopeless procedures of the previous regime. Earle Lewis did not have to be asked to resign from his box office post; he announced his intention of retiring on our first meeting. To replace him, I assigned the management of the box office to Francis Robinson, as southern as George Sloan (they were both from Nashville), a gracious, stage-struck former newspaperman who had been Katharine Cornell's press representative and had come to the Metropolitan with the Sol Hurok organization when Hurok was managing the annual spring tour. Later, Robinson would assume the public relations post at the

Metropolitan, and it is as assistant manager in charge of public relations that he continues from my regime to that of my successor.

Perhaps the most urgent immediate need was someone who could tame the wild dragons of the technical staff, the stage crews, and the physical productions they manipulated (or manhandled). I asked around discreetly, and someone recommended Horace Armistead, an experienced stage designer who was also reputed to know the ins and outs of American union rules and regulations. Perhaps he did; his problem was that he himself belonged to the wrong union (he was a "stage designer" rather than a "stage employee"), and his very appointment made an uproar. The fact is that he never took hold, though Fritz Stiedry after our opening night said in tribute that in his work on our first production "Armistead did absolutely not badly." He was especially unable (as I was myself) to get any control over our chief electrician, a man named Jacob Buchter, who gave heart attacks to every director and designer I brought so long as he was there. For Buchter, nothing could be done at the Metropolitan that had not been done before. He was the only man who had keys to the electrical room. Once, when there was a strike threat, I asked him to make a copy for me, so I could get in if he were gone, and he refused . . .

I needed another man. I had known Rudolf in Darmstadt, and we had never fought about anything, but we had not been friends. (During our years together at the Met, we would become friends and I would come to treasure Max's spirit as well as his judgment.) Entering what looked like—and was, and still is—an immensely dangerous lion's den, I felt that I needed one man on my staff on whom I could rely at all times for complete and unflinching personal loyalty. John Gutman had been a rising musicologist and a critic on good Berlin papers when I was at the Städtische Oper, and was now in New York—

in fact, he was one of the people I looked up in the first days of my visit for Glyndebourne. He was wasting his training, talents, and time working for a company that manufactured venetian blinds. I asked him to come to the Metropolitan as my personal assistant, expecting we could create some American equivalent for the European Dramaturg, the man responsible for the literary aspects of opera. During the early years Gutman did a great variety of jobs for me, from handling negotiations with music publishers to auditioning singers to translating operas into English; in the later years, he gave most of his time to the Metropolitan Opera Studio, an organization that brought along younger singers and put on performances in schools, etc. But for almost twenty-three years he was available for help in any emergency; and in the early years, when there were plenty of emergencies, he was invaluable.

It seemed to me unwise for me to have an office amongst the offices of the men who were running the house while I was merely an observer, and after a few days I asked for and received a suite in the "studio building," an office block built onto the northeast corner of the opera house. (There was a door from the studio wing into the orchestra level of the auditorium, but it was always locked, and for those who didn't have a key, which included nearly all the tenants in the office block, there was little difference between the Metropolitan studio building and lots of other 1880s-vintage office buildings on Broadway.) My secretary was a very bright young lady named Louise Florian, who later became an artists' manager.

On five evenings a week I was at the opera house, watching performances, judging productions and performers; and I spent most of my days meeting with my newly appointed staff or with people I wished to engage for the next season. One of the first artists I hired—for fear someone in Europe would hear this remarkably beautiful voice and steal the man away—was Richard

Tucker. We had a minor disagreement about fee, winding up our negotiations with $50 per performance still separating us. I foolishly suggested that we toss a coin. We did, and I won, and he never forgot it; he would remind me of this episode in all subsequent negotiations over a period of twenty-odd years, and accuse me of using his coin and pocketing it at the end.

I decided quite early that I wished to open my first season with Verdi's *Don Carlo*, which had not been done at the Metropolitan since 1922—and had not been much of a success then (only eleven performances in three years) despite the presence of Chaliapin, Martinelli, and Ponselle. People thought this an extremely adventurous choice; what I knew that they did not was that during the late 1920s in Central Europe we had learned how to do these later Verdi operas so that they made their proper effect. But part of the approach was the quality of the staging: I would need a first-class director for *Don Carlo*, and I would need the entire cast in New York working at the task for three weeks before opening night.

Stage direction was the key to the ways my management was to differ from previous managements of the Metropolitan. The house in its history had enjoyed the services of singers as great as or greater than any I could ever hope to recruit; and even in the immediate past the conducting staff had been of a quality my administration was unlikely to surpass. But staging of the first order the Metropolitan had never known, and my experience with Ebert had convinced me that staging was more important in opera than most people connected with opera had ever believed.

To conduct *Don Carlo*, I had Fritz Stiedry, who had launched Ebert's management of the Städtische Oper in Berlin with *Macbeth*. He was an outstanding personality and musician, though not a great conductor. He had a strange physical problem—his elbows went up when it should have been his

[ 148 ]

baton. (He had interesting troubles with English, too. Once there was some problem about the members of the cast laughing at him; but I couldn't blame them—he had sternly told a soprano, "Don't *rush!* You're *dragging!*") To sing the title role, I had Jussi Bjoerling, already at the house. For the baritone lead, I wanted Leonard Warren, but he would not commit three weeks for rehearsing, and we were lucky enough to have two great American baritones at the Met: Robert Merrill was second only to Warren, and would have been first anywhere else in the world. An excellent young American bass, Jerome Hines, was available for the Grand Inquisitor. For the rest, I wrote and telephoned abroad—Boris Christoff, a Bulgarian, to sing King Philip; Delia Rigal, an Argentinian, for the Queen; Fedora Barbieri, an Italian, for Eboli, all in debut appearances. Another debut was arranged for the smallest of the solo roles: Lucine Amara, a San Francisco girl who came recommended by Pierre Monteux and Carl Fbert, then running an opera program at the University of Southern California, would make her first appearance at the Metropolitan as the Celestial Voice at the end of the auto-da-fé scene.

My first choice to direct anything that year was inevitably Tyrone Guthrie, but Tony was too busy in England. I believe it was he who recommended Margaret Webster, who was at first extremely reluctant to try something so foreign to her experience as opera. But I pointed out that Ebert himself had never had anything to do with opera before he took over in Darmstadt, and that the effects we wanted were essentially Shakespearean—the opera was set in what were for the English Elizabethan times, and both Schiller (on whose play the libretto was based) and Verdi had been firm Shakespeareans. What we had to offer her, unfortunately, was nothing but an exciting opportunity: her total fee for directing *Don Carlo*, including expenses, was $2,500. Rolf Gérard agreed to design the sets and costumes, months of work for so lavish an opera, for $4,000. Including these fees, and extra payments for rehearsals, I budgeted *Don Carlo* at $65,000, which Mrs. Nin Ryan raised, as I have recounted, by selling one of the family Rembrandts. This production, which several members of the board considered desperately extravagant (it did run over budget), must now be counted one of the bargains of operatic history: counting the performances in my final season, the Metropolitan has done this *Don Carlo* more than eighty times, and the sets and costumes were sufficiently well-made to need no more than an occasional freshening. A *Don Carlo* of this substance would cost perhaps $250,000 in 1972—but, on the other hand, the Rembrandt would probably fetch even more than $250,000 now.

The other centerpiece of my first season would be *Fledermaus*, the brilliant Johann Strauss operetta which we would do in an English translation, hoping to draw to the Metropolitan a new audience that usually went to the theaters a few blocks away rather than to the opera house. Here again I had something close to an ideal cast easily available: Ljuba Welitsch for Rosalinda and a pretty young American coloratura, Patrice Munsel, for the servant Adele; the ever attractive Risë Stevens for Prince Orlofsky; Richard Tucker for Alfred; Set Svanholm, a much better actor than those who had seen him only in Wagner could realize, for Eisenstein; and John Brownlee, who had been with us at Glyndebourne and was now a fixture at the Metropolitan, as the stage-managing Dr. Falke. The selection of Fritz Reiner to conduct guaranteed that everyone would take the work seriously as music—and it deserves to be taken seriously as music. Reiner, though not among the naturally light at heart, knew the Viennese spirit and could be counted on to give us a first-class musical performance.

Here I wanted a Broadway or Hollywood director to ensure

that the adaptation met local taste. My initial choice was Rouben Mamoulian, but he was committed to a new Maxwell Anderson-Kurt Weill musical, and could not shake free. (Then Weill died, and there was no musical; and, indeed, Mamoulian faded from the Broadway scene.) Someone proposed Garson Kanin, who came to my office with his splendid wife Ruth Gordon to tell me that the whole idea was nonsense, he knew nothing of operas and opera houses, but ultimately agreed to take on the job. He recommended the musical comedy lyricist Howard Dietz for the translation. Again, I asked Rolf Gérard to design.

The other two productions could not bear the same personal stamp of the new management. I thought I should do something by Wagner to balance the new Verdi production. There had been no new production of *Der Fliegende Holländer* at the Metropolitan since 1930, and the opera would make a fine showcase for the debut of Hans Hotter, whom I wished to bring over from Germany. I hoped also to have Welitsch as Senta, but she could not come on time; in any event, we had excellent substitutes in Astrid Varnay and the American soprano Margaret Harshaw. Herbert Graf was available to direct. I had been investigating American theatrical designers, and had found Robert Edmond Jones to be perhaps the best regarded. He took quite a lot of persuading, and then had reason to regret his acceptance, because he became seriously ill during that summer (he died shortly thereafter); his designs had to be executed by Charles Elson, who later became one of the most useful men around the house, revising and repairing large numbers of productions I could not afford to replace but flatly refused to put onstage in their existing condition. We coined the new verb "elsonize" to describe what he did for the Metropolitan.

Finally, I owed the New York public a new staging of an Italian warhorse, and one of the productions in the worst shape was that of the old twins, *Cavalleria* and *Pagliacci*. Not much money would be left for these, and I put the designing task in the hands of Armistead, who wanted to continue with his professional work as well as supervising our backstage. To direct, I first tried Vittorio de Sica, whose films were then an international sensation; denied there, I turned to Hans Peter Busch, Fritz Busch's son and an old colleague of mine at Glyndebourne (from 1935, when we were both listed as "Assistant Producer"), who had become a professor of opera production at Indiana University.

Neither of the conductors of Italian repertory then on the Metropolitan staff were to my taste. To replace them, I hired my old friend Alberto Erede from Glyndebourne days and Fausto Cleva, who had been for years the Metropolitan's chorus master, but had left the house to make a career in Europe as a conductor. And I claimed the promise of Bruno Walter that he would help me if I came to New York. He agreed to conduct *Fidelio* and the Verdi *Requiem*, which I wished to use as a replacement for the tired old *Parsifal* the Metropolitan traditionally did in Easter week. Typically, Walter had one question about *Fidelio*: "Who," he said nervously, "will sing the First Prisoner?" The big things the management would have to take care of in its own interest; Walter wanted to make sure he was protected on the small things.

For the two works Walter would conduct I re-engaged two prominent sopranos who had been under contract to the Metropolitan in years past but had not appeared on this stage in recent seasons. One was immensely important to the work of the house in the following years, but her re-engagement occasioned little notice; the re-engagement of the other caused a huge furor.

The first was Zinka Milanov. Someone, I believe Max Rudolf, told me of this wonderful soprano whose contract had been allowed to lapse for reasons no one understood, and I went to Hartford, Connecticut, to hear her sing in *Un Ballo in Maschera*. It was a performance the like of which I have rarely seen. The sets must have been borrowed from a *Hansel and Gretel* of a previous Christmas; chorus and orchestra rarely agreed on tempi, the other soloists were third-rate provincial and obviously had never seen the sets before, much less rehearsed before them—but there in those preposterous surroundings was a voice of such beauty that I felt I had never heard anything like it before. She would sing in my first season, among other things, the soprano part in the Verdi *Requiem*.

And the other soprano I re-engaged was, of course, Kirsten Flagstad. I went to hear her at a recital in Carnegie Hall, and satisfied myself that the voice was still among the treasures of the age. Then I began to make inquiries as to the extent to which she had in fact been involved with the Nazis. I wrote to the U. S. Ambassador to Norway to make sure of feelings about her in her home country, which had probably suffered more grievously than any other, except perhaps Poland, from the Nazi occupation, and was the most violently anti-German place in Europe. I wrote to Chuck Spofford in Germany to find out what the Allied Military Government thought. And I had assistants check the archives for what information they contained.

Miss Flagstad's husband had worked for and with the Nazis, and after the conquest of Norway she had returned home to be at his side. But throughout that time she had not sung in public. It seemed to me peculiar that an artist like Erna Berger—who had sung all through the war for the pleasure of the Nazi bigwigs in Berlin—could be acceptable at the Metropolitan, while Miss Flagstad had to be banned. Only one item damaging to her came out of the search—after the invasion of Norway, while she was still in America, she had sung a recital in Washington at which the German Ambassador was present. But she was a guest of the United States, which was still at peace with Germany, and she might well have thought it rude to bar anyone from her audience. Anyway, it was long ago, and trivial. I had lived with the Christies long enough to know how foolish non-political people could be in the face of a Nazi menace they did not begin to understand. Miss Flagstad was obviously a non-political person, and the time for punishing her for her husband's misdeeds had ended. I asked her to return, to sing Isolde under Fritz Reiner, and Leonore with Bruno Walter— who was acting again as my one-man de-Nazification court. Asked by the press to justify my action, I said simply that the world's greatest soprano should sing in the world's greatest opera house.

My announcement that Miss Flagstad would return unleashed a torrent of vituperation, especially from a vicious little man named Billy Rose, who had been a Broadway musical impresario and considered himself an expert on opera, and now suggested in a newspaper column he was writing that I might hire Ilse Koch (the concentration camp monster who had lampshades made of human skin) to be the wardrobe mistress and Hjalmar Schacht (Hitler's finance minister) to be the Metropolitan's chief accountant. Though it was the negative reactions that made the news, I also had a stream of approving letters, and a reasonable degree of support from my board.

In fact, when Miss Flagstad appeared the next year, she was welcomed with overwhelming warmth by the Metropolitan audience—but in a sense the damage had been done, because the board the next year, fearing a repetition of the denunciations in the press, rejected my request to hire Wilhelm Furtwängler as a conductor at the Metropolitan—the only time in twenty-two years that I was told whom I could or could not hire. What is so odd about this incident in my recollection is that I was personally extremely sensitive to the question of whether or not an artist had collaborated with the Nazis, and there were many I flatly refused to hire because of my feeling that they had taken sides against the decent people of the world. But others chose not to make rational judgments but to condemn all they could reach.

The rumors that I was about to engage Miss Flagstad, and the fact that I had already re-engaged some of the singers on the Italian side, provoked a difficult incident with the Metropolitan's reigning Wagnerian duo, Melchior and Helen Traubel, both of whom announced they were resigning from the company. Melchior's announcement followed an ultimatum delivered to me at eleven o'clock on the morning of a day I was to go to Philadelphia with the company, that if I had not re-engaged him by noon he would quit. I had not known, frankly, how to handle the Melchior problem, how to make him a responsible artist rather than a disturbing artistic influence in the house; his telegram now told me how. Miss Traubel, however, I needed not only for roles she sang very well but also to avoid any appearance of pushing Americans out to take Miss Flagstad in. Fortunately, it was possible—by offering her alternate placement in Miss Flagstad's roles plus a choice role she had never done before, the Marschallin in *Der Rosenkavalier*—to reconcile Miss Traubel with the new management, at least temporarily. Eventually, she decided that she found nightclub work more rewarding and less debilitating than opera, and changed the focus of her endeavors.

In the meantime, I was constantly writing Europe, for various purposes. I felt that I still had vestigial responsibilities at Edinburgh and Glyndebourne, and maintained correspondence with both Ian Hunter and Moran Caplat. For Hunter, I suggested and arranged a performance of the Virgil Thomson *Cello Concerto* by Pierre Fournier and Sir Thomas Beecham, and made a deal for Leonard Bernstein to conduct two festival concerts (for a flat fee of $1,000). Caplat, the files reveal, wrote me about whether he should hire the mezzo Blanche Thebom, a regular at the Metropolitan, and I was pleased to be able to reply, "I think she is most suitable in every respect: excellent voice, talented actress, and beautiful to look at."

But most of the letters to Europe were an effort to establish lines of communication that would enable me to learn quickly and accurately about artists working thousands of miles from New York. The key man in Europe for me was Alfred Diez, a Viennese artists' manager resident in England, whom I had come to know in London. For years Diez kept me informed of all newsworthy developments on the European operatic scene, found answers to questions I sent him, and arranged my annual visits to Europe north of the Alps. South of the Alps, unfortunately, Diez was much less useful, and my original contact in Italy, an amiable old bandit named Liduino Bonard, soon turned out to be less than useful. On my first trip, he set up auditions for me in Rome—thirty or thirty-one singers, each worse than the one before. I said to him, "Would you have introduced these fellows to Ghiringhelli? [the head of La Scala]?" He threw up his hands: "Oh, *no*," he said.

I asked Alberto Erede what I should do, and he introduced me to Roberto Bauer, an independently wealthy enthusiast born in Milan to German parents, who had one of the world's greatest collections of vocal recordings and was on good personal terms with most of the best singers in Italy. He put himself at my disposal. I would send him names that had been recommended to me, by agents or tourists or other artists, and he would screen thousands of singers and write back—unnecessary, unnecessary, unnecessary, this one you must hear, and so forth. Then he would organize my time in Italy, would say, "Come to Milan for five days, Rome three days, Florence three days," and set up the auditions for me. Almost every Italian artist of real importance during my time at the Metropolitan came to us through Bauer—Tebaldi, Corelli, Cossotto, Pavarotti, Siepi, Scotto, Corena, Freni, Valletti, Bastianini, and many others.

I trusted Bauer's ear and his judgment, and perhaps even more important, the singers trusted him. We certainly could not have held onto Franco Corelli without Bauer, who would come over with him to New York and hold his hand whenever he was threatening disaster. The key was that he worked for the Metropolitan, not for the singers: from 1952 to his death in 1970, we paid him a retainer, plus a small sum for every contract signed through his efforts. There is no doubt he saved us very much more than we paid him—one year I was able to tell the board that I had budgeted $30,000 to $40,000 additional to pay Italian singers in a rising market, but would be able to hold the extra payment to $2,000 because of Bauer's negotiating abilities. He became a great friend, an immensely helpful and substantial collaborator, and his death was a great loss to me and to the Metropolitan Opera.

For my first annual European trip in spring 1950, however, I was very much in Diez's hands, apart from the excursion to Rome. Before leaving, I tidied up in New York with a number of announcements. Opening night would be *Don Carlo;* it would be withdrawn from the Monday subscription and offered together with the first *Fledermaus* and the Walter-Flagstad *Fidelio* as a package of "Three Firsts" at a $50 top. The number of operas to be performed would be reduced from twenty-four in Johnson's nineteen-week season to twenty (counting *Cav* and *Pag* as one) in my twenty-two-week season, giving more time for the rehearsing of each. That also meant, however, that some operas would have to be repeated in a season-long subscription series. Subscribers were therefore offered half-season, alternate-week as well as full-season, every-week subscriptions.

I hoped to be able to offer subscriptions on this basis to some of the Metropolitan's waiting list, but unfortunately 95 per cent of existing subscribers took the every-week subscription, even though it meant they would get repetitions. A worse failure was my decision, also announced at this time, to get the Metropolitan out of the ballet business and turn over all opera ballets to Antony Tudor and the Ballet Theatre; this arrangement would last exactly one year.

Discussing my plans during the intermission of a broadcast of a New York Philharmonic concert, I said I planned to engage black artists at the earliest opportunity, which provoked another storm. (In fact, I had already asked Max Rudolf to sound out Marian Anderson on the possibility of singing Azucena in *Il Trovatore* for us, but nothing came of it.) In general, however, my announcements at the end of the observation year were well accepted by everyone except Melchior, Johnson, Billy Rose, and Walter Winchell. I could go off to Europe confident that the new team was ready to function.

# 16

Traveling as general manager of the Metropolitan Opera was a new and strange experience. I would arrive in a city and be surrounded from the moment I left the plane—reporters, photographers, singers, and agents. I would hold auditions all day, and go to performances at night, and meet with the agents somehow in between, trying to remember what we needed now, what we needed later, what we could afford. When I knew I wanted an artist, my basic principles were two: artistically, I needed rehearsal time as well as performing time (as I said in my first statement to the New York press, I wanted "an ensemble of stars, not of comets"), which would normally mean at least ten or twelve weeks; and institutionally, I needed an option on the spring weeks when the Metropolitan toured the country, because we were committed to give the host cities the same performances we gave in New York. European artists have never liked the tour, and I must say I can't blame them, but only a handful have tried to avoid the obligation once they agreed to undertake it.

Of the artists I heard in that first spring tour in 1950, I engaged only one for the next season—Victoria de los Angeles, whom I heard in Paris. (In the fall, before the Metropolitan season began, I went to San Francisco on a combined courtesy call and audition safari and heard Mario del Monaco, whom I not only engaged for fall 1951 for opening night but also invited to do a rare one-night "guest appearance" in Puccini's *Manon Lescaut* on his way home in fall 1950. It was a mistake: the critics resented the idea of a guest, and I got him to do it too cheaply; I paid him $150 or $250 for the evening, I've forgotten which, and he never forgave me for it.) With very few exceptions, and most of those to cover emergencies, I engaged foreign artists only after I heard them abroad; and Diez and Bauer served as early warning posts, telling me which artists I should audition on these flying trips, rather than as authorities telling me which artists I should engage. Some artists, of course, I found in New York itself: in my first month as general manager, Roberta Peters had to be called upon to make a sudden debut as replacement for Nadine Conner in *Don Giovanni*. Few artists have survived being thrown on the Metropolitan stage without warning; Miss Peters became a star.

Because there was little time between the Metropolitan tour and the end of the European season, all those trips were frantic, much too crowded and busy. My wife either stayed in Paris or went ahead to establish our hold on whatever resort hotel we would stay at that summer. To save my life, I cannot remember in which year I first heard which artists, or under what circumstances. One of the few auditions I remember vividly is that of Tito Gobbi, who had completed his Rome season a day or two before I arrived and was already too eminent an artist to participate in the day-long series of auditions held for me at the Teatro Argentina. But he graciously agreed that I should hear him before offering him an engagement, and he told me he had a large enough room at home. I went to his house and settled down on a couch to listen, and just as his pianist struck the first chord his pet lion came in through a swinging door and started straight for me. I am extremely fond of animals, and this was only a baby lion, but I must admit it was a distracting experience. Gobbi kept singing, and before the lion reached me across the big room his little daughter came dashing through the same door, grabbed the lion by the tail, and dragged him back where he had come from. Eventually we did engage Gobbi, but that audition did not speed the process.

In those early years, we divided our summer between Bad Ischl in Austria and Monte Pana in the Dolomite Alps. I made it a point to get to Salzburg, where the Festival had been revived, and there in summer 1950 I had the first of what would be several long and ultimately fruitless talks with Wilhelm Furtwängler. I was quite certain that Furtwängler had never been a Nazi or a Nazi sympathizer, and I had the testimony of Yehudi Menuhin, whom I trusted absolutely, that he had worked hard on behalf of Jewish members of the Berlin Philharmonic. But it had not yet been possible for him to conduct in America because of agitation against him, and in summer 1950 all we could do was agree to wait until we learned how the New York public accepted the return of Kirsten Flagstad.

When I returned to New York in the fall I settled into the general manager's office on the ground floor of the "old yellow brick brewery," at the Thirty-ninth Street and Seventh Avenue corner. The Opera was almost exactly one mile from our apartment at the Essex House, and I enjoyed the walk down Seventh Avenue, through the garishness of a Times Square which was just shabby and dirty in the morning light. In bad weather, I took the BMT subway, which had entrances only a few hundred feet from the Fifty-eighth Street door of the Essex House, and only a few score feet from the Metropolitan.

The anteroom through which I or anyone else had to walk to get to my office was the general switchboard of the Metropolitan telephones, and contained the main bulletin board on which notices to the company were posted: it was the nerve center of the house. One could tell a great deal about the emotional condition of the theater on any given day—and theaters have emotional conditions, which change from day to day—simply by walking into one's office, and sniffing the air en route. I retained Edward Johnson's secretary, Reva Freidberg (who in 1972 still worked for me part-time, from her home, organizing the lists of guests I invited to share the general manager's box at each performance). Her office was to the left off the narrow corridor between the general anteroom and my office. A step beyond and a step down and I was "home," in a very cozy place, not large, with a rather low ceiling, furnished in soft colors and soft fabrics, a relaxed place for a most unrelaxed job.

I found Gérard well advanced with both the *Don Carlo* and the *Fledermaus* sets, the *Dutchman* somewhat delayed by Jones's illness. Peggy Webster had been meeting with Fritz Stiedry to find out what she had to know about *Don Carlo*, and Garson Kanin had been firing off suggestions to Fritz Reiner based on his researches into and sparkling thoughts about *Fledermaus*. The *Fledermaus* situation was blowing up not one but several storms.

The worst problem was Reiner's recording contract with RCA Victor. I was counting on revenues from a recording of our production of *Fledermaus* to help pay the Metropolitan's bills, and the house was midstream of a four-year exclusive contract with Columbia Records. During the summer, it came to our attention that Victor, with Reiner, Risë Stevens, and Pat Munsel under contract, planned to issue a *Fledermaus* of its own, which would severely undercut the market for our Columbia recording. I went to General Sarnoff and was referred to George Marek, the head of the Victor division, to whom I proposed a "triple entente" of Victor, Columbia, and the Metropolitan, to make recordings of many Metropolitan productions, give the record buyer the best possible performances, and guarantee the opera house the revenues it needed so desperately. This suggestion was apparently taken seriously at Victor, but I soon discovered that under cover of their negotiations with me the Victor people were making additional contracts with other artists we had hoped to use for our authorized recording.

Goddard Lieberson of Columbia Records was legitimately distressed by this turn of events. He had guaranteed the Metropolitan $25,000 a year in record royalties, and we were not earning it; *Fledermaus* was his best bet to recoup on the contract, and our best bet to show additional recording revenues. If Victor and Reiner could go behind my back, I could go behind theirs. I wrote Sir Thomas Beecham, whose recording contract was with the English company then affiliated with Columbia, asking him to come and take over our *Fledermaus*, but he couldn't.

We had already gone through a considerable hunt to find the right comedian to play Frosch, the jailer, in the last act. In the spring I had announced that I was trying to get Danny Kaye, who had given me some reason to believe he could clear the time. When he finally found he could not, Garson Kanin and I kept exchanging names of men who might do the job: I tried Milton Berle; he tried Groucho Marx and then Zero Mostel; I suggested Bert Lahr and Bobby Clark; he suggested James Barton (from *Tobacco Road!*) and Fred Allen. The man we hit on, Jack Gilford, lacked the celebrity of these men but had the great advantage of being available for the entire season and for the tour, and the further advantage of doing the act extremely well. Later it would turn out that his presence had some disadvantageous aspects, too—not his fault, but a serious problem for the Metropolitan both on tour at the end of this season and, as shall be noted, in the next year.

Relations between Kanin and Reiner deteriorated throughout October, because Kanin was an enthusiast and Reiner had not an ounce of that quality in his tightly controlled personality. In one week in October, Kanin sent Reiner five separate letters, with suggestions for the production, to which Reiner replied:

> Your five letters of last week reached me, after a detour to Westport, finally at my winter quarters, the Hotel Marguery.
>
> Re—Conducting the Overture facing the audience; Sorry but for various reasons not feasible.
>
> Re—Repeat of 'DUI-DU': I prefer not to tamper with the original score.
>
> Re—'Acceleration Waltz'—I will play 'Southern Roses' because I like it better.
>
> Re—Using a gypsy band for the 'Czardas': not impossible but 1) Music material (orchestration) would have to be arranged by say Robert Russell Bennett or Don Walker to make it sound satisfactory. 2) Musicians on stage will have to play by memory (major problem). 3) Would add to cost of production.
>
> Re—Using BELOW, BELOW, BELOW instead of MERCI, MERCI, MERCI—I will respect your wish and Mr. Dietz's.

Reiner sent me a copy of this epistle, to which I replied:

> Thank you for sending me a copy of your letter to Mr. Kanin dated October 31st.
>
> Frankly, I don't think that letter emanates your usual charm and it doesn't strike me as a very happy attempt to establish a friendly relationship with a guest stage director; but no doubt you have your own way of handling your collaborators.

Toward the end of November, I had occasion to write Reiner again about the staging problem: "You yourself anticipated that further trouble would blow up in the near future between yourself and the stage director and if you persist in the attitude so far displayed I have no reason to doubt your prophecy." But by then, I must admit, the war between Reiner and Kanin had become a matter of some satisfaction to me, because I was deep in negotiations to replace Reiner on the podium in *Fledermaus* with a conductor who would later be able to make a Metropolitan Opera recording for Columbia Records. I had not seen Eugene Ormandy since the Hugo Heller days in Vienna, when I had arranged his Viennese debut as a violinist. Now he agreed, subject to the approval of the Philadelphia Orchestra board, to make his debut as an opera conductor with our *Fledermaus*.

The day before Thanksgiving, Ormandy's board did approve, and on the holiday I left in Reiner's mailbox a note telling him that considering all the circumstances I thought he might be relieved to learn that I had decided to give the *Fledermaus* conducting assignment to someone else. Then I abandoned my office for the day and retired to my old suite in the studio building, while Reiner raged through the house trying to find out who his replacement would be before I announced it to the press. Our relationship had never been based on friendship, anyway, and he was not going to sacrifice the chance to conduct Flagstad in *Tristan* to get even with me over *Fledermaus*: I was in no serious danger of losing the services of a man who was, after all, a great conductor and a great builder of orchestras. Meanwhile, I had protected our stage performance of *Fledermaus* (which sold out nineteen evenings at the Metropolitan and twelve evenings on tour in that 1950–51 season) and guaranteed Columbia the advertised "Metropolitan" authenticity of its recording.

My *Don Carlo* troubles were more intractable—not to say frightening. That fall, over the veto of President Truman, Congress had passed the McCarran Act, which prohibited the issuance of visas to anyone who had ever been associated with any totalitarian party, Nazi, Fascist, or Communist. The McCarthyite witch hunt had begun, directed initially at foreigners. Fedora Barbieri was detained by the immigration authorities when she arrived, but our lawyers were able to get her out. Boris Christoff, however, was not allowed to come at all. There are few operas where the bass is the key figure, but *Don Carlo* is one of them. I cabled to the American Embassy in Rome:

BORIS CHRISTOFF THROUGH HIS AGENT INFORMS US DIFFI-CULTIES OBTAINING AMERICAN ENTRY VISA STOP HE IS SCHEDULED IMPORTANT ROLES OPENING AND EARLY PER-FORMANCES NEW SEASON DUE TO LEAVE SOUTHAMPTON OCTOBER SEVENTH STOP HIS DELAY WOULD PRACTICALLY WRECK OUR SEASON AND CAUSES SERIOUS DIFFICULTIES WOULD BE GREATLY OBLIGED IF YOU CAN FIND IT POSSIBLE TO GRANT VISA SPEEDILY AND ADVISE US OF POSITION.

On October 2 a reply was received:

. . . FOUND INELIGIBLE TO RECEIVE A VISA UNDER THE ACT OF OCTOBER 16, 1918, AS AMENDED, WHICH RELATES TO ALIENS WHO BECAUSE OF THEIR BELIEFS, ACTIVITIES, MEMBERSHIP IN OR AFFILIATION WITH CERTAIN ORGANIZA-TIONS ARE EXCLUDABLE FROM THE UNITED STATES.

Christoff himself sent a frantic cable to his manager, Sol Hurok:

NEVER HAD ANY POLITICAL IDEA NEVER BELONGED TO ANY POLITICAL PARTY.

But it did no good; none at all. At the very last moment, I was confronted with the need to find a King Philip. There was a brief hope that the Hungarian bass Mihaly Szekely, who had been at the house before, might be able to fill in; but just as the Americans would not let Christoff in, the Hungarians now would not let Szekely out. Diez from London proposed Gottlob

Frick, but his Nazi associations were too blatant for me, even if they could have passed the immigration authorities (which I doubted). I wrote Diez, asking him to locate Cesare Siepi, whom I had heard the previous spring; and I groaned when he replied that Siepi's address was the Via Moscova—the authorities might well bar entry to anyone who had the bad taste to live on Moscow Street. Siepi as a young man during the war had fled Mussolini's Italy and lived in Switzerland, and it seemed impossible that there could be any real objection to him, but we had to pull strings all over Washington before we got a quick clearance for his visa. Even with a quick clearance, he missed the first rehearsals; but he did come, and made an overpowering debut and a well-deserved great career at the Metropolitan.

Bjoerling, too, missed rehearsals, but not because of visa problems. On October 21 I sent him a letter:

My dear Mr. Bjoerling,

I cannot tell you how upset and discouraged I am. You were one of the first with whom I discussed my hopes for some more teamwork and some more rehearsing and I was happy and encouraged by your reactions; and now look how the thing starts!

Right from the beginning the artistic discipline is undermined. The Italian artists are here for every rehearsal on the dot and have to rehearse ensembles, duos and everything without a tenor . . .

You must know how much I have been looking forward to our collaboration and what enormous value I put on your artistic service to this house, but it simply cannot go on like this. Please let us avoid a major trouble which will no doubt arise unless you can see your way to attend rehearsals without fail and punctually. It is one of the foremost objectives I have in mind, to establish real rehearsal discipline in this house and however great my regret may be, I cannot abandon that policy

[ 167 ]

whatever the consequences may be. So please cooperate as you have so kindly promised only the other day again.

This despairing letter made its effect, and Bjoerling did indeed attend rehearsals; but he grumbled about it, and later in the season began to talk about being "unable to afford" to continue singing at the Metropolitan. He did continue, but his participation in our efforts to improve staging was always grudging, as little as he could get away with. He was, unfortunately, a very irresponsible artist. One of the most astonishing things I ever saw on an opera stage was the last act of Puccini's *Manon Lescaut* during my observation year, on a night when Bjoerling, as Des Grieux, was troubled with a backache and didn't feel like getting up to fetch some water for the dying Manon. The ever obliging Licia Albanese, at his suggestion, got up and fetched the water for him . . .

Meanwhile, there was the new *Flying Dutchman* to put onstage, only three days after our opening-night *Don Carlo*. (Two new productions in the same week did not make quite the crisis they would have made in later years, because we could leave the house dark for the three nights between; today, union costs are so enormous the Metropolitan cannot sacrifice the revenues from the sale of tickets on any night.) With the dress rehearsal for *Don Carlo* on November 4 (opening night on November 6), we gave the stage to *Holländer* for scenic run-throughs on November 2 and 3. I had to write some memos to Herbert Graf:

FIRST ACT "HOLLÄNDER"
   1. My urgent suggestion is to kill the storm drop. It is practically invisible and only becomes visible, and to my mind rather distracting, when you see something strange being pulled up. In addition to that it has the enormous risk of getting stuck as it did on the two occasions when I saw it.

34. Playing chess with Richard Tucker on *Rigoletto* set in Boston, 1952

35. Left to right: Edward Johnson, Mrs. August Belmont, Rudolf Bing

36. Left to right: Sir Tyrone Guthrie, Rolf Gérard, Margaret Webster, Rudolf Bing

37. Anselmo Colzani, Gabriella Tucci, Franco Zeffirelli, Rudolf Bing

38. Seated left to right: Herbert Graf, stage director; Mrs. John Barry Ryan; Mrs. August Belmont; Rudolf Bing; Standing left to right: Rolf Gérard, Max Rudolf, John Gutman

39. Sir Tyrone Guthrie, Fritz Reiner, Kurt Adler (chorus master), at *Carmen* rehearsal, 1952

40. En route to the Old Met

2. I have asked Mr. Armistead . . . to look into the possibility of an improved wind machine. What I heard is not loud enough.

3. I think we require heavier chains for the anchor chains and possibly more of them. I think the noise of the rattling should go on for a little longer than this short chain today provided.

4. Will you remember, if possible, to have the extremely "obliging" rock-steps covered up a little so that they don't look as if they were in the Waldorf-Astoria . . .

7. Dutchman boat appearance: obviously it should go smoother . . .

SECOND ACT "HOLLÄNDER"

1. The fisher net either wants some light or isn't rough enough. From the 4th or 5th row onwards it already looks like a thin veil rather than a real fisher net.

2. The rock projections look very well from the back of the house but deteriorate the more forward one comes. Why? , , Also the wrinkles on the cyclorama on the u.p. side affect the rock badly . ,

THIRD ACT "HOLLÄNDER"

2. Disappearance of Dutchman boat and appearance of the model in the distance: Please make sure that the Dutchman boat does not begin to disappear before the Dutchman has actually gotten off stage as it happened in this morning's rehearsal. May I rely on it that the appearance of the model will at least be timed accurately in such a way that it arrives at the assigned spot at the right moment and need not wait as it did today. We will have the house roaring with laughter if a boat in full sail suddenly stops dead in the middle of the ocean . . . Incidentally, I think the sinking today was a bit slow, quite apart from the fact that it moved back in the process of sinking . . .

Finally, to mixed feelings of relief that it would soon be over and regrets that we didn't have three more days to make everything perfect, November 6 came. My guests in the general manager's box were the British ambassador and his wife, Sir Oliver and Lady Franks; and Mr. and Mrs. Henry Luce. All the work that Stiedry and Webster and Gérard and our great cast had done came together in a truly excellent performance of what was revealed as a masterwork. The audience was impressed and moved; the critics were pleased; I was worn out and ecstatic, and ready to start planning my next season.

# 17

Surveying the results of the first weeks of my first season, and looking ahead to the rest of it, I saw one great weakness that seemed unlikely to be remedied without drastic action: conducting. I suppose the occupational syndrome of the new general manager anywhere is the belief that somehow if he plays his cards right he can get a number of great conductors to work in his theater. My dreams in the fall of 1950 included the return of Arturo Toscanini to the Metropolitan Opera podium, and I wrote his son Walter a letter inviting the Maestro back on whatever terms he chose to set. The letter was never answered. As noted, I asked Beecham for *Fledermaus,* with no results. The more I examined our condition, the more concerned I became about our musical leadership.

Reiner was jealous of my long acquaintance with Stiedry and furious about losing *Fledermaus,* and in any event it seemed evident to me that he considered the Metropolitan little more than a stopgap before he proceeded to the leadership of one of America's great orchestras. (In fact, Reiner stayed with me for three seasons before the Chicago Symphony offered him three times what we were paying him; and he was by far the leading musical figure in the house in all three years. We parted amicably in April 1953, with a ceremonial drink at my office, both our wives present at the little party, after the *Carmen* which was to be his last public appearance at the Metropolitan.) Stiedry, while an excellent musician and a fine human being, could not carry the burden of inspiring a house. Walter was well into his seventies. In my letter to Erede in December 1949, offering him a post at the Metropolitan, I had noted that "There is no principal conductor here. All conductors are on the same level, and their positions entirely depend on the personal success they can make for themselves." By that standard, it was clear early in the 1950–51 season that neither Erede nor Cleva could be the source of major musical excitement at the Metropolitan.

Toward the end of November 1950 I wrote to Alfred Diez to invite Erich Kleiber to the Metropolitan:

> While I cannot at this moment offer the official position of a "generalmusikdirektor," I would like to point out that this position has not existed at the Metropolitan in decades. Not even Bodanzky had ever officially held such a position; only he had been at the Metropolitan for many years, he had devoted practically his whole time and energy to the Metropolitan and as a result naturally his words and views weighed heavily with the management. Exactly the same may be the case in the future. If Mr. Kleiber should agree to join us, if he then gives us sufficient time and really throws in his lot with the Metropolitan there is not the slightest doubt that his views will weigh heavily with me and although in the last resort I am responsible and, therefore, must reserve the right of final decision, there is no question that . . . a conductor of Kleiber's eminent standing, experience and ability [would be] my closest and most valued musical adviser . . .

Naturally if a man like Kleiber joined us he would be consulted in case of new engagements for orchestra, chorus and solo singers, though again in these respects I must reserve the right of final decision quite apart from the fact that we have to observe quite a number of union restrictions and regulations. Naturally, the repertory would have to be jointly discussed and the distribution of works among the various conductors must also be discussed . . . Altogether I feel that all these matters are largely questions of mutual understanding and goodwill. If these two qualifications are lacking no contract on earth can make the thing work. If on the other hand people try to get on with each other on fair and reasonable terms, I think, while far from minimizing difficulties, that they can always be overcome . . .

Would you ask Mr. Kleiber whether he is interested at all and whether he would be available to us for the whole next season . . . Perhaps Mr. Kleiber may feel that I have gone too far in this letter, but I don't believe in the old-fashioned "diplomatic way of careful soundings." I am quite clear in my own mind that subject to certain clarifications I want Mr. Kleiber to come and, therefore, I do not see any reason why I should not say so and I hereby do . . . I know I can rely on you and Mr. Kleiber to treat this invitation—and it is an invitation—in absolute strict confidence . . .

This proposal was a gamble: Kleiber had once said in Berlin that to work successfully in an opera house a conductor had to "get his claws into it." But a manager must expect to pay a price in discomfort for the best. The letter to Diez put me in contact with Ruth Kleiber, the conductor's wife, who at first thought it might be possible for her husband to make a flying trip to New York to discuss the matter with me, and asked advice on questions like which concert management he should seek to associate himself with in America. But after a few letters back and forth it became clear that Kleiber was too committed to his work at Covent Garden in London and on the Continent to wish to accept anything remotely like what I was offering him. Six weeks to two months was the maximum he could consider giving to the Metropolitan, and I was still committed in those days to engagements of at least half a season for anyone undertaking the immense responsibilities of an opera conductor.

Mrs. Kleiber kindly passed on to me the names of three men her husband had suggested as possible substitutes for himself, none of them anywhere near his stature. One of the three was an old acquaintance. "This gentleman I know well," I wrote Mrs. Kleiber, "and I was engaged with him for at least two years at the Städtische Oper in Berlin. He is a mediocre conductor but was an outstanding Nazi. I am only prepared to consider the opposite mixture: a mediocre Nazi who is an outstanding conductor."

Planning my second season, then, I had to go with what I had in stock, so to speak—Cleva for an opening-night *Aida* that would again link the talents of Gérard as designer and Peggy Webster as director; Erede for a new production of *Rigoletto* to be designed by Eugene Berman (who had never done sets and costumes for an opera before) and directed by Herbert Graf; Stiedry for a *Così Fan Tutte* which Gérard (who had already set this opera for me in Glyndebourne's Edinburgh season) would design and Alfred Lunt, another newcomer to opera, would direct; and Reiner for *Carmen*. Not having a French conductor for *Carmen* I was extremely anxious to get a French director, specifically René Clair, whom I had come to know in London; and when Clair proved impossible I tried Jean-Louis Barrault, who was also unavailable. Luckily, Tony Guthrie was able to clear the time. We wanted Oliver Messel to design it, but when he proved unable to commit himself to either a yes or a no this assignment too, with Guthrie's strong endorsement, went to Gérard.

Before the opening of that season, I decided to try to persuade my board to accept Furtwängler, on the grounds that the house needed him. I wrote a long letter to Mrs. Belmont, expressing my sense that the Metropolitan simply had to have "an outstanding conductor-personality of an even higher rank than we have now." I ran down the list of possibilities: Victor de Sabata, "extremely difficult and unreliable, so unreasonable in his not facing inevitable facts and limitations . . . One cannot have arguments with de Sabata, one either gives in or has an explosion, and both these alternatives do not seem too attractive to me." Walter was seventy-five. Kleiber was about to work in East Berlin (he left a year later, finding he liked Communists no better than he had liked Nazis), which probably made his immigration case impossible: "a brilliant conductor; but he is apparently in the process—if he has not done so already—of throwing in his lot with the Russians." Clemens Krauss was politically unacceptable; the year before, Diez had offered him to me and I had replied, "I would not wish to have [him] *near* my house. It is typical of the Viennese to accept him back with all honors." Then, I added in my letter to Mrs. Belmont, "Of the younger set, there is Herbert von Karajan . . . whom I, personally, would not propose to invite." I had gone after both Guido Cantelli and Hans Knappertsbusch, but neither was available. Furtwängler was.

A month later, I summoned a meeting of the production committee of the board and laid out the case for its members—Mrs. Belmont, Lucrezia Bori, Wadmond, and Carleton Sprague Smith of the New York Public Library. I had checked with Spofford in the American Military Government, and had been told that Furtwängler "is clear with the present West German government and with our High Commissioner and staff. There would be no difficulty in obtaining an exit permit from Germany. Since Furtwängler was never a member of the party . . . there would be no McCarran Act difficulties . . ." Mrs. Belmont offered to lobby with Arthur Hays Sulzberger of the New York *Times,* and suggested that I have a session with C. D. Jackson of Time, Inc. But in the end the board still thought the engagement of Furtwängler too risky, especially at a time when the finance committee had to plan a major fund-raising drive.

Not until my fourth season, 1953–54, was I able to make a major addition to the Metropolitan conducting staff, but then it was a wonderful recruit: Pierre Monteux, an astoundingly youthful seventy-eight, who returned to the Metropolitan podium after an absence of almost thirty-five years. This was the result of just trying: he had retired from the San Francisco Symphony, and I wrote him a letter to his Maine home in October 1952, not even mentioning any specific opera. Three days later he sent the reply: "I would be enchanted to renew my association with the Metropolitan Opera." For 1953–54 he undertook three big French operas for us: *Faust, Pelléas et Mélisande,* and *Carmen.* Meanwhile, Reiner having departed, I was able to bring George Szell back for Wagner's *Tannhäuser.* But the situation still made me nervous. In March 1953 I wrote to George Sloan:

> The question of Metropolitan Opera conductors is one of the many problems that worries me a good deal. I am aware that next year's arrangement with the eighty-year-old Mr. Monteux and the badly overworked Mr. Szell can only be an interim solution. In the season after next we simply must have, at least for a good part of the season, an outstanding conductor of international reputation. I have little hope in the present difficult situation that faces us with regard to Italian artists of obtaining the services of Sig. de Sabata and I feel, there-

fore, once again, that I ought to concentrate on Dr. Furtwängler . . . I am now talking of the season 1954-55 . . . Would
you very kindly consider the matter and let me know whether
you are prepared to authorize me to go ahead . . .

In fall 1953, finally, the board did approve an approach to
Furtwängler—with Sloan warning me in an aside that friends
of his in Vienna had said the conductor was ill. This information was untrue but prescient, for the next spring Furtwängler
did begin to fail (at the age of sixty-eight), and by November
1954 he was dead, never having appeared at the Metropolitan.
By then I needed him worse than ever, because the romance
with Szell had lasted only four performances. Szell fought with
Herbert Graf, he fought with Gérard about details of the sets,
he fought with the cast—too many of whom, I must admit, had
never sung the work before at the Metropolitan. He blew up in
the press and, for the second time, walked out on me (Max
Rudolf took over the performances he abandoned). I remember
somebody once said to me, "George Szell is his own worst
enemy." I said, "Not while I am alive." Personally, toward the
end of his life, we did make it up. He saw several performances
at Lincoln Center as a guest in my box, and I had the pleasure
of giving him a tour of the technical wonders of our new
theater, always the sort of thing that captivated him.

The man who came to us in 1954-55, providentially, was
Dimitri Mitropoulos, conductor of the New York Philharmonic,
whose contract there left him not only open weeks when he
could give all his time to the Metropolitan but also occasional
open evenings during the weeks when his primary responsibilities were at Carnegie Hall. He was honest and decent and
helpful, a wonderful person. A little to his own surprise, he
found that he loved working in an opera house, and he was
happy at the Metropolitan. Everything he did was personal to

him. With his big bony bald head and huge hands, he didn't look like anyone else in the world, and his musical ideas were often as original as his appearance. The orchestra was devoted to him as perhaps to no one else who has stood in that pit in my time.

For five years Mitropoulos was my senior adviser; I could discuss anything with him, singers, orchestra personnel, musical editions, knowing that he would never be spiteful. As time passed, he cut down more and more at the Philharmonic, planning to turn over its leadership to Leonard Bernstein and give us the bulk of his time. In 1958 Bernstein took over at Carnegie Hall and Mitropoulos agreed to be at the Metropolitan for nearly the entire season, conducting no fewer than seven operas, including new productions of *Macbeth* and of *Cav* and *Pag*. Alas, less than halfway through the season he suffered a heart attack, and while he returned to us the next year (and conducted the new production of Verdi's *Simon Boccanegra* that gave Leonard Warren his final triumph at the Metropolitan), his strength had been greatly diminished, and he died in Milan in fall 1960 before he could rejoin us for that season. Too many people in New York took him for granted; his death was a terrific loss to the Met and to me.

By then several others who would be stalwarts of the house were working in the pit—Karl Böhm, who would leave us to be Generalmusikdirektor in Vienna and then return; Erich Leinsdorf, who would leave us to be conductor of the Boston Symphony Orchestra and then return; Thomas Schippers, who made his debut at the Metropolitan at the age of twenty-five in 1955, and reappeared in almost every subsequent season, taking off a year now and then to work at La Scala. Monteux after three seasons did become a little too old to assume the burdens of opera, but we acquired a plausible substitute (if not a replacement) in Jean Morel, a fine French conductor then at the top of his form.

In 1954–55 and 1955–56 we enjoyed the services of Rudolf Kempe, who led the New York premiere of Richard Strauss's *Arabella* (the work I had heard him conduct in Munich two summers before, when I decided to engage him). The next summer he was ill, and in the fall of 1956 he became involved in matrimonial tangles. Like the soprano Sena Jurinac, he was always either too happy to come or too unhappy to come.

Not long after Kempe's departure, on one of the saddest days of my life, I was compelled to tell Fritz Stiedry that he could no longer conduct at the Metropolitan. For several seasons, he had been growing increasingly deaf without being conscious of it, and performances under his direction had become increasingly perilous to all involved in them. He could not accept the fact of his physical infirmity and felt that I had betrayed him; and we never spoke or met again. Not long after he died, however, his widow, also an old friend, came to us in Italy in the summer for several weeks, and told us that it had been his deteriorating health that had prevented him from replying to any of my attempts to repair contact with him.

Among the productions left conductorless by Mitropoulos' death was Puccini's *Turandot,* for which I had engaged the Japanese director Yoshio Aoyama (who had done an outstanding job for us on *Madame Butterfly*) and the designer Cecil (now Sir Cecil) Beaton. My choice for a replacement was Leopold Stokowski, a decision I soon regretted. He went around the house correcting the way people pronounced each other's names, interfering with the director—Aoyama took sick and Nathaniel Merrill had to finish the job—and trying to give orders to Beaton. He was especially concerned with the lighting, and how it might affect the appearance of his hands while he was conducting. At performances, he often just luxuriated in his role, failing, for example, to tell his soloists when to end a sustained high note which the score allowed them to hold ad lib.

In Boston, on tour, this situation exploded. In the second-act finale, Franco Corelli ran out of breath while Birgit Nilsson was still sustaining her tone, and he just walked off the stage. I was not in the hall: an emissary came to me in the lobby and said, "Mr. Bing, we are losing our tenor." I went backstage, and even before I neared Corelli's door I heard him screaming, his wife screaming, the dog barking. He had slammed his hand on the dressing table, and had picked up a miniscule splinter. There was a drop of blood on the table, and Mrs. was calling for an ambulance. I calmed them down as much as I could, and suggested to Corelli that in the love scene in the next act he could get even with Miss Nilsson by biting her ear. That cheered him up a great deal; in fact, he liked the idea so much that he told Miss Nilsson about it, which gave him all the satisfaction of actually biting her without doing it, thank God. Meanwhile, I went to Stokowski's dressing room to apologize to him, and found him entirely unconcerned. These are nerve-wracking experiences; Stokowski was not invited again, except for the last night in the old house, when he abused our hospitality by launching a crusade to prevent its necessary destruction.

Through the triumphs and trials of conducting at the Metropolitan in the 1950s, there runs a disastrous thread of gradual but steady diminution in the time the house could demand from the best men. The star system, bad enough when it compels changes in the singing cast from performance to performance, had come to the podium, to the great detriment of opera production everywhere. As early as 1952, I dined with Carlo Maria Giulini in Milan, and talked to him about the possibilities of his conducting at the Metropolitan Opera. But he had two young sons, and was simply not willing either to take them away from their home for months at a time or to spend months away from them; the most he was ever willing to offer me was six weeks.

In six weeks a conductor can prepare one new production and, perhaps, one revival, and give at most the first four or five performances of each. He cannot leave his stamp on the theater, and he cannot even assure a standard of performance for the productions he launches on the world—once he departs, other conductors must take over, producing a loss of quality if they are routiniers (as they probably will be, because except for a near-saint like Mitropoulos the best conductors are unwilling to assume responsibility for work prepared by others) or a change of conception if they are musicians of high individual ability. Sometimes one just gets a kind of competitive nastiness, as when Schippers prepared a new *Luisa Miller* for us and made a number of insubstantial cuts, and Cleva as the price of taking over insisted on reopening the cuts, which was a nuisance to the cast, the chorus, the orchestra, everybody. Then at the end of the season Schippers returned and again imposed the cuts.

By the 1960s I had lost the war to secure the best conductors for long seasons, and finally I became more than willing to take even six-week commitments from conductors like Georg Solti, Leonard Bernstein, Herbert von Karajan and Colin Davis. The days when a Busch would commit himself for eight months at Dresden, or a Walter to six months in Vienna, or a Kleiber to seven months in Berlin, had vanished in the jetstream of modern aircraft. During his first season, my successor will actually have a music director who can commit only six weeks to the Metropolitan; and the 1972–73 season opens with a new production that will have to be turned over to a substitute conductor less than a month after its premiere.

The costs of this modern madness are heavy everywhere, even in the Italian *stagione* system, in which productions are mounted for only a month at a time and then go out of repertory; individual productions suffer less, but the orchestra and the tone of the theater are damaged by the shuttling about of musical leadership. In the northern European repertory system the flightiness of the conductors becomes ruinous, and nowhere more ruinous than at the Metropolitan, which is uniquely burdened with an annual spring tour. The cities to be visited on the tour naturally wish the most publicized new productions. Even if these productions were first presented in the early fall, they must be brought back in the spring to be polished for tour use. The conductors who created them will only rarely return for this purpose—and today they will rarely make the tour. New York often, and the tour cities too often, must make do with substitute conductors from the Metropolitan's staff of assistants and associates.

I have been blessed with a corps of unusually able assistant conductors at the Metropolitan. If there had been no Hitler and no war, men like Jan Behr, Martin Rich, George Schick, Ignace Strasfogel, and Walter Taussig would have been Generalmusikdirektor in Wiesbaden or Aachen, even Darmstadt or Bremen—but one must face the fact that they would not have conducted in the great houses, Vienna or Berlin or Hamburg or Munich or Dresden. It is a legitimate criticism of the Metropolitan in the last decade that very many performances have been conducted by such substitutes. The tour cities especially, asked to guarantee $50,000 a night for a Metropolitan Opera appearance, have had reason to be irritated at the conductors who have led the performances they receive. Fortunately for the Metropolitan Opera, much of the Metropolitan audience and even more of the audience in the tour cities are more interested in hearing great voices than in experiencing the dramatically unified musical performance that only a great conductor can sustain.

The shortage of conductors is not the Metropolitan's problem alone—look at who actually conducts most of the performances at Covent Garden or La Scala or Vienna. The usual criticism that the Metropolitan has not had great conductors in my time is both unfair and uninformed: apart from Giulini (who had announced a desire to stop conducting operas by the time I became willing to offer six-week engagements) and perhaps Boulez (who has conducted less than half a dozen operas in his life)—and among the younger generation perhaps Carlos Kleiber (Erich's son, who doesn't answer letters sent to him)—every truly important opera conductor of the last twenty years has in fact worked at the Metropolitan Opera. Many of them, moreover, have given us substantial numbers of performances. In spring 1971 one of the New York critics sneered that the great conductors like Böhm spend little time at the Metropolitan, but Böhm in 1970–71 conducted no less than twenty-seven performances at the house, which is a very large number (and very expensive, not only because Böhm gets the top fee but also because he demands many rehearsals with the orchestra and the full cast and chorus). Nevertheless, I must admit that the great weakness I was concerned about after only one month as general manager continued to be a problem for the house throughout my tenure. If I don't feel particularly guilty, it's because I can't think of anything I could have done to improve the situation that I did not actually do.

# 18

My second season had several landmark events. On opening night, Janet Collins, a black ballerina, became the first of her race to appear as a featured solo artist in a Metropolitan Opera production. Zachary Solov, who had become our ballet director on the departure of Antony Tudor and the cherished scheme to have Ballet Theatre handle our dance problems, came to me in the spring to tell me that he had a wonderful girl for the triumphal scene in *Aida,* but there was a problem—her color. I really had some trouble understanding what he meant, because the dancers are supposed to be Nubians: everyone in the corps de ballet puts on dark body paint for the scene. I never had the slightest question about engaging Miss Collins, and I told the board about it after the contract was signed.

The hit of the 1951–52 season was Mozart's *Così Fan Tutte,* which had received only twelve performances in the entire previous history of the Metropolitan. I am convinced *Così* was the success it was because of the way Alfred Lunt came out onstage just after the house lights went down and the gold curtain rose, revealing a smaller false proscenium with a delicate WAM monogram on the interior curtain. Lunt entered in eighteenth-century costume, lit the candles at the side of the proscenium, and then bowed to Stiedry as if to say, "You may start." In that brief moment, his grace and carriage and understanding of courtly style set the mood for the entire performance to come.

Lunt had worked extremely hard on this production. He virtually memorized the Glyndebourne recording of the opera, and long before he got together with the cast he had some friends from the theater out to his house to try out for him some of the attitudes and gestures he wanted the singers to assume. The opera was done in English, with an English-speaking cast (Eleanor Steber as Fiordiligi, Blanche Thebom as Dorabella, Patrice Munsel as Despina, Richard Tucker as Ferrando, Frank Guarrera as Guglielmo, John Brownlee as Don Alfonso), and Lunt convinced them they were going to be part of a theatrical, not just an operatic, presentation. The critic Virgil Thomson, who was by no means happy with all aspects of my management, headed his review, "Lunt Makes History," and offered a pious injunction: "Not ever again, let us hope, will conduct on the operatic stage be left to the improvisation of the singers." To make my board's cup run over, Gérard brought in the light and airy, entirely suitable physical production for less than $25,000; and we were still using it in 1972.

Another notable new production was Tony Guthrie's staging of *Carmen,* which Mary Garden later told me (and the press) was the best *Carmen* she had ever seen or heard. (She came to my box, an old lady in a remarkable strapless gown, and one of the even older men said to her, "What makes that dress stay up?" She said, "Your age, sir.") Again, Reiner found himself working with a director who had strong and non-traditional ideas about a piece—among other things, Guthrie wanted to cut the chorus of boys in the first act: "Dramatically, it is corny to the point of suffocation," he wrote me, "and, practically, I do not believe you will ever get real boys who can make themselves adequately heard; and I simply cannot bear to think we must fall back on the last resort of Opera Houses, namely, the employment of the chorus ladies with the smallest behinds: that, in my opinion, is the ultimate in opera bathos." (The Metropolitan, of course, has a chorus of clearly audible boys.) But Guthrie handled Reiner better than Kanin had—or maybe Reiner handled Guthrie better—and there were no fights. Both men were dazzled by Risë Stevens's willingness to restudy her role though she had established herself, years before, as the world's leading Carmen. Reiner's ability to make something both authentic and personal of Bizet's overfamiliar score was for me one of the greatest of all his triumphs at the Met, very satisfying to a general manager who had gambled on the superficially unlikely assignment.

Probably the best-remembered performance of this season was that of Ljuba Welitsch as Musetta in *La Bohème*. Ljuba had not done nearly as well at the Metropolitan as I had hoped and expected. Her Salome was still quite successful, and she had scored as Rosalinda in *Fledermaus*, but there were too many roles for which she was simply not so attractive a choice as the triumphant Zinka Milanov or the rapidly improving Eleanor Steber. I wrote to Diez: "The cruelty and speed with which the New York public forgets is extraordinary." Deprived of opportunities she thought she should have, Welitsch hung on my ear with insistence that one of her greatest successes had been made at Covent Garden in the role of Musetta.

Meanwhile, I was having the most ghastly troubles with Pat Munsel. Pretty and bright, with a sweet voice, she had made a Metropolitan Opera debut some years before at the age of seventeen, setting a record for youth that one hopes will never be beaten. On this endowment, she had become what the press liked to call a star of stage, screen, and radio—and, at the Metropolitan, not one of our leading coloraturas. There are some singers who can achieve authentic stardom in the soubrette, however, and Miss Munsel was one of those. By casting her as Adele in *Fledermaus* and Despina in *Così*, I had made her a much more important artist than she had ever been before. My reward was a threat that if I did not give her a Mimi she would abandon the parts in which I needed her, and skip off to musical comedy or whatever.

I very grimly agreed to give Miss Munsel a Mimi, and then called Ljuba and told her she could have her Musetta. This performance would have to be thrown onstage, with nothing more than an opportunity for the principals to meet in the afternoon, but both artists agreed to the conditions. Miss Munsel did not know who was to be Musetta in her *Bohème* until the day of the performance, and when she learned she virtually fled the country. Dorothy Kirsten gallantly filled in for her. Welitsch then produced a performance which could be said to define the difference between a mischievous courtesan and a raucous whore. She jumped on the tables and danced, forced her Marcello (Paolo Silveri) to carry her on his shoulders around the stage, elbowed everybody out of the way, and just misbehaved shockingly. I never regretted it too much: the performance served its purpose, and the audience, which must have been enormous (everybody now says he was there), obviously got its money's worth. Many years later during a radio interview I was taxed with this example of mistaken casting, and I muttered something about the soprano who wished to be Mimi when I thought at most she might be a passable Musetta herself. Irving Kolodin in his history of the Metropolitan comments that "This must have been interesting news to the Mimi, Dorothy Kirsten, who was still a member of the company." The full story has been told here to set that record straight: my feelings for Miss Kirsten, not only on that occasion but on many others, were those of gratitude.

The significant departure from the Metropolitan this season was that of Kirsten Flagstad, who received a twenty-minute ovation after her final Alcestis. The individual performance I remember best was that of Ramon Vinay as Otello; it was the two hundredth time he had sung the role, and never in my life have I heard it sung and acted so perfectly. Perhaps the most important debut was that of Eugene Berman as an opera designer: his Renaissance *Rigoletto,* solid and superbly detailed, heralded a long relationship with the Metropolitan. It was almost always a difficult relationship, because Berman believed that he should have first call on any new production I planned, and also that every effort made to reduce costs was aimed straight at the heart of his artistic integrity. But at its best Berman's work was worth all the trouble—most particularly, I think, in the *Don Giovanni* of 1957, for which he not only supervised the painting of the scenery but actually did a good deal of it himself. There are only a handful of opera productions of which one can say that the designer rather than the director was responsible for the dramatic mood and tone, but this *Don Giovanni* was one of them.

The significant debut on opening night was that of George London, whose strong voice filled the Metropolitan for the first time as Amonasro in *Aida.* His was undoubtedly the dramatic triumph of the evening. Neither Miss Webster nor Gérard had been able to grasp the antique-Egyptian of Verdi's opera for Cairo with the same strength of purpose they had found for the exotic-Spanish of Verdi's opera for Paris, and neither Miss Milanov in the title role nor Mario del Monaco as Radames had the temperament or sheer body control to profit by Miss Webster's acting lessons.

Both London and I were lucky, in different ways, in the circumstances of this debut, because originally I had penciled in the role for Robert Merrill, in honor of his great success with Posa the year before. (Merrill was not, however, planned for Escamillo in *Carmen*, despite speculation to the contrary: Guthrie had written that "unless he can look reasonably like a toreador, and unless he is a very vital and sexually attractive man, the part means absolutely nothing at all; and the whole romantic story of the opera is invalidated . . . As everyone knows, the tessitura of the big song is extremely awkward, and practically nobody makes a success of it solely vocally, but it can, I suggest, be put over (pardon the vulgarity of my vocabulary!) as a 'point number' by a man who is not a great, or even a very good, singer but who has what it takes in personality and as an actor." This was Guarrera from the beginning.) But Robert Merrill was not on the Metropolitan roster at the beginning of the 1951–52 season: I had suspended him for failure to meet his contractual obligations on the spring tour. He had gone off to Hollywood to contribute to the national culture by performing in a film entitled *Aaron Slick from Pumkin Crick,* and not until he made a formal written apology, which he did just under a year later, would I agree to accept him back on the Metropolitan Opera stage. We lost a year's services of a great baritone, but we sustained a principle without which there could be no hope of first-class opera productions ever.

Most artists, including some of the most notoriously temperamental, are in reality very scrupulous about living up to the terms of their contracts, and I like to think I have done something over the decades to reinforce everyone's natural sense of obligation. For people on the top levels there are of course great temptations: when an artist was offered $7,000 to appear four minutes on "The Ed Sullivan Show" (in years when our absolute top fee was $1,000 per performance), it was hard to force her to a dress rehearsal that conflicted with a Sullivan run-through. That show is now out of business, but it is too late for me. And there are also disappointments that cannot be avoided. Among the young artists I had signed during my first season at the Metropolitan was the mezzo Mildred Miller, but plans for her debut had to be postponed when I received a deeply apologetic and unconsciously funny letter from her husband (now chancellor of the University of Pittsburgh) informing me that my Cherubino was pregnant. (One can just imagine the conversation that preceded this letter—"*I'm* not going to write him; *you* write him!") But Miss Miller did indeed arrive, only a year late, and in 1972 I had the pleasure of attending a ceremony at which she was presented with a silver clock to commemorate her twentieth season with the company.

Beyond such heaven-sent events, singers are necessarily people who live under tension, risking their professional lives every time they step onstage. The common cold is a threat to their very existence as artists, and often for reasons as much psychological as physical they cannot sing when they have so much as a sniffle. Sometimes it is part of a general manager's job to nurse along high-strung major artists who cannot face the idea of public performance on any day when they don't feel *simpatico* with the world—keeping Franco Corelli cheerful, for example, long seemed to me one of the things for which I was paid (in this instance, grossly underpaid). There are other artists from whom one demands a doctor's certificate whenever they call up to make excuses—usually a hopeless demand, because it is no trouble at all for a singer to procure from a doctor a letter reading "Mr. or Miss So-and-So is under my care"; but the act of demanding the letter is satisfying, and sometimes the implied distrust jolts a singer into re-examining his own condition and discovering that he can sing after all.

One of the most erratic artists with whom I had to work at

the Metropolitan Opera was also one of the most gloriously talented: Giuseppe di Stefano. The most spectacular single moment in my observation year had come when I heard his diminuendo on the high C in "Salut! demeure" in *Faust*: I shall never as long as I live forget the beauty of that sound. For my first season, I was counting on him to do a number of Alma-vivas in *Barbiere*, and ultimately he did do most of them, but we never knew from day to day whether he would show up. Once his wife called on the afternoon of a performance to tell me how sick he was, and I said that if he was that sick he should not be permitted to remain at home, I would immediately call an ambulance at the expense of the Metropolitan Opera. In an hour he was at the theater.

The story of how di Stefano's career at the Metropolitan was interrupted illustrates concisely one kind of catastrophe a general manager of an opera house must expect to face once in a while. This incident also had, as will be seen, some larger implications. Both the story and the implications can be presented entirely in the documents of the period, without any intrusion of hindsight. The occasion for the trouble was our forthcoming new production of *La Bohème* in 1952–53, but its formal beginnings were in a letter I wrote while putting together a cast for the new *Faust* which Pierre Monteux would conduct more than a year later to open the 1953–54 season:

October 1, 1952

My dear Di Stefano,

I hope you had a very good summer and that you and the family are well.

We are now beginning to discuss plans for the 1953–54 season and you are practically the first artist whom I am approaching on that subject. May I ask you to keep everything in strict confidence.

[ 191 ]

I am thinking of opening the season with a great new production of Gounod's "Faust" and surely I would like you to do Faust in that production, for which I am searching the world for a great designer and a great stage director. It must be very different from what "Faust" was at the Metropolitan Opera for the last fifty years and you will have to work hard in that production.

. . . You know that our openings are always somewhere before the middle of November which with the inevitable rehearsals for a new production means that you would have to be available from about the middle of October. I shall be grateful if you will let me know by return whether that project interests you . . .

In reply the next week, di Stefano told me my letter had thrilled him and that he would indeed come to the Metropolitan in 1953–54, because of his great respect for me. But he had money worries. Scala had offered him a chance to sing a few extra performances if only he could skip the first two weeks of our rehearsals for the new *Bohème* in the current season. The performances at Scala would give him glory in his own country, and some extra pennies.

October 13, 1952

My dear Di Stefano,

I am afraid your letter of October 7th is extremely depressing to me because in spite of all our conversations it shows clearly that you still have no conception of what I mean when I talk of "new productions and a new approach to the dramatic aspects of opera." I had hoped that you, as one of the best young tenors, would wish to take part in a new development of American opera but it seems that you are perfectly happy with the ridiculous antics that usually pass on our stage for acting.

I told you that this year "Bohème" will be done in a new production for which I have engaged one of the outstanding

41. Rudolf Bing, Anthony Bliss, and Mrs. August Belmont on her eightieth birthday

42. Conducting the National Anthem, 1955

43. Left to right: Rudolf Bing, Sir John Falconer, Nina Bing, Lord Harewood, Miss Diana Falconer, at Edinburgh Festival Club, 1957

44. Carl Ebert, stage director; Rudolf Bing, general manager; Dimitri Mitropoulos, conductor; discussing *Macbeth*, 1958-59 season

45. With Maria Callas backstage

film directors of our day. The fact that you have done "Bohème" so often makes the situation much worse because if this production is to be a good one I do not believe that anything of what you have done so far in the way of acting will be acceptable. Of course, this does not apply to you only but to practically the whole cast. Therefore, you will have to unlearn what you have done and to learn new ways of moving and acting on the stage. I had hoped that you would be interested in such possibilities, which could lift you from being a very good singer to becoming a very good artist, but apparently you are only thinking of making a few extra dollars at the Scala and trying to cut rehearsals. You know that I have promised you a substantial extra payment for your being available on the agreed date—I did not do that just to please you; I did that because the minimum of rehearsals which would thereby be made possible is the minimum that you will need to be integrated into the new "Bohème" production. I am awfully sorry I cannot under any circumstances agree to your arriving later and I must warn you that the consequences will be serious.

Now, as to next season your letter does not give me a clear answer. Again, I can only use you for a new production of "Faust" if you are ready and willing to forget completely what has so far happened on the Metropolitan stage which made me blush every time the curtain went up on "Faust." In spite of your exceedingly beautiful singing, what went on on that stage during a "Faust" performance was about the worst I have ever seen anywhere in the world and it will have to be changed from top to bottom. Do you want to be part of that or not? If yes, you will have to work hard. If not, say so frankly . . .

Please let me know clearly and unmistakably: a) that you will arrive ready and available for rehearsals on December 22 as agreed; b) whether or not you would accept an offer for the season 1953–54 . . .

I hope you realize that this whole letter, although it may displease you in certain aspects, is really a great compliment because if I did not think so highly of you I would not take the trouble to write so fully. Also, you are so much younger than I am I feel that I have not only a right but almost an obligation to try to put you on the right way—believe me, you are not quite on the right way yet. I know that you are an excellent singer, I know that you are a successful singer and I know that you earn a great deal of money—but this is not all. You could be a great artist and in the long run make an even greater career and earn even more money . . .

Di Stefano wrote that he was disappointed, but would abide by his contract, and would talk about 1953–54 after his arrival in New York. But that was far from the end of it:

6 NOV 1952

RUDOLF BING:

WOULD LIKE TO ASK ALSO IN NAME MAESTRO DESABATA TO ALLOW TENOR DISTEFANO TO REMAIN HERE UNTIL DECEMBER 30TH STOP DISTEFANO WOULD FLY OVER IMMEDIATELY AFTER THANKS REGARDS

GHIRINGHELLI

NOVEMBER 7, 1952

GIUSEPPE DISTEFANO:

CAN AGREE YOUR ARRIVING HERE SUNDAY DECEMBER TWENTYEIGHT LATEST AVAILABLE MORNING REHEARSAL TWENTYNINE PROVIDED YOU AGREE REDUCING EXPENSES PAYMENT TO ONE THOUSAND

BING

NOVEMBER 7, 1952

GHIRINGHELLI:

VERY LATEST I CAN AGREE DISTEFANO ARRIVING NEW YORK

[ 194 ]

SUNDAY DECEMBER TWENTYEIGHT AVAILABLE FOR MORNING
REHEARSAL TWENTYNINE REGARDS

                                           BING

                              NOVEMBER 17, 1952
RUDOLF BING:

OWING TO YOUR KINDNESS WHICH HAS BEEN HIGHLY
APPRECIATED DESABATA AND I RESOLVE TO ASK YOU ALLOW
DISTEFANO SING SCALA EVENING DECEMBER 28 AS WE AS-
SURE HIS DEPARTURE 29 BY PLANE STOP THIS PERMISSION
WOULD AVOID US VERY SERIOUS TROUBLES THANKS IN AD-
VANCE KINDEST REGARDS

                                      GHIRINGHELLI

                              NOVEMBER 18, 1952
GHIRINGHELLI:

DEEPLY REGRET CANNOT POSSIBLY EXTEND DISTEFANO PER-
MIT MUST INSIST HIS AVAILABILITY MORNING REHEARSAL
DECEMBER TWENTYNINE VERY SORRY REGARDS

                                           BING

                              NOVEMBER 18, 1952
DISTEFANO LA SCALA:

VERY SORRY BUT MUST INSIST YOUR ARRIVING HERE DE-
CEMBER TWENTYEIGHT AVAILABLE MORNING REHEARSAL
TWENTYNINE REGARDS

                                           BING

On December 21 di Stefano cabled that he would arrive as
agreed on the twenty-eighth. On December 27 he cabled
that he was awfully sorry but because of a sudden illness he

had been forbidden by his doctor to fly to New York, and he was looking for a reservation on a ship.

DECEMBER 29, 1952
ROBERTO BAUER VIA MAGGIOLINI 2 MILANO:

CAN YOU STRICTLY CONFIDENTIALLY ASCERTAIN WHETHER DISTEFANO IS REALLY ILL WHEN WAS HIS LAST PERFORM-ANCE MILANO GREETINGS HAPPY NEW YEAR

BING

DECEMBER 29, 1952

BING:

DISTEFANO SINGS TONIGHT

BAUER

DECEMBER 30, 1952
DISTEFANO CORSO GENOVA 6:

REQUEST NAME ADDRESS YOUR DOCTOR WILL ASK AMERICAN CONSUL TO INSPECT DOCTORS CERTIFICATE STOP WILL YOU SUBMIT EXAMINATION DOCTOR DESIGNATED BY AMERICAN CONSUL

BING

DECEMBER 30, 1952
GHIRINGHELLI:

ACCORDING MY INFORMATION DISTEFANO PERFORMED LA-SCALA LAST NIGHT THEREBY VIOLATING CONTRACT AND IN-VALIDATING HIS CLAIM TO BE SICK STOP GRATEFUL FOR YOUR CONFIRMATION WHEN HE SANG LAST AND WHETHER FUTURE PERFORMANCES PLANNED

BING

December 30, 1952

Dear Mr. Bing,

I was certainly surprised when I received your wire this morning . . .

As far as I could ascertain DiStefano never was ill at all and he sang very regularly his performances here in Milano. He started on December 15th in *La Bohème,* repeated it on December 18th and sang a matinee of it on the 21st. And then came *Gioconda.* The premiere should have been on the 24th, but then they postponed it to the 26th. But as far as to my knowledge this was due partly because it was Xmas evening and besides that technically the performance was not completely ready. In any case he sang on the 26th, repeated it on the 28th and is singing tonight . . . He is announced also for the *Gioconda*-matinee on the 1st of January . . .

Roberto Bauer

JANUARY 2, 1953

RUDOLF BING:

IN SPITE DISTEFANOS ILLNESS WHICH PREVENTED HIS DEBUT IN GIOCONDA DECEMBER 24TH HE FACED PERFORMANCE 26TH IMPOSSIBLE FOR HIM TO TRAVEL HE USED HIS TIME SINGING OTHER PERFORMANCES REGARDS

GHIRINGHELLI

That same cable delivery brought one from di Stefano, too, giving me the name of his doctor and demanding that we immediately deposit $2,000 to his account in New York to pay for his steamship tickets . . .

January 8, 1953

Dear Mr. Di Stefano:

In view of the information received about your activities in Milano, we consider you in breach of contract which is hereby terminated . . .

A few weeks later I wrote a letter to Clare Boothe Luce, then the U. S. Ambassadress to Italy, suggesting the idea of a Metropolitan Opera goodwill tour of Europe, and also telling her about some of the ill will that was being generated between ourselves and La Scala. Returning from a European trip, George Sloan asked me irritably why I was against the Marshall Plan . . . Nevertheless, some good seems to have come of it. Scala engaged Leonard Warren for what was for us an awkward part of the Metropolitan season, and also lured Risë Stevens to Milan for part of that next year. (Her Scala schedule was such that she had to go straight from the airplane to her dressing room at the Met for a broadcast *Carmen*.) But they did not try such outright piracy again. Bjoerling took the role I had set aside for di Stefano in *Faust*.

Our case to bar di Stefano from American stages was scheduled for a hearing at AGMA (American Guild of Musical Artists) in late November 1954. Early that month I heard from Joseph Gimma, Wall Streeter, Opera Club member, and husband to Licia Albanese, that he had been asked to act as di Stefano's agent in America. We drew up a new contract at the same rates as the one that had been broken, withdrew the AGMA charges (and allowed di Stefano to break our *new* contract to fulfill an engagement he had carelessly entered into with the Lyric Opera in Chicago), then presented di Stefano as Don José in 1955–56. Then he was gone for good, except for one attempt at a comeback in a disastrous *Tales of Hoffman* in 1965. As I had feared, his lack of self-discipline soon harmed what might have been a career men would remember with Caruso's—but it was not to be.

# 19

Planning the schedule is the opera manager's expertise. There is an almost endless chain of considerations before firm decisions can be made. The first step is to look at the two preceding seasons and decide which operas you wish to repeat and which you don't, considering primarily the success of the productions and how often a particular work has been done in the past. Then you look at what hasn't been done and deserves to be done, either as a revival or as a new production. In my twenty-two years at the Metropolitan I had an average of about four new productions a season, involving something like eighty operas—*Aida, Carmen, Cav* and *Pag, Faust, Fidelio, Otello, Traviata,* and *Tristan* were each given two new productions in my time.

You must ask how many different productions you need, which is partly a function of the works chosen. If you have *Pelléas et Mélisande* or *Wozzeck* on the list, you know that you cannot schedule twelve or fifteen performances of it, because the public will not come. Every *Pelléas* or *Wozzeck* must

[ 199 ]

be balanced by a *Traviata* or a *Bohème*. You must ask, have I got a cast? Special problems arise: for years I felt the Metropolitan could not do *Falstaff*, because I could not imagine either a *Falstaff* with Leonard Warren or telling him that we were going to do it without him. Once an artist forced me to give an opera by refusing to accept an engagement unless that work were scheduled—Renata Tebaldi simply had to sing the glamorous actress Adriana Lecouvreur in New York. (Then she took sick and canceled, and we had to do the wretched opera *without* Tebaldi.) Once an opening night had to be changed late in the planning process, when Joan Sutherland decided she was not yet ready to attempt *Norma*. More commonly, the problem is simply the availability of a necessary star: there is very little chance of doing *Carmen* successfully at the Metropolitan unless you have under contract at least one, and preferably two, internationally known Carmens.

The need for "covers" complicates planning at all stages. In Frankfurt, if someone is ill, the manager can put in a call to Hamburg or Cologne or Munich or Zurich at two in the afternoon, and borrow a mezzo-soprano for the night. I could call Hartford, Connecticut, until I was blue in the face without finding a possible Carmen. And an opera like *Carmen* is easy, because there are only a few difficult roles to cast. Consider *Die Walküre*, with its eight Valkyries in addition to the principal singers; to cast *Die Walküre*, the Metropolitan should have sixteen of them. The Three Ladies needed for *The Magic Flute* become six ladies at the Metropolitan. In my early years, most singers came by the week, and were permitted to take outside engagements only with the consent of the management; they could cover performances they were not scheduled to sing. But now nearly all even slightly important singers are engaged on a per-performance basis. You have someone who sings Wednesday whom you would like to have as a cover for a role on

Saturday; but he takes an engagement in Philadelphia on Friday, and that's that.

Important artists hate to cover, and do so only when there is a husband or a lover or a baby in New York to make the sacrifice of pride seem worthwhile. Among my most unpleasant duties during my last years at the Metropolitan were the annual negotiations with Lucine Amara, who was invaluable for this purpose: a well-trained artist with an accurate, flexible voice, she could be counted on to manage at least acceptably most of the soprano roles in the Italian repertory—but somehow she had never acquired the projection of a star. In return for her courtesy in covering, she was entitled to whatever courtesies I could offer and when a role suited to her low-profile temperament came up in a new production—Ellen, the schoolteacher, in *Peter Grimes*—I felt obliged to assign it to her, even though Georg Solti, who was to conduct, had a rival candidate for the role and left our roster when Miss Amara was chosen.

Quite apart from such moral obligations, you must ask yourself *practically*, to whom do I owe a new production? In the normal course of events, most artists couldn't care less about new productions: they would just as soon not rehearse. But starring in a new production has become a status symbol, and all the artists fight for the roles. Indeed, they even fight to have the first night in a revived older production, because the critics come to the first nights. Fortunately, we have two plums on the tree, because the broadcast rates almost as highly as the premiere in the status it confers.

Once the new productions are determined, you must put together the team of conductor, director, and designer who can bring about the result. Bringing together director and designer is one of a general manager's hardest jobs, for these two must work on terms of complete conceptual harmony. One of the outstanding accomplishments of my time at the Metropolitan was the development of the team of Nathaniel Merrill and Robert O'Hearn, who gave us superb (and on-budget) productions of *L'Elisir d'Amore*, *Samson et Dalila*, and *Die Frau ohne Schatten*, among others. (In *L'Elisir*, I had troubles with conductor Fausto Cleva, who insisted Dott. Dulcamara could not arrive in a balloon, at the featured moment of the staging and of the score. He never explained *why* this could not be done, and I told him finally to go along with the director.) Occasionally a director and designer would agree on something I disliked, in which case I usually gave them their heads, sometimes mistakenly—Eugene Berman's sketches for *Barber of Seville* in 1954, for example, I considered much too heavy for the work, but Cyril Ritchard was pleased, so I permitted Berman to proceed. The critics agreed with Ritchard, but the ticket-buying public, unfortunately, agreed with me. Some combinations are natural, like Yoshio Aoyama and Motohiro Nagasaka to direct and design a 1958 *Madame Butterfly* in which both the Japanese and American characters moved and looked authentic (and non-Italian). Some combinations must be fought for—it took me literally weeks to persuade Otto Schenk that he wanted Boris Aronson as the designer for Beethoven's *Fidelio* in 1970, but I did it, and I was right. Only Aronson of all available designers would be crazy enough to agree with Schenk, and by being crazy together they (with Karl Böhm) brought us a magnificent production for the bicentenary year.

Having chosen repertory, you must decide where on the year's program to place each opera. The first problem is opening night. Certain operas, in general the most popular, lend themselves to opening nights, and others do not. *Pelléas* is impossible—it's not an opera where people go off to Sherry's in the intermission and don't come back for the next act. Ordinarily *Don Carlo* would not be a good opening-night opera, either, but we got away with it, twice.

Placement of operas must be governed by the availability of singers. Corelli comes for perhaps three months, and will not sing more than six times a month. (Planning seasons in the 1960s, I always talked first to Corelli, and always signed him last. He would say yes, then no, then I don't think so; he would come in and talk out his troubles, and I would say, "Well, Franco . . .") Miss Nilsson comes for less than two months; certain Wagner operas have been all but unthinkable without her, though the new management will have to start thinking. Miss Price, having accepted a silly theory about the dangers of overexposure, may be available as little as three or four times a season. Miss Sutherland will sing only if her husband conducts. The sequence in which roles appear is important in determining whether an artist can undertake two parts: a soprano needs more time to go from *Aida* to *Traviata* (lightening the voice) than to go from *Traviata* to *Aida*.

You must worry constantly about the subscribers. People have to get a mixture—a certain number of Italian works, a certain number of German works, a French opera, a Mozart if there is one, a modern if they're unlucky. Each subscription series justly demands its share of the electrifying artists and of the new productions. Obviously, rehearsal schedules must be meshed with performances. You find you cannot do *Tristan* on the night you had planned because that day you need a stage rehearsal of *Turandot*, and Miss Nilsson can't do both. Indeed, technically, the stage itself can't do both. Some days (if Karajan is in the house, it may be four or five days for a single production) the stage is unavailable to performers, because the designer needs it for lighting rehearsals. At the new house in Lincoln Center the machinery is so complicated that whole days must be reserved for its maintenance. Now that we make all our own sets, and nearly all our own costumes, there are other scheduling needs, for the shops must never be without work: designers must deliver their designs according to a prearranged schedule that may have relatively little to do with when the opera is to be put onstage.

Then there are the union contracts, which become more burdensome with each renewal. What were once "weekly artists" who sang comprimario roles as needed are now "plan artists" who can be asked to sing twice and cover three times or sing once and cover four times, according to complicated formulas. You write in Velis for a role, and the watchdogs come and say, "That takes him over his number for the week, it will cost X dollars penalty," and you take Velis out and put in someone not as good.

Under the 1969 contracts, the chorus cannot be asked to sing more than five performances a week without the imposition of heavy overtime penalties. Making the final plans for 1971–72, back in 1970, we had everything lined up just so—Nilsson's dates and Corelli's dates, Böhm's dates, Colin Davis's dates, the new productions, the rehearsals, the covers, the plan artists, the balance among the different subscription series—and suddenly somebody looked at the list and said, "Oh, my God, there's no chorus-free opera that week." And somebody else—I think it was I—said, "Oh, forget it; that's just tough." Someday, I am told, all these things will be done by computer; I have no desire to see it.

A season is like a watch: all the parts have to be in place before it operates. In the early years, I found myself inconvenienced by the fact that artists had already made commitments to other opera houses before I asked them, and as time passed I began to plan seasons further and further in advance. Each time I lengthened out the planning period, we managed for a while to get first pick of almost all the people we needed; but then Vienna and La Scala and Covent Garden would see what was happening to them and make their own plans further and further in advance. When I came to New York in October

1949, I was still in plenty of time to plan a season to open in November 1950. Goeran Gentele was appointed to succeed me in December 1970, and I had to tell him that there were few changes that could still be made in the 1972–73 Metropolitan season, 80 per cent of which I had already been obliged to lock up. In fact, if he wanted to have a first-rate company in 1973–74, he could not afford to delay decisions until he came to New York in fall 1971 for the same sort of observation year I had undertaken under Edward Johnson.

Yet despite all this complexity, I believe we created at the Metropolitan Opera an atmosphere in which people worked effectively and cheerfully. Our plans almost always held up. In twenty-two years, the Metropolitan missed only three and a half performances—one in the power blackout, two in the aftermath of the assassination of President Kennedy, and one half when Leonard Warren died onstage in the middle of a performance. Conductors and directors both almost always received as many rehearsals as they said they needed (as early as 1953, I was able to promise Monteux no fewer than eight orchestra rehearsals for *Pelléas et Mélisande*); and the fact is, despite much apparently authoritative statement to the contrary, that the average Metropolitan Opera performance has more rehearsal hours behind it than the average performance at any other opera house in the world. Moreover, everyone in the house knows long in advance exactly what will be expected of him —not only the performance schedule but the full rehearsal schedule is fixed many months ahead.

How quickly my new system caught on at the Metropolitan is expressed for me by the contrast between two letters I received during the early years, the first from Peggy Webster shortly after *Don Carlo:*

> The first question all of us freshmen ask is, "Who is the Stage Manager?" and there is no clear answer; from this ensues

endless dropped threads and confused responsibilities and lack
of co-ordination and waste of time and effort . . .

I made the "ritratto di Carlo" with my own hands, out of a
colored postcard and the back of a miniature of my grand-
father!!! which one expects to do in a summer theatre, but not
at the Met! . . .

The second came from Peter Brook a few weeks after the
first performance of *Faust*, three years later:

Now that I am at a safe distance away, and before I get
immersed in things here [London], I must write to tell you
how tremendously impressed I have been with your theatre
and the work you do there. Quite apart from my own production—and I think I have made it clear how much I have enjoyed that, and how grateful I was for all your support and
backing—I have been most struck in the last two weeks by the
remarkable standard both of singing and of production in what
I have seen of your repertory. I am sure that no other opera
house is presenting such striking casts, and if you carry on like
this, there is maybe a glimmering of hope that the opera war
may eventually be won and we can all work in sane and reasonable conditions.

So whether we manage to arrange anything for next year or
not, my experience of this year will remain a most happy one,
and I certainly wish you and your charming colleagues a very
successful season . . .

Two special problems faced me in planning repertory in the
first decade. One of them went away; the other, if anything,
grew steadily more troublesome.

The problem that went away was opera in English. In the
Austria and Germany of my youth, of course, virtually everything was done in German; at Covent Garden at the time when
I left London, virtually everything was done in English. It
seemed to me arriving in New York that our best hope for
building a bigger and younger audience was to give opera in

the language the whole audience could understand. *Fledermaus* and *Così* encouraged that belief; both were excellent translations, of comedies. Flagstad sang *Alcestis* for us in English. In 1952–53, however, the translator of *Fledermaus* returned to attempt *La Bohème*, and the results were disastrous, doggerel verse totally unsuitable for the tragic play and by no means perfectly fitted to Puccini's phrasing. (This translation also started a long and nasty fight between the Metropolitan and G. Ricordi, proprietors of the surviving Puccini copyrights and sole possessors of many of the Verdi parts. Once again, the precipitating factor was the desire of RCA Victor to do a recording, with Metropolitan artists, of something the Metropolitan would be publicizing, thus freezing out Columbia Records, with which the Metropolitan still had a contract. We had extraordinary difficulty getting from Ricordi vocal scores with the translation we had commissioned: "It once again shows how extremely clever you are and how inefficient I am," I wrote to Franco Colombo of Ricordi, "that I could be persuaded to sign a contract not stipulating the date by which the scores would have to be available . . .") The Metropolitan had long done *The Magic Flute* and *Gianni Schicchi* in English; as time passed, we added to the English-translation list *Boris Godunov*, *Arabella* (both done by our own John Gutman), *Eugene Onegin*, *Queen of Spades*, *Martha*, and operettas which we hoped, in vain, would duplicate the success of *Fledermaus*— Offenbach's *Perichole* and Strauss's *Gypsy Baron*.

What made opera in English translation so difficult for us was, of course, the international casts; one can get away with mispronunciations of a language not that of the audience (Glyndebourne did, for years), but when the whole audience knows that the word is being mispronounced the damage to dramatic viability is great, even in comedy. Too often, moreover, because the prosody has been applied after the music, the words may be incomprehensible however well pronounced. In every translation, too, something of the original phrasing is necessarily lost. A decade or so after my arrival at the Metropolitan, I had a questionnaire distributed, asking the audience at a performance of a *Marriage of Figaro* whether they would rather have the opera presented in English or in Italian. The preference for Italian was overwhelming, and we gradually returned works like *Zauberflöte, Così,* and *Schicchi* to their original languages. Only the operettas continued to be presented consistently in English translation, though the Russian category varied according to the apparent linguistic abilities of the season's cast.

The problem that grew ever more difficult was contemporary opera. Here, too, I had been brought up in a school where it was a matter of routine to present premieres every season, and in England I had co-operated wholeheartedly in launching Britten's *The Rape of Lucretia* and *Albert Herring.* During my observation year I tried to bring Aaron Copland, who I had been told was the best American composer, together with Thornton Wilder to produce a new opera for the Metropolitan. But Wilder wrote to Copland:

> I'm convinced that I write a-musical plays; that my texts "swear at" music; that they're after totally different effects; that they delight in the homeliest aspects of our daily life; that in them ever the life of the emotions is expressed "contra musicam" . . . They are homely and not one bit lyrical.
>
> But I'm delighted that you are applying yourself to opera and the musical play and very proud that that born impresario Mr. Bing has expressed this good opinion of me. Give him my regards.

I wrote to Copland, who had sent a copy of this letter to me, "for once I do not agree with Mr. Wilder"; but there was nothing to be done. There is no doubt that Wilder's work lent itself later to musical comedy: *Hello Dolly* was based on a Wilder play.

William Schuman, then president of the Juilliard School, came to the Metropolitan board in the early years with a proposal for a $100,000 fund to commission a number of American operas, and I was asked to calculate how much subsidy the actual production of such operas would require. About the best I could do was to examine how the Metropolitan box office had behaved in 1947–48 and 1948–49, when Benjamin Britten's excellent *Peter Grimes* had been presented. The results were discouraging. After two performances at 93 per cent of capacity in its first year, *Grimes* had dropped to 70 per cent and 71 per cent later on; in its second year, the work had topped out at 84 per cent and fallen as low as 71 per cent. Even these figures were deceptive—the 84 per cent top in the second year, for example, represented 73 per cent of the house by subscription series and only 11 per cent by single sale at the box office. In those days, new productions cost us $65,000 or so to mount for the first time, and another $5,000 to $10,000 for repairs when they were brought back in a second season. Using the *Grimes* figures and early 1950s box office prices, Reginald Allen worked out a loss of $26,500 for nine performances (as compared with what a conventional opera would take in), and I informed the board that the Metropolitan should try to fund any contemporary American opera for at least $100,000 before attempting it.

At about this time, George Antheil offered me his opera *Volpone*, and I wrote to him that given the recurrent financial crisis of the house "it would be utterly mad and indeed unjustified if the management was contemplating spending a great deal of money on the production of an opera which, however good or interesting, will most likely not be a box office success . . . If and when the Metropolitan will be on a financial basis that it need not look to the box office every night for survival, then the time will come to further contemporary works and, of course, in that line, predominately American works. At the moment, there is nothing left for me but to say clearly and unmistakably that there is not a ghost of a chance."

In my third season, 1952–53, we gave Igor Stravinsky's *The Rake's Progress* one of its earliest productions after its premiere at the Venice Biennale. At the composer's request, Fritz Reiner was the conductor and George Balanchine the director; Stravinsky had also asked for Eugene Berman to do the decor, but his librettist W. H. Auden was for some reason opposed to Berman, and in the interests of a necessary harmony I took the blame and assigned the work to Horace Armistead, whose settings did not harm it, though I would have to agree that they did not help it either. Critics complained about the casting of Hilde Gueden as Anne Trulove in an English-speaking opera, but Stravinsky's request, which I refused to meet "for reasons I would rather not discuss in writing," had been for Elisabeth Schwarzkopf; and Miss Gueden seemed the closest to what he wanted.

I thought it was an outstanding performance of the opera, much better than others I have seen elsewhere, but I must admit I absolutely hated the work, both the words and the music. I do not consider myself a prude, but a woman with a beard I think goes too far. The early box office was most encouraging (it was during those first weeks of *The Rake* that what I called "the Schuman plan" received its most careful consideration), but later performances were played to many empty seats and in the next year the subscribers were furious—people literally spat at the box office, and we couldn't give tickets away. We offered to send heated cabs, but nobody would come.

The first world premiere under my management was of Samuel Barber's *Vanessa*, in the 1957–58 season. I rather liked it despite its dull libretto (by Gian Carlo Menotti); we gave it a first-class production, Mitropoulos conducting, Menotti himself directing, sets and costumes by Cecil Beaton; Eleanor Steber, Nicolai Gedda, Giorgio Tozzi, Rosalind Elias, and Regina Resnik in the cast. It had what I and my colleagues called a "cocktail party success"—the first performances were filled by friends of Sam and Gian Carlo who had to say at cocktail parties that they had seen it, and then the house was empty except for some long-suffering subscribers. Nevertheless, when the new theater was to be opened in Lincoln Center, we went back to Barber for a new opera; but the story of *that* disaster is associated with the new house rather than with music, and shall come later. The only other world premiere in my time was Marvin David Levy's *Mourning Becomes Electra*, which was of interest mostly because of the strength of the Eugene O'Neill play and the splendidly realistic direction of Michael Cacoyannis.

The one complete success we had with a modern opera was the revival of *Peter Grimes*, in which the direction of Tyrone Guthrie and the conducting of Colin Davis combined to convince even our more skeptical subscribers that they were in attendance at a great performance of a wonderful opera. Attendance at *Grimes* held up in our second season of the work, too. *Wozzeck*, which is not, of course, a contemporary opera—it will be fifty years old soon—was a disappointment to me at the box office. On my arrival in New York, I gave the New York *Times* a list of my ten favorite operas, and one of them was *Wozzeck*. Under the leadership first of Karl Böhm and then of Colin Davis—with superb performances by Hermann Uhde as Wozzeck (until his death), Eleanor Steber as Marie, Karl Dönch as the Doctor, Paul Franke as the Captain, and Kurt Baum as the Drum Major; and in English translation, hoping to heighten public involvement in what is a true *Gesamtkunstwerk*, a union of the theatrical and musical arts—our *Wozzeck* seemed to me a superlative production. I brought it back for three revivals, each time at increasing losses.

Twice, with money from the Ford Foundation, we commissioned American composers to write operas for us but did not stage the results—once because there were no results (Marc Blitzstein was bizarrely murdered in the Caribbean before completing any but a fraction of *Sacco and Vanzetti*), once because, frankly, we did not like the results (Virgil Thomson's *Lord Byron*, performed in spring 1972 for the first time by the Juilliard School). And we virtually shared with Paris, coming in a close second by prearrangement, the launching of Menotti's *The Last Savage*, charmingly set for us by Beni Montresor, an anti-modern modern comic opera of which I suspect we soon heard the last.

Some day a new operatic genius will arise whose works draw the public, and when he does we shall all know about it. Failing such a genius, I was not wildly interested in presenting contemporary opera at the Metropolitan. My colleague in Hamburg does contemporary opera after contemporary opera and the press loves him, and he plays to empty houses, and the state pays. But in America the state does not pay. I dare say that if I had done three more world premieres in my twenty-two years the Met would not have gone broke, but the finances would have been that much more difficult, and except for two or three reviewers nobody would have thanked me. The audience certainly would not have thanked me. I had only four new productions a year, and a necessity to give plums to singers; if I had taken more of those new productions for contemporary opera the singers would not have thanked me. You can't get a Tebaldi or a Callas (we tried Callas, for *Vanessa*) or a Nilsson or a Corelli or a Tucker to sing contemporary opera; you're lucky if you can get a Lear. I am always being told that opera will die unless the new works are performed; it seems to me that these days a better case can be made for the proposition that opera will *never* die unless the new works are performed.

# 20

I wonder whether anyone could run today's Metropolitan Opera, with its $50 million theater and $20 million annual budget, its year-long season, and nearly a thousand regular employees, the way I ran the old building in my first half-dozen years as general manager. They say President Truman had a sign on his desk reading, "The buck stops here"; I could have put that sign on my desk, too. Every decision relating to the artistic operation of the house was my decision—indeed, all casting decisions down to the Third Orphan in *Rosenkavalier* continued to be mine to the very end of my administration—and I also shouldered the burden of routine daily supervision. I used to say in those days that an opera house had to be organized as a militant democracy, in which one man ruled.

Nobody who has not worked at an opera house can imagine the sheer number of things that go wrong, and the number of occasions requiring the intervention of a general manager situated as I was in the 1950s—with an inherited operating staff that had fallen into disgraceful habits through lack of supervision over the years. Perhaps a sampling of the memoranda I sent during those years will convey some flavor of what it meant to sit down in the morning, having worked all day the day before and worried through a performance the previous night:

To: All Assistant Conductors
From: Rudolf Bing

It has come to my attention that Assistant Conductors in an effort to see the conductor are pulling aside the house curtain near the stage manager's desk.

This is a very undesirable practice because (a) in due course it will ruin the curtain and (b) it makes [backstage lights] visible from the auditorium.

. . . This leads me to the general suggestion that you should please avoid using the Stage Manager's Desk as a "meeting place." Even though you conduct your conversations in whispers, it is a dangerous spot for voices to be carried into the auditorium, it may distract the person responsible for cues and it may even block downstage entrances to the stage. I am sure that this little reminder is all that is necessary . . .

To: [Business Manager and Comptroller]
From: Rudolf Bing
Subject: Typewriters

I appreciate the importance of this type of equipment. At the same time I think the purchase of 15 new typewriters in 5 years is a pretty substantial investment and even though it is perfectly true I don't think we can keep harping on the shocking state of affairs of this type of equipment when my management took over.

I really don't think we should at this present moment buy 8 typewriters and I hope that by hook or by crook you could

manage with acquiring 3 or a maximum of 4 . . . Let me
know what you decide . . .

To: [House Manager]
FROM: Rudolf Bing

The last few performances I sat for quite a while in one of
the House seats in order to check on complaints that have
reached me from patrons sitting on the corridor aisles, particularly on the 39th Street side. Unfortunately, I found it quite
true that these unhappy people, who are paying $8 [sic!] just
like everybody else, are badly disturbed by late coming patrons
and ushers talking in the corridor.

I would be grateful if you would please issue very strict instructions—and have it checked occasionally by your assistants
or yourself that these are observed—that ushers should not only
themselves speak very softly in the corridors immediately ad-
joining the auditorium, but in addition that they must use polite but firm initiative in getting late coming patrons to behave
quietly and show some consideration for those who came earlier
and do not wish to be disturbed . . .

To: [Chorus Delegate]
FROM: Rudolf Bing

I would be grateful if you would please ask the gentlemen
of the chorus when after a chorus scene or act they crowd
in front of the elevator that they would be good enough to look
out for the principal artists and see that they are not "crowded
out."

It seems unreasonable that Mr. del Monaco and/or Mr.
Warren after very heavy scenes would have to walk up three
flights because they cannot get quickly into the elevator and I
am quite sure that it only needs a reminder to our always helpful chorus gentlemen to give the principal artists the courtesy
of letting them ride with them with as little delay as possible . . .

[ 215 ]

To: [Comptroller]
FROM: Rudolf Bing

Tonight, during negotiations with the Concessionaires Union I discovered that a current contract with that union was not available. On inquiring, Mr. [          ] said he thought the contract had been sent to Mr. Lauterstein [the Metropolitan's lawyer] and, apparently, had got lost. He did not know when it had been sent. I, frankly, think this is an intolerable situation . . .

To: [Stage Manager]
FROM: Rudolf Bing

Will you please immediately obtain a suitable knife with a rubber blade for use in Act IV of "Carmen." I would like in any performance in which Mr. Tucker or Mr. Vinay appears to use the real knife as so far; but in any performance in which Mr. del Monaco or Mr. Baum appears as Don Jose I would like them please to use the rubber knife. They have had less rehearsal in the part . . . [In fact, Miss Stevens was terrified of the way both del Monaco and Baum threw themselves into their role . . .]

To: [House Manager]
FROM: Rudolf Bing

At least ten days ago I asked that a little stool be placed in the new elevator as I see no reason at all why the old man running it should be expected to stand all the time. I consider this very bad employment tactics to force an employee to completely unnecessary strain and I would like this situation to be remedied at once.

To: Rudolf Bing
FROM: [House Manager]

I respectfully request that you reconsider your directive of

[ 216 ]

46. Francis Robinson, Rudolf Bing on tour, 1958

47. Rudolf Bing in the
Old Met. His brother
commented—"No
wonder you have a
deficit!"

48. Right, with Mr. and
Mrs. Herbert von Karajan,
Salzburg Festival, 1960

49. Below, with Renata
Tebaldi at Sherry's
Restaurant in the Old Met,
1963

50. Sir Rudolf Bing

51. Right, Rudolf Bing with
Mrs. John F. Kennedy, 1965

52. Below, Bing, Balanchine,
Bernstein on balcony of the
New York State Theater,
New York, 1966

53. Front row: Bodo Igesz, assistant stage director; Back row (left to right): Günther Rennert, director; Marc Chagall, designer; Rudolph Bing; watching the rehearsal of *Die Zauberflöte*, 1966-67 season

this date ordering a movable stool in the new 39th Street elevator for the following reasons:

I have consistently refused to allow stools or chairs in any of our elevators although there has been a long and constant arbitration for them. This refers to the two backstage cars, the Studio Building car, and the Storehouse car on W. 40th St. Our elevator operators are relieved at regular intervals and they also have a seat in the hall to which they can go during non-busy periods. During the busy periods I do not approve of an operator running the car from a stool as it reduces his efficiency and promotes carelessness . . . A stool is in the way, is a tripping hazard, and if we concede a stool in the 39th Street car it will open anew the problem of stools in the other cars. Furthermore, it becomes a direct challenge to my authority when the men can go over my head and obtain things which have been denied them for a good reason.

To: [House Manager]
From: Rudolf Bing

Nobody has approached me at all. I myself asked why the man had no seat and was merely told that they had none. Until I talked to Mr. Allen I had been unaware that you did not want it.

I cannot really accept your reasoning in this case. The position of the new 39th Street elevator is different from any of the others inasmuch as it is in much more continuous use. If you tell me that the others are in continuous use then I think it would be perfectly right for them to have little stools also. I ride in elevators in every part of the City every day and I have never yet seen one without a stool for the operator. I have not heard of any particular accidents or carelessness arising from these stools and I cannot, therefore, see why they should apply to our elevator operators . . .

To: [All Senior Staff]
FROM: Rudolf Bing

I am afraid it appears that papering the house, when this seems desirable, with our own personnel turns out to our disadvantage: immediately the rumor spreads that box office receipts are bad and this or that opera is a financial flop. I would be grateful, therefore, if all of you to whom this note is addressed would not only be extremely careful yourself but also encourage your staff never to talk pessimistically about the box office—"Everything is doing just fine!"

If we must paper, let us consider it and I think students and soldiers would be more advantageous than members of this company who apparently, if quite unconsciously, are spreading bad propaganda. On the whole I think an occasional bad house is less dangerous than papering because people are less inclined to tell stories about a bad house than about having received complimentary tickets which may constitute quite an event.

To: [Stage Manager]
FROM: Rudolf Bing

Please remember that the promise of supering is an important feature in our ballet school publicity. Any type of supers that the ballet school can reasonably be expected to supply should be taken from the ballet school and only such supers, subject to occasional important exceptions, should be taken outside the school that the school cannot supply, like old men or old women or very special types . . .

To: [Business, Box Office, and House Managers]
FROM: Rudolf Bing

Honestly, I am beginning to get seriously concerned with the nature of complaints about the rude, unfriendly behavior of various employees who are in constant touch with our patrons. As you know, it concerns the box office and I think we know that it rather concentrates on one member of the box office. It lately also includes the libretto table and this, frankly, I am not prepared to tolerate at all. I will be grateful if you would take that up immediately and most seriously . . .

The next group are the ushers. I have occasionally talked to Mr. [          ] about it and at various times have been assured that matters will improve and nothing happens. The point has now been reached when at the next complaint I will see the ushers myself and Mr. [          ] will not like it because there will be a hell of a row and a few of them may be dismissed . . . I am getting fed up with the attitude that the patrons are a nuisance disturbing our personnel . . .

To: [Stage Manager]
FROM: Rudolf Bing

Please remind all artists and tell the new ones that, as last year, I shall be grateful if they would keep "hands down" in front of the curtain and would not resume the practice of congratulating each other.

To: [Chief Electrician]
FROM: Rudolf Bing

I hear that a special effect machine for "Don Giovanni" that was estimated to cost $50 has now turned out to cost $220.

I am very sorry but I am unwilling and unable to purchase the machine for that price which was never authorized. Will you please, therefore, return the machine . . . and work out another way of achieving the effect . . .

To: [All Solo Cast]
FROM: Rudolf Bing

Despite the Management's continued efforts to do away with

the claque in this theater this regrettable institution has by no means disappeared, and in fact it would seem that in recent weeks it has shown up with particular virulence. The Management has received an ever-increasing number of letters by subscribers who complain—and quite rightly—about this unbearable nuisance.

Nothing is, of course, more desirable in an opera house than applause and enthusiasm in general. Both artists and Management would certainly rue the day, if it ever came, when there would be silence after a great aria or at the end of an act. However, it seems to me, and I do think that it should appear to all real artists, that paid applause is a reflection on rather than a sign of artistic merit . . .

To: [House Manager]
FROM: Rudolf Bing

According to Mr. Lauterstein, we are perfectly entitled to refuse to sell tickets to anyone except for reasons of race, color or faith. Therefore, if you know the identity of one or two or three of the worst offenders in standing room, it would be most helpful indeed if you could stop the box office from selling a ticket to the person in question. I wish we could stop selling tickets to the heads of the claque, but I understand that they never themselves buy their tickets . . .

[but, on the other hand . . .]

To: [Business Manager]
FROM: Rudolf Bing

Again and again in sleepless nights I am thinking about the standing room position next year and if I still had need of any prodding last night's performance of "Aida" would have provided it.

I think we are making a very serious and very great mistake in cutting standing room. It is practically the only source of real enthusiasm in the House which, whenever genuine, is infectious. There may have been a little claque last night but no claque can produce the amount of heartwarming and really exciting ovations that rang through the House from beginning to end last night. Every time it comes from the standing room, it infects the rest of the house but is kept up by the standing room, it sets the tone of the evening, it inspires the artists and, consequently, it contributes to the spirit and level of a performance . . .

To: [Business Manager]
FROM: Rudolf Bing

As you know, the fire officers last night found 7 men smoking onstage during the performance. As you also know, the Metropolitan will be summonsed and it may cost us several hundred dollars.

I have now practically for three years tried to stop this criminal carelessness by being friendly and almost jokingly attempting to stop stagehands every time I see anyone smoking. I have put notices on the board and I have done everything short of having a terrific row and firing people. Unfortunately, the honor system and friendliness do not seem to work and this matter must be stopped now regardless of what means we have to employ . . .

To: [Box Office Manager]
FROM: Rudolf Bing

I received a letter today from a gentleman in San Francisco who while in New York last week inquired at the box office whether "Boris Godunov" would be performed some time later during the season and was told—according to his letter—that there was no way of obtaining this information except by following the weekly announcements in the New York paper.

I have no reason to assume that this gentleman just invented the story and if the statement is correct it really alarms me as a sign of particular unhelpfulness on the part of our box office staff. Of course everyone in the box office knows or should know that the complete repertory for the season is established: that we could if we wanted to give out the whole season's repertory for every single night with complete casts but that for certain reasons well known to you we refrain from so doing. [In the late 1960s we did begin to hand out complete season's schedules at the beginning of each year.] However, there is no reason on earth why we should not tell a customer whether or not a particular opera will be given later in the season and of course it must be known to the box office that "Boris Godunov" is not in this year's repertory . . .

To: [Permanent Conductors]
FROM: Rudolf Bing

May I draw your attention to some of the House Rules and requests that were issued in the early part of the season after discussion with AGMA.

I am particularly referring to those rules which, except in cases of utmost emergency, deal with the scheduling of rehearsals. I had lately quite a few complaints, some of them I know justifiable, that artists were pressured by individual conductors to stay at rehearsals or come to rehearsals when they were not, in accordance with the regulations, obliged to do so and were also asked for special rehearsals which had not been scheduled officially by the rehearsal department.

I shall be grateful if you will please realize that for any such violation the Management gets into serious trouble and that indeed, we, all of us, will have to pay dearly in the future . . .

To: [Orchestra Manager]
FROM: Rudolf Bing

I recall that the orchestra agreed last year that every one of them would stand up the first time the conductor enters the pit at the beginning of a performance. Last night in "Forza" this apparently was overlooked and I would be grateful if you would kindly remind the orchestra as I would very much like them to resume this practice which does not seem a great hardship and at the same time is a gesture of respect and discipline which can only be of advantage to the standing of the orchestra and to the House in general.

To: [Assistant Stage Manager]
FROM: Rudolf Bing
SUBJECT: Canary for "Pagliacci"

I took special trouble at the last performance to watch the bird in its cage and found that it is quite impossible to realize whether it is alive or stuffed. I suggest, therefore, that we should not harass the poor animal any further by carting it up and down in the cold and that it should be given to somebody who wants it and assures you that he will treat it well and keep it in a warm, brightly lit room . . .

If there had been sparrows, I am sure that as part of the role I played at the Metropolitan during that first decade, I would have noted every time one of them fell.

The problem of the claque was persistent, and did not yield to occasional memos. I came finally to the opinion that so long as a house has Italian artists there is no way to eradicate the claque: the artist receives someone at home, that someone buys standing room tickets, people present themselves at the door with valid tickets . . . The worst offender in my time at the Metropolitan held occasional parties at her apartment for the claque, and even sang a song or two for them. (She called them "my children.") I have never been completely opposed to claques. At our lovely production of Massenet's *Werther* in 1971 I felt that an expert claque could have helped both audience and cast by signaling the correct moments for applause in a work that had not been done in New York in sixty years. But a claque hired to promote one artist soon becomes a threat to those who do not pay, and the same standees who shouted their approval of Miss Milanov began to yell insults at her tenors and at others. I hired a private detective to join the line waiting to buy standing room, issued various threats, even announced (but then did not enforce) the cancellation of standing room at the house.

If we could not eliminate the claque, we could control its opportunities. Solo bows before the curtain at the end of each scene or act were an obvious invitation to artists to compete against each other for volume or duration of public favor, and I determined to forbid solo bows and make the whole cast come out at once and accept public acclaim as a group. I wrote to Lord Harewood, then at Covent Garden:

> I wonder whether you could do me a great favor. At the Metropolitan for decades there has been a terrible habit that after acts and at the end of a performance artists first go out in front of the curtain as a group and then individually with the star as the last person out. This of course makes it very easy for the claque, paid and unpaid, to show their preferences. I think it is a most undignified procedure with the artists standing behind the curtain listening to who gets a little more applause than the others, and, as I said, awakening the low instincts of the public.
>
> I would like to abolish this and would be grateful if you could confirm to me that solo curtain calls, with very few exceptions, are not the practice at Covent Garden . . .

But, alas, Harewood cabled back:

WHILE IN FULL AGREEMENT YOUR SENTIMENTS REGRET SOLO CURTAIN CALLS PRACTICE COVENT GARDEN OPERA AND BALLET.

So I did it on my own initiative.

Many problems it will always be impossible for a general manager to escape. Only the general manager can tell Lily Pons that she mustn't wear black tights as Gilda in *Rigoletto*. Keeping artists comfortable can be delegated only up to a point, and retaining their confidence cannot be delegated at all. When the Metropolitan did *La Sonnambula* for Joan Sutherland in 1963, Rolf Gérard designed a suspension bridge over which the sleepwalking heroine would pass, to the horror of all the little Swiss villagers on the ground. Though I have no special liking for heights, and the bridge looked actually dangerous to me, I felt I should sleepwalk across it first myself, to assure Miss Sutherland that we were looking out for her interests. To the last day, I felt that anyone in the company who felt a need to see me had the right to do so, even though in nine cases out of ten the need was a grievance that could make nothing but unpleasantness for me—especially when the grievance involved, as it often did, somebody on a management level who was outraged by the idea that a person in his department would go over his head.

But in 1953, very luckily, two young men who would have the capacity to handle all the problems of running the house came onto the Metropolitan Opera staff. One of them was Captain Charles Robert Herman of the U. S. Army, who had been a pupil of Carl Ebert's at the University of Southern California, and had worked with Ebert on productions at Glyndebourne. He wanted to be an assistant stage director, which was what Ebert had recommended him for, but the open slot in our organization was for an assistant stage manager, responsible for getting the physical production rather than the people into the right place. We compromised, and he undertook both responsibilities. From his first days as an assistant, it was clear that Bob Herman was a man of extraordinary efficiency, capacity for detail, and clarity of mind. Any production on which he was assistant stage director came onto the boards with a perfect "book," telling exactly what the original *régisseur* wanted everybody to be doing at each moment. When the director left, which often happened the morning after the first performance, a production on which Herman had been the assistant survived virtually without loss of dramatic quality, because Herman could supply a blueprint for every substitute who entered the cast.

The other newcomer was Herman E. Krawitz, who arrived under what were for me less promising auspices. Our backstage difficulties had been growing increasingly serious under Armistead's weak control, and Anthony Bliss, as a relatively new member of the board, suggested that a foundation set up in memory of his father might contribute the salary of an expert in backstage organization, to work at the Metropolitan for eight to ten weeks or so. Krawitz, who was still in his twenties, came recommended by the Broadway producer Richard Aldrich; most of his experience had been in summer theaters on Cape Cod. I found it quite awkward to have this outsider poking around the house, and I thought some of his reports presumptuous: I wrote to Bliss after one of them,

> I don't think it is any of Mr. Krawitz's business to pass judgment on the Comptroller's Department, on the Stage Management and indeed on the Management, etc. . . . Naturally, Mr. Krawitz is perfectly entitled to his views and I daresay some of them are reasonably correct. You or any other Director may in conversation ask him for such views; this naturally is your privilege. I don't think I will ask him because I don't wish to hear him criticise people who are either his superiors or at any rate are not to be under his control. Even though Mr. Krawitz writes very generously about me in his paragraph "The Management" I feel I do not like that either. I do not wish to be either criticised or praised by Mr. Krawitz . . .

Yet the fact is that (apart from any judgment of kind words about myself) nearly everything Krawitz reported back to Bliss *was* right, and when he completed his consulting studies I asked him to work for the Metropolitan full-time. He saved us almost all his first year's salary at once, by awarding a contract for cable work on the stage to a new company rather than to the one we had done business with before; the new company did the job well for half the price. "In my opinion," he wrote, "[the new company] was in here to do a job the best possible way at the lowest cost, and [the old company] had been in here to see how much money could be given to the stagehands over the longest period of time . . ."

The realization by the stagehands that their work was to be examined by somebody who knew stages provoked a strike threat when it was learned we were hiring Krawitz. The men announced they would not work that evening's performance of *Tannhäuser*, and we determined to put it on anyway. I was prepared to man the curtain myself, and came to the theater in a sports jacket, to work with my hands. (When the men decided they *would* fulfill their obligations that night, I went to my box as usual. In the hall, I met one of the Misses Wetmore, an elderly lady who was among the social pillars of the theater, who looked at me with amazement and inquired in a choked voice why I was not "dressed." I said, "If anyone asks you, tell them you don't know . . .") To the honor of Richard Walsh, president of Local 1 of the stagehands' union, he refused to countenance such a strike, and though the men did not work the next day's dress rehearsal (when I did operate the curtain, nearly decapitating Zinka Milanov by releasing it a shade too soon), the crisis passed.

In the history of the Metropolitan Opera, the 1954–55 season is of course the year of three debuts—Marian Anderson, Renata Tebaldi, and Dimitri Mitropoulos. The appearance of Miss

Anderson on the Metropolitan stage, as the first featured black singer in the history of the company, was among my proudest moments at the house. It was something I had wanted to do from my first year with the company, but it was not until 1954 that we had the right part—Ulrica in *Un Ballo in Maschera*, which demanded little acting and little rehearsal time from a fiercely busy concert artist and could be managed within the confines of a voice past its prime. Even so, her engagement was made possible only by the lucky chance that I found myself seated beside her at a party given by Sol Hurok for the Sadler's Wells Ballet. We discussed her engagement there, and it was set within a few days. The Metropolitan Opera board was not among the many organizations that sent congratulations when the news was announced . . .

But for all the pleasures and importance of that event—and of the later introduction of Miss Tebaldi, who would be the darling of the house for more than a decade—the most significant development of 1954–55 at the Metropolitan may have been the development of the administrative cadre that would see the house through the next seventeen years. Rudy Kuntner, in 1972 the over-all chief of stage work, became our chief electrician; Lou Edson, who stayed with us through the opening of the new house, became chief carpenter. And Bob Herman and Herman Krawitz began their rise within the management structure. By 1958 they would both be assistant managers of the company, Reggie Allen having gone to work for Lincoln Center and Max Rudolf having become conductor of the Cincinnati Symphony. They were an indispensable support to all my efforts.

Krawitz, despite the difficult beginnings, developed extraordinarily good relations with all our backstage people, guaranteeing good pay and fair working conditions to one side of the inevitable conflict, good work and willing co-operation to the other side. His tone of camaraderie goes down well with all the crafts, and relieved our stage situation of tension. Under his supervision, the Metropolitan organized to manufacture its own productions in its own "factories," rather than farming out the work (at much greater cost) as always in the past. In addition to his flair for theatrical matters, Krawitz has a strong sense of quality, and when he saw quality—in a Chagall, a Zeffirelli, a Karajan—he broke his back to provide the right conditions for its display.

Bob Herman first called attention to himself as the only assistant stage director the Metropolitan has ever had who knew the union rules well enough to warn a visiting director in time that a mandated break was coming up. He has an uncanny brain for detail, for record keeping, for making and keeping charts. And he was invaluable in union negotiations because he could *immediately* grasp the implications of granting a demand—he would say, "That will mean so-and-so many hours of overtime." Obviously, he became unpopular. To this day, I fail to understand how such able men as the top leadership of the Metropolitan Opera board have failed to see Bob Herman's outstanding qualities, and have allowed themselves to be duped by some disgruntled artists, like chorus and comprimario people who know Herman's work has deprived them of overtime.

Over nearly twenty years with the house, Krawitz and Herman proved themselves totally loyal to myself and to the organization. They relieved me of most of the burden of detail, simply by handling it so well that few problems survived to cross my desk. On larger matters, they always had their own ideas, but when my word went against them they carried out my decisions without question. When I determined to resign, I suggested to the board that, at least for an interregnum, a triumvirate of Krawitz, Herman, and a music director should run the house. The idea was never even considered. I am still surprised that my successor lacked the judgment to recognize the outstanding ability of these men—or, if he judged them correctly, lacked the strength to stand up against the board members who were prejudiced against them—and allowed the Metropolitan to suffer the major disadvantage of their departure.

# 21

I first heard the name of Maria Callas in 1950, and it was attached to unbelievable stories about the range of her voice and the variety of the roles she played. I had not yet met Roberto Bauer, and could not trust anyone I knew in Italy; and Diez in London was not a useful source of views on Italian singers. In November 1950 I wrote to Erich Engel at the Vienna State Opera:

> . . . Do you know Maria Callas who, I understand, sang in Buenos Aires and who is now recommended to me as the best existing Aida, etc. and even suggested for the Queen of the Night. Could you very kindly drop me a confidential note advising me whether in your view Miss Callas is vocally really as outstanding as I am led to believe. How would you compare her vocal qualifications for instance with Ljuba Welitsch? I gather she does not look well and is an uninteresting actress. Does the beauty of her voice make up for all these defects? I should be most grateful to hear from you as soon as possible.

Engel was very positive: her performances at the Colón were considered worthy of the highest attention; her coloratura technique as Norma had been regarded as astonishing. Moreover, her repertory was incredibly varied—she had been praised in various houses as Turandot, Norma, Aida, Fidelio, Kundry, and Isolde. She was considered an unusually intelligent artist, with a great career ahead of her. Moreover, the Colón was a big house; if she had filled that one, she could probably sing anywhere.

I had had my fill of Liduino Bonard on the previous spring's trip to Italy, and Max Rudolf wrote to him about Miss Callas. Bonard replied, "This artist will be very glad to get in touch with you to sing at the Metropolitan Theatre, as such an important one. She would prefer to come to New York for the opening of the season, and to stay for a month. During this month the artist would like to sing 8 performances with a fee of 700 Dollari each performance and the travel-expense."

This was now a matter I had to handle, and I turned wearily to negotiations with Bonard, by mail. We would need twelve to fourteen weeks, I wrote him, and for an artist unknown in America I could not offer more than $400 per performance. The reply arrived within ten days:

> I have spoken with the artist *Maria Callas Meneghini,* who is very glad to agree with you to stay in New York longer than two months, if necessary.
>
> Regarding the conditions is alright 600 Dollars each performance; but I retain to reduce the conditions to 500 Dollars.

Again I offered $400, and presently received the surprising reply:

> Maria Callas Meneghini is very anxious to be in the company of this very well known Theatre and she agrees to accept 200 Dollars each performance.

Of course she would like very much to know how many performances she could have during the two months of her staying at the Metropolitan. Also she is asking in which operas she will sing, and, if possible, the opera of her debut.

This was more serious—maybe. I wrote Bonard to remind him that we had offered $400 and would stay with that figure despite his remarkable reduction in price, and to offer Miss Callas our opening-night *Aïda* in 1951 if she would guarantee us three weeks of rehearsal and twelve weeks of performances thereafter. She would also have to return in the spring for the tour. In return, I would guarantee twenty performances in the first twelve weeks, with an option for the same length season, at $500 per performance, in 1952–53. As an illustration of how little was known about Maria Callas in New York in 1950, I ended my letter by asking her nationality.

This letter went unanswered for three weeks, and then I received an acceptance of the offer, with its terms altered—ten days instead of three weeks of rehearsal, *two* return tickets Milan–New York, and in addition to *Aïda* "one or two of the following operas: *Norma—Puritani—Traviata—Trovatore.*" The question of the tour and the 1952–53 option Miss Callas would discuss with me on her arrival in New York.

But we were not doing any of the four operas Miss Callas wanted during the time we wished her to be in New York, and I could not wait for her arrival to tell the tour cities whether they would hear her or not. Nor was I willing to reduce to ten days the rehearsal period before our opening-night *Aïda*—or to give Miss Callas, alone among all our European artists, transportation for spouse as well as self. The arrangement, if there ever was an arrangement (nothing ever came of my dealings with Bonard), foundered in an exchange of negative telegrams. But Bonard agreed to set up an audition for me in the spring, when I would be in Florence while she was engaged for the Maggio Musicale.

The lady I saw in Florence in spring 1951 bore only a slight relationship to the Maria Callas who later became world-famous. She was monstrously fat, and awkward. I wrote Bonard:

> . . . I heard her and had a long talk with her. She has no doubt remarkable material but has still a lot to learn before she can be a star at the Met. We had quite a friendly discussion but did not get very far . . . In September or October I will write and let her know whether and what I can offer her for the Season 1952–53, and she will then have to make up her mind whether she can accept my offer . . . Let's wait for a few months . . .

Eventually, we did offer her *Traviata* in 1952–53, and we believed she was coming; and then we received a letter to the effect that our failure to procure a visa for her husband, Battista Meneghini, made it impossible for her to come to New York. As I speak no Italian, and Meneghini spoke no English, Max Rudolf called across the ocean to find out what was going on, but all we ever found out was that she was canceling her contract.

By now I had signed Roberto Bauer as our Italian representative, and we could hope to operate on a more businesslike basis with the Meneghini-Callas family as with others. Bauer arranged with Miss Callas to reserve time for us in January and February of 1954, and I wrote from Italy to Max Rudolf: "Can we use Callas in January and/or February for some performances: *Lucia!! Traviata, Aida. (Norma,* of course, unless that would upset Milanov, which I want to avoid—she is still better than anyone here . . .)* Send me your views urgently." Rudolf, still annoyed by the telephoning and cabling of earlier that season, doubted that we should take the trouble, and I agreed by mail from Italy—in a letter announcing an offer to the baritone Ettore Bastianini and praising a rehearsal of *Forza* I had just heard, especially the Leonora of Miss Tebaldi, who "really is wonderful; the only voice in Europe that can compete with Zinka."

During that summer, Miss Callas lost at least fifty pounds, and became the astonishing, svelte, striking woman who conquered the operatic (and more than the operatic) world. It was like Andersen's fairy tale. She showed none of the signs one usually finds in a fat woman who has lost weight: she looked as though she had been born to that slender and graceful figure, and had always moved with that elegance. Now it became urgent for the Metropolitan to have her. I wrote to Bauer:

> What is the situation? Any reasonable chance of having her next season at last? Could she be available for rehearsals as from November 8 and debut in *Traviata* during the week beginning November 15? She could do Santuzza possibly the following week and Tosca a little later . . . We could guarantee her a minimum of 12 performances in 10 weeks or 15 performances in 12 weeks, provided that in addition to the above-mentioned operas she is prepared to sing at least two or more of the following parts: Aida, Gioconda, Amelia (*Ballo in Maschera*), Madeleine (*Andrea Chénier*).
>
> As to fee, I await your suggestion. I would not like to have to pay her more than $750 per performance but if she at last agrees—finally and irrevocably and without any strings attached as to visas for husbands, friends or concubines!—I would be prepared to go up to $800 per performance . . .

But instead Miss Callas signed to sing at the Chicago Lyric Opera, both in 1954 and in 1955, for very much more money than we were prepared to offer her. Then in the spring of 1955 she and I finally did reach agreement, on an opening-night *Lucia* in 1956–57, to be followed by a Queen of the Night in

*The Magic Flute.* But nothing was signed; Miss Callas complained of our choice of conductor for *Lucia:* she and Cleva had fought about something at a rehearsal in Italy. I wrote to Meneghini: "Surely Signora Callas is a big enough artist and great enough personality to let the past be forgotten. Frankly, I don't know how I can get over this difficulty unless Signora Callas is prepared to be of sufficient greatness of mind to ignore an incident of the past . . . Please do not ask me for a change of conductor because that is one wish that, with the best will in the world, I cannot fulfill." Then she refused to sing *The Magic Flute* in English, even though I agreed to take the second-act aria down a whole tone for her. We still had no contract when she passed through New York that fall on her way to Chicago.

Contrary to press report at the time, the problem was never money. A year before, Wadmond had denied my request to lift the top fee from $1,000 to $1,200, and Miss Callas signed for $1,000 a night—to which we added $2,000 for transportation (in effect paying Meneghini's way, too). I added a typed clause to our printed contract: "Artist agrees to comply with the rules and regulations of the Metropolitan Opera Association management, in particular as far as punctual attendance at rehearsals, the wearing of approved costumes and accessories, practices about curtain calls, etc. etc. are concerned." When she actually came to New York in 1956, the board had relaxed the maximum fee rule, and we added another $3,000 to her contract for "expenses" for her twelve performances during the nine weeks of her stay.

To sign that contract in 1955, we had to take the mountain to Mahomet: Francis Robinson and I flew to Chicago, where the managers of the Lyric Opera, Carol Fox and Lawrence Kelly, were not pleased to see us. (They feared, correctly, that once Callas signed in New York, Chicago would hear her no more.)

We heard Miss Callas sing in *Trovatore*, with Bjoerling as Manrico, and I remember saying that during "Ah si, ben mio" in the third act it was Callas' quiet listening rather than Bjoerling's voice that made the dramatic impact: "He didn't know what he was singing, but she knew." Then we went backstage, where I offered my very best version of the kiss-the-hand routine I had learned as a child, and the picture got into all the papers—and, finally, the Metropolitan signed Maria Callas to a contract.

Before she actually came, all the roles changed: her opening night was *Norma*, and her other roles were Lucia and Tosca. In the meantime, a new kind of problem had arisen. Backstage in the opera house, at the last night of her Chicago season, Miss Callas had been served with a summons by Richard Bagarozy, who claimed that during her stay in New York in the 1940s (when she took lessons from Bagarozy's wife Louise Caselotti) Miss Callas had signed an exclusive management contract with him, pledging him 10 per cent of all her earnings as a singer for ten years. This had mounted up (eventually Bagarozy would claim no less than $300,000), and he wanted to be paid. Miss Callas exploded with rage, and accused Kelly and Miss Fox of failing to protect her. It was understood that in New York the Metropolitan would have to protect her.

The best our lawyers could work out, after consultation with the lawyers in Chicago who were handling the case for Miss Callas, was an agreement to deposit the money for her appearances in a Swiss bank, which meant that she would have no salary in America for the Bagarozys to attach. We perfected this arrangement in great detail, but Meneghini rejected it. In fact, Meneghini rejected all arrangements that did not involve payment to him *in cash*, before the curtain rose, of his wife's fee for each performance. Toward the end, I had him paid in five-dollar bills, to make a wad uncomfortably large for him to carry.

We gave Miss Callas treatment no other artist has ever received. She was met at the airport by Francis Robinson and a lawyer (in case process servers were around), escorted to and from her hotel, attended by Robinson at all her interviews. After one of them, he came back to my office bursting with the story of one of her replies. A lady reporter had said to her, "Madame Callas, you were born in the United States, you were brought up in Greece, you are now practically an Italian. What language do you think in?" To which Miss Callas replied, "I count in English."

But all of this, like everything I have read, conveys a very wrong impression of the Maria Callas I had come to know during the previous year's meetings and correspondence. What almost everything written about Miss Callas fails to catch is the girlishness, the innocent dependence on others that was so strong a part of her personality when she did not feel she had to be wary. Her letters to me in 1955 and 1956 are full of these moments. "Is New York," she wrote in one of them, "anxious to hear me?" Indeed it was: her opening night was undoubtedly the most exciting of all such in my time at the Metropolitan. But what with the tension and the heat of a New York Indian summer (we had moved to a twenty-four-week season for the first time since the Depression, and our opening was in October), Miss Callas was not in her best voice for her Metropolitan debut. Later that season she scored a great triumph in London, and when I cabled to congratulate her on it she wrote back, "I am still trying to discover what happened in New York. I am only sorry I couldn't give you personally what other theaters have. I hope next year."

Two moments of terror remain in the memory from that first Callas season. The Saturday matinee following her debut, she sent word from her dressing room during the overture that she would be unable to go on. I literally ran to her room, and found her genuinely ill, with Meneghini and a doctor in solicitous attendance; by the time I got there, I suppose, I looked sicker than she felt, and after a few encouraging words from me she agreed to go on, saving us from what would have been a riot. (It was at the close of this performance that some idiot threw radishes on the stage; fortunately, Miss Callas was so short-sighted she thought they were tea roses.) Then, in a *Lucia*, an Italian baritone held a high note beyond the value Donizetti had given it, making Miss Callas, who had sung her part of the duet correctly, look short of breath. She said, *"Basta!"* (which was misinterpreted by the audience in the orchestra rows that heard her); and so did I: I ordered the balance of the baritone's Metropolitan contract canceled. He got on the front page of the newspapers tearing up her picture, and then booked space on the plane that was taking her back to Italy. She said, with her typical honesty, "I don't like this man taking advantage of my publicity." During her nine weeks she canceled only one performance, which is at least par for the course in a New York winter.

We agreed by mail (she held the contract ten weeks before signing it, shortening my life) that she would return for the latter part of the 1957–58 season, though not for the tour, adding *Traviata* to the previous season's Lucia and Tosca, at $1,500 per performance. Meanwhile, she was to sing late that summer with La Scala in a visit to the Edinburgh Festival and early that fall with the San Francisco Opera. La Scala without her agreement added an extra performance of *La Sonnambula* to its Edinburgh season, and she did not appear in it. (The role was one she did not like, anyway: she had written me a year before that it was "very difficult because you have to control yourself so much and sing very softly throughout.") Unfortunately, while Scala was playing a Callas-less *Sonnambula* in Edinburgh, Callas herself was at a party given in Venice by

Elsa Maxwell, who announced proudly that her pet diva had canceled an Edinburgh appearance in order to come to the party. Almost immediately thereafter, she canceled her San Francisco Opera appearances, too, and San Francisco, not unreasonably, went into shock. I wrote Maria:

. . . The situation created by your cancellation at San Francisco is full of danger for your future career in America and particularly to your association with the Metropolitan, which I trust you value. Naturally, San Francisco, doubting the good faith of your cancellation, is outraged, and Mme. Stella's cancellation following a day or two after yours has not improved matters. It should not surprise you to learn that San Francisco is making every effort to prove that both you and Mme. Stella are in breach of contract. If they succeed, we are informed that they are determined to file charges with AGMA, and under the circumstances and in the light of the unreliability of certain European-based artists in contract matters, AGMA may have no alternative but to take action. If they should terminate your membership or suspend you for any period of time, your Metropolitan appearances will probably be impossible. You must know that your appearances in this country depend upon your remaining an AGMA member in good standing. I need not tell you how terribly upsetting this would be, not only to our whole repertory planning but also personally to me. I was looking forward so much to your return and I felt that your next performances here would be almost more important than those last year. I was hoping for your new immense success which would really then have established you finally.

Naturally any professional activity on your part during the period covered by your doctor's certificate or by your contract with San Francisco would necessarily be considered by San Francisco and by AGMA as proof that your cancellation of your San Francisco contract was not in good faith, with the results I have mentioned.

I might add that Miss Maxwell's gossip that you broke your Edinburgh contract in order to attend her party in Venice will be no help to you under such circumstances.

I should be most grateful for a line from you assuring me that you will take my warnings seriously . . .

This letter she answered quickly: she *was* sick, and she would *not* be singing during the period of her San Francisco contract (and she didn't). "If [others] get away with all they did not being ill," she wrote, "and I being ill be condemned, then I really will be sure the world is crazy." And she kept her contract for *Medea* and *Traviata* in Dallas, where Larry Kelly, having broken with Carol Fox and Chicago, was starting a short celebrity opera season with deficits for three weeks that approximated ours for thirty-one weeks.

The previous June—eighteen months ahead of the performance, on the lengthened "lead time" for opera planning—Maria and I had agreed on her 1958–59 season, which was to feature our new production of Verdi's *Macbeth,* plus more Violettas and Toscas. When Miss Callas passed through Idlewild Airport on her way back from Dallas to Italy, Francis Robinson went out with the contract to get her to sign it, which she wouldn't, and again there was the long interval of worry (spiced on this occasion by a scene in Rome when Miss Callas walked out at the end of the first act, with the President of the Republic in the audience!). But she came to us for her February and March season, scored the complete triumph that she had just missed the year before, and signed her contract for 1958–59. This contract included the tour: I simply could not go to our tour cities for a third year and say they would have to do without our most publicized star.

Lady Macbeth is an extremely difficult role, much heavier than Violetta, and Miss Callas was concerned about mixing the two. I did not worry about it too much, because she had mixed

Violetta and Medea, just as heavy as Lady Macbeth, in Dallas the year before, and was now returning to Dallas to mix Medea with Lucia, which is even lighter than Violetta. Our schedule, moreover, allowed her no fewer than *eight* days to lighten the voice down from Lady Macbeth to Violetta, and four days after the Violettas to prepare for the next Lady Macbeth. I simply could not believe we had any serious problem, until Miss Callas and her husband passed through New York en route to Dallas in early October, and I lunched with them and heard their long list of complaints.

Some of the complaints were entirely valid. The *Lucia* in which Miss Callas had been appearing was one of our oldest and poorest productions still on the boards (it had also served the year before for a twenty-fifth Metropolitan anniversary appearance by Lily Pons, who had also complained bitterly about it). *Norma* was scarcely better, in terms of physical production. Our *Traviata* was a new production, but the premier had been done by Renata Tebaldi; and it was common knowledge that we had originally planned the opening-night *Eugene Onegin* of the 1957–58 season for Miss Tebaldi, who had very successfully sung Tatyana at La Scala but ultimately backed away from our proposal because she did not wish to attempt an English translation. *Macbeth* was to be Miss Callas's first new production at the Metropolitan, and she would have to share the spotlight with Leonard Warren. Moreover, she did not like either Rolf Gérard's sets for *Traviata* (especially the second act) or what remained of Tony Guthrie's direction (which had been frustrated from the start by Miss Tebaldi's always pleasant but always firm refusal to do anything other than what she had always done).

I came out of that luncheon meeting knowing that something was very seriously wrong, but not knowing what. Some of my associates later came to believe that Miss Callas was afraid of

Lady Macbeth, a terrifying role rising to a D-flat, which of course she would have to sing herself (one could not imagine a chorister supplying a high note for Maria Callas). Much of the press later supported her published position that the mix of Violetta and Lady Macbeth was unbearable, though at the lunch all she actually insisted on was a minimum of three days after a Lady Macbeth before a *Traviata*, and I was giving her eight days. I have always felt that the basic dissatisfaction was the tour, where she would have to sing in many cities off the international publicity circuit, under conditions she knew would be undesirable. She and her husband complained about the tour requirements at lunch: the hotels would be inadequate, the planes wouldn't take their poodle Toy, the trains were smelly, the schedule was too strenuous. At the least, Miss Callas said, she wanted a couple of weeks off to return to Italy between her last appearance in New York and the start of the tour—but I knew perfectly well that once they left the country they would not return for the tour.

In Dallas, Miss Callas was *prima donna assoluta* to a degree all but unimaginable in New York—an entire opera company had been built around her. Everyone told her that she should never do anything she didn't wholeheartedly want to do: she was Maria Callas, and the world would have to follow her lead. She wrote me canceling the *Traviatas*, a most remarkable letter, *in Italian*:

. . . You have told me that Tebaldi, last season, demanded categorically that I should not take over her *Traviata*, because if you did not accede to this request she threatened not to return to the Metropolitan. You also told me that you replied with great firmness and annoyance to such an absurd request, and that Tebaldi would have to submit to your reasons and decisions.

However, you also told me, a few days ago, that Tebaldi has

refused to sing *Traviata* this year, although she was committed to do so, and that you, for the sake of peace, have accepted this. It is therefore logical that I should not perform this role either, since Tebaldi has dared to impose the above-mentioned cancellation on you; . . .

I want to mention still another matter. Last spring, after my engagement at the Met, we talked about the next season. I said that among the roles you suggested for me, I would have liked to add Butterfly. Why did you not do it?

The fact is: you assured me that you would do it. Is it perhaps because my Butterfly disturbed Signorina Tebaldi, who— although (it is true) in a grave moment—left you completely in the lurch last season, and is it perhaps possible that she has once again imposed on you, as in the case of *Traviata?* . . .

The "grave moment" of the letter was the death of Miss Tebaldi's mother, who had been her constant companion on all her travels throughout her career. Nothing else in the letter made any sense at all. I replied, "Frankly, knowing and admiring you as I do, I cannot for the life of me see why an artist of your stature should be guided in any of her decisions by whatever another artist might or might not do. I feel your refusal to do *Traviata* to be unnecessary and deliberate unfriendliness which I deeply regret; but if you insist on it I will accept it." Instead, I offered to substitute *Lucia,* which she was alternating with *Medea* in Dallas; but I added regretfully that "your letter . . . sounds more the Maria Callas of whom I have been warned than the Maria Callas I know, like and respect . . ."

Miss Callas was displeased ("the most stupefying is that you do not recall what you told me clearly regarding the request of Signorina Tebaldi in connection with my taking on *Traviata*"). John Gutman had a most unpleasant telephone conversation with her husband. Our season was beginning (Miss Tebaldi did an opening-night *Tosca,* which probably did not help our bargaining position); we had to know Maria's plans. "I cannot," she wrote, "put myself at the disposal of the Metropolitan for the old standard routine." On November 6 I sent her a telegram demanding an immediate confirmation of her acceptance of the three *Lucias* instead of the three *Traviatas* called for in her contract. On November 7 the newspapers carried banner headlines: BING FIRES CALLAS! She gave a number of interviews: "Those lousy *Traviatas* that he wanted me to do—they're lousy, really lousy." I gave a few interviews myself: "Madame Callas is constitutionally unable to fit into any organization not tailored to her own personality." It was all very unfortunate.

I engaged Leonie Rysanek to make her debut at the Metropolitan in the *Macbeth* Miss Callas had abandoned (our most expensive production to that date, by the way; the first to break the $100,000 barrier). It was an impossible assignment even for a great artist. For the only time in my career, I interfered with public behavior at a performance: I hired a claqueur to station himself near the front of the house and at the moment of Miss Rysanek's entrance to call into the auditorium, at an angle which would minimize the chance of her hearing it, the words "Brava Callas!" I counted on the American love for the underdog to resent this intervention, and to balance the scales a little for Miss Rysanek—who did indeed rise to the occasion with a splendid performance, the first of many, in many different roles, the Metropolitan would receive from her.

For a long time, Miss Callas and I were at daggers drawn. Once I was in Milan when she was scheduled to do a *Traviata,* and she actually canceled the performance—the house was dark that night—for fear I would be in the audience. I was admitted to a recording session, hidden high in the balcony, threatened with being thrown off it if I came far enough forward for anyone to have the slightest chance of seeing I was there. But gradually these fires, like others, ran out of fuel, and after she discarded Meneghini we became friends again. The French artists' agent Michel Glotz reintroduced us at a lovely lunch at the Pré Catelan Restaurant in the Bois de Boulogne; Onassis came by for coffee. Even the feud between Callas and Tebaldi ended in New York in 1968, when Renata sang an opening-night *Adriana Lecouvreur*, and Maria was a guest in my box. At the end I asked Maria if she would like to go backstage. She nodded, and I knocked at the door of Tebaldi's dressing room: "Renata, I have an old friend here to see you." Miss Tebaldi opened the door, and the two sopranos fell into each other's arms, crying.

Once I went to hear Miss Callas sing *Norma* in Paris, and she broke on a high note as I have never heard a professional singer break in public. The house fell into an uproar, half the audience booing, half cheering. She raised her hand, and there was silence. She motioned to the conductor to start the aria again, and this time she did not break—and there was pandemonium. I went backstage to her dressing room afterward, and I didn't know whether to refer to this episode or not—it's like a woman wearing a very low-cut dress, you're not sure whether it's more rude to look or not to look. I decided not to mention it, and she never mentioned it, either.

Miss Callas returned to the Metropolitan for two perform-ances of *Tosca* in 1964–65. She did not sing well but it made no difference whatever—never had there been such a *Tosca*. Nearly everything she ever did spoiled that opera for me; I never fully enjoyed any other artist in one of her roles after she did it. Just the line of her arm when she struck the gong in *Norma*—what volumes it spoke! A few motions of her hand did more to establish a character and an emotion than whole acts of earnest acting by other singers. She and Herbert von Karajan were the complete artists of my time at the Metropolitan, and I can criticize myself most effectively by complaining how few performances we had from either—from Callas, only twenty-one altogether, seven of Lucia, six each of Norma and Tosca, two of Violetta.

Yet the fact remains that I could not have yielded to her urgently expressed whims and continued to keep the Metropolitan going as an artistic enterprise. When the photographs of our contract signing in Chicago appeared in the papers, I had to badger my press department to place pictures of my signing Miss Tebaldi and Miss Milanov, neither being exactly a news event. Any special favor extended to her (even an escort from rehearsals to lunch, to protect her from process servers —del Monaco instantly demanded the same escort for himself) would have required equal favors to others who were almost as indispensable as she was, beyond the point where I could have held the company together.

I don't think I have been vain in my relations with singers. I made a ritual of getting thankfully on my knees on the annual occasion of Birgit Nilsson's return to the house. (After I was knighted in 1971, she commented, "You do that much better since you practiced it for the Queen.") Once Bob Herman and I both went on our knees to beg Franco Corelli to cover for an ailing Carlo Bergonzi in a performance in Cleveland (but it turned out we knocked on the wrong hotel door, and an elderly lady looked out in amazement to find two men kneeling on the carpet outside her door). I permitted Joan Sutherland to dictate her husband as conductor, and allowed Renata Tebaldi to force us into a production of *Adriana Lecouvreur*, an opera I detested. (Miss Tebaldi was always very sweet and very firm; I used to say she had dimples of iron.) I cannot describe the combination of blandishment and threat I had to use on Franco Corelli after his debut at the house, which unfortunately occurred on the same evening as Leontyne Price's debut, which meant that the press paid virtually no attention to him. "I don't want to sing with that soprano again," he said the next day at my office . . . but he did; and he stayed more than ten years, giving us one wonderful performance after another, while I and my staff serviced his every need.

But there comes a place where a concession is not part of compromise and negotiation but a sign of subservience; and any management that allows itself to be bullied into that place can no longer command the respect or the best work of the artists in the house. Meneghini and Miss Callas had pushed me to the edge of that place; in the interests of the Metropolitan, I could go no further.

# 22

The tour is the albatross hung around the neck of the manager of the Metropolitan Opera. Eventually, I suppose, it will simply fall off from sheer economic weight. Even now, when the tour cities pay $50,000 a performance, the tour is a damaging loss. A sold-out house in New York also yields about $50,000, and can be gained without the expense of carting about costumes and scenery and paying transportation plus a $25-a-day per diem to 300-odd members of the company. Until quite recently, the bookkeeping of the tour was handled in such a way that it seemed to show a profit, because tour receipts were not asked to cover any portion of the company's overhead or the wear and tear on the productions (even though the need to pack the costumes into trunks immediately after every performance, despite their sweated-through condition, undoubtedly shortens their life more than a number of uses in New York). Now, however, everybody knows that the tour loses money. The cities the Metropolitan visits say they cannot be asked to put up anything more; they are hard pressed. And, of course, they are. We are all hard pressed.

In this one way, Miss Callas was a typical rather than an extraordinary artist: she fought against the tour. It was always difficult for me to get commitments from foreign artists to extend their American stay—or return to the United States— through the month of May. Even a rootless opera singer likes to be home in springtime, and most European companies have their high season in spring. During the early years of my regime, the travel itself was frightening, with weeks divided between places with mysterious names that were farther apart than Paris and Berlin. During the later years, I was often asking artists to take for the privilege of touring with the Metropolitan fees lower than they could earn by staying home. As Birgit Nilsson wrote in 1959, when (prior to her Metropolitan debut) I tried to engage her for *Tristan* and *Turandot* on our 1961 tour, "I am quite well-informed about your seven weeks' tour . . . I find that it is impossible to accept your offer to sing Turandot and Isolde on this tour. I am afraid it would be too hard a job, and a fee of 1500 Dollars does not at all cover what I can get for that time from other companies."

I felt the strongest kind of obligation to the tour cities. We said we were bringing them the Metropolitan Opera. We could not hope to bring the theatrical values of our best productions in New York, because their theaters were simply not equipped to handle our solid sets—in fact, once we began taking our stage responsibilities seriously in New York we had to prepare special inexpensive "tour sets," painted drops that could be hung on the wretched stages we played during the tour. Our best conductors usually would not make the tour, and nothing I could say would change their minds. All we had to offer out of town were singers of Metropolitan caliber. There were a few occasions when I even engaged European artists of some celebrity

[ 250 ]

for our tour alone, to replace artists I had been unable to sign up for those weeks.

In the days before year-round contracts, the first function of the tour was to extend the working season for our employees: when we ran only twenty-two weeks in New York, a seven-week tour added almost one third to the income an artist could receive from the practice of his or her art. We traveled about the country in special trains, the biggest thing after Barnum & Bailey, except that giraffes don't get hoarse. In 1959 we needed no fewer than twenty-seven seventy-foot boxcars with us for the physical productions. From Boston to Atlanta was two nights and one day on the train. We all ate in the same dining cars. I never knew what went on all night, the comings and goings between the compartments.

Some, indeed, looked forward all year to the party atmosphere of the tour, for there were (and are) parties everywhere, often rather wonderful parties, including much of the performing company (but only rarely the members of the orchestra, who grow resentful). There were happy surprises, like Justine's in Memphis, the best restaurant in the United States. Members of our board used to go to the cities with the best parties, and especially to Atlanta, with its truly gracious style of living. For years, Atlanta paid us a fraction of what our performances cost us to give, because the board, otherwise so worried about money, would not authorize me to demand a higher fee from such nice people.

I must admit I enjoyed the visits to Atlanta. Never have I known a place to become so excited about opera: work stopped, sleep stopped all over town while the Metropolitan was there. (Work stopped for the company, too: Tullio Serafin once called a rehearsal in Atlanta, and his soloists turned up with voices like frogs. "Remember," Serafin said, "we are here also to sing.") They sold out the theater months in advance; people lined up for miles and fought to get in. We played in an old movie theater, which had an impossible stage, but it was all red and gold, and had style and grace and good acoustics. I was particularly fond of it, because the hotel where I stayed was right across the street, and I could sit on the porch in a rocking chair and still be "on duty": if anything happened in the theater, I could be summoned almost as quickly as if I were in the audience. Now, alas, Atlanta has built a new Civic Center, with a hall almost as impractical as the old movie house (the orchestra pit is far too small), much less attractive, and far from my hotel.

The organization of the Metropolitan's visit to Atlanta is entirely amateur, done by the Junior League. Among my tasks in the early years was convincing them that they could take a full week, which they finally agreed to do; should the tour survive, my successor will have the task of convincing them to take the company for two weeks. I have no doubt that these busy ladies could sell even more than two weeks if they set their minds to it. On one of my earliest trips, I found myself at dinner beside a very attractive young lady who was identified as the president of the Junior League, and I said to her, "Tell me, what does the Junior League *do?*" She thought for a moment and then said, "It seeks to make working women out of butterflies." I said, "I think it should be abolished forthwith."

One of my strongest memories of Atlanta is of an incident during a performance of *Lucia*, with Lily Pons, who was in her time a great artist, but whose time had passed even before I ever came to the Metropolitan. I was sitting out in the lobby, trying to recover from three cocktail parties and four dinners, and there was a commotion by one of the doors. A little black boy had somehow got into the orchestra section, and was being pushed out by an usher. I took him by the hand and told him that if he wanted to listen he could stand in the aisle just by the door. He went in, and after about three minutes he came out, and said, very politely, "Thank you; I've had enough." I thought to myself, This race will go far . . .

But the race question on tour in the early years was not a joke at all; and much as I loved the graciousness of Atlanta I hated the prejudices of the South. One of the worst moments of my life was walking into my first southern railroad station and seeing the separate washrooms, one for "White," one for "Colored." (One year when Pierre Monteux toured with the company I took him for a drive into the countryside around Atlanta, and we stopped for tea at a simple place by the road. A fat old black lady came out and said she couldn't serve us: "We only serve colored." Monteux said with that wonderful smile under the wonderful white mustache, "But *we* are colored; we are pink.") We took *Aida* on tour to Washington after my second season, and I was told that our ballerina Janet Collins would not be welcomed at the cast party at the Mayflower Club given by the local society sponsoring our tour. So I said I wouldn't come, either, and I gave my own party. When we included an opera starring Leontyne Price in our Atlanta season, I made it a point to take Miss Price to dinner with me at my hotel the night of our arrival, and as we walked in there was a sudden hush, which I greatly enjoyed.

After my first year, I learned that the Capitol, the theater we played in Washington, had segregated seating; and I informed the sponsors that we would cancel that part of our tour unless they persuaded the theater to change its policy. They did. Eventually we had to cancel Washington anyway, for economic reasons, but not before one memorable evening when President Eisenhower came to our performance of *La Bohème*. The Secret Service men interrogated me before his arrival:

"We hear the girl dies. How is she killed?"

[ 253 ]

I said, "She dies of consumption. It isn't contagious at a distance."

They told me that the President would arrive in a limousine, and that I was to escort him very quickly into the theater. I said, "Do you mean you're afraid someone will shoot at him?" They just looked at me, and I suggested that if it was so dangerous perhaps I would wait for the President *inside* the theater and they could escort him across the sidewalk themselves. The President himself had only one question for me: "Whatever happened," he inquired, "to that fat fellow?"

I said, "Do you mean Melchior?"

"That's the name," the President said with some pleasure.

I said, "He's no longer with the company."

Incidentally, I do not believe opera can be completely color-blind. I say I am responsible for casting "down to the Third Orphan in *Rosenkavalier*" because I once did intervene to change the assignment to that role: it struck me as improper for an aristocratic Viennese widow to have two white children and one black child. In Boston in spring 1971 I raised the roof because three of the supers for the parade of Nubian slaves in *Aida* looked white. "But Mr. Bing," I was told, "these men are black." I said, "I don't care what they are; they can wear dark make-up like everybody else."

As the years passed, we made the tour more and more efficient. Tony Bliss soon after coming onto the board prepared a report on the economics of the tour, pointing out that we were then (in 1953) carrying sixteen operas out of town, because our policy had been to supply anything in our current season that the tour committees requested. Gradually, we cut back on what we would offer, and eventually we required every city that wanted the Metropolitan to take a full week of performances, reducing some of the frenzy of moving around. In 1972 we traveled with eight productions (seven of them scheduled, one as a spare).

Instead of riding the rails, we chartered two planes from Eastern Airlines, and sent the productions on trucks. With the virtual perfection of air travel, we could arrange to have soloists fly in and out for their performances, and we did not have to take as many cover artists with us. The cover arrangements called for the artists to wait in New York, being paid something considerably less than their usual fee for holding the night free, something more than their usual fee if in fact we had to call on them.

These plans do not always work. Franco Corelli has a dog that must go with him everywhere. The dog can ride with us in the chartered plane, but on a scheduled flight it must go in a container and the container must go in the luggage compartment. Even with my connections with the president of Eastern Airlines (which gave us $500,000 toward the cost of a *Ring* cycle), there is nothing I can do. So Corelli had to stay with the company and fly our chartered plane, which he didn't want to do. After a performance in Cleveland, without telling anybody, he hired a car and drove off at midnight. He found to his great surprise that it took him nine hours to drive to New York. Then he couldn't fly to Atlanta, because he couldn't take the dog, so we arranged for him to take the train. I had him picked up by limousine, because otherwise he couldn't have found the station, the track, the train, or the compartment. They arrived with two minutes to spare, and Mrs. Corelli found she had forgotten the holy water. My boy, with great presence of mind, pushed Corelli into the compartment with the dog and took Mrs. Corelli home to get the holy water—without the dog, *she* could fly to Atlanta. If I hadn't put up with this sort of thing, somebody at another opera house would have, and would have paid Corelli a higher fee, too.

Whatever we do, the tour is artistically a scandal. There is not one single house we play in that is acceptable, still less good. Most places we must play in multi-purpose houses, which have elephants early in the week and then a sales convention, and then over a weekend are turned into an opera house. The War Memorial in Boston was so unsuited for opera that the first year we were there the only way to get from one side of the stage to the other without walking across it was to go *outside*. Our half-nude ballet girls had to go out in what could be a pretty cold night in Boston to enter from stage left if they had departed from stage right. The supers must assemble in a stage space smaller than my office to pick up the standards for *Aida*, and all the banners get tangled. It's a shambles, but nobody notices, nobody cares.

In Cleveland the house is even worse. It seats nine thousand, and we have to use amplification. One of the *maestri* sits out in the hall and turns dials. If he turns the wrong dial, suddenly the soprano is screaming all over the theater. The orchestra sits on the auditorium level. The intermissions are endless because the stagehands have to hand things through holes in the wall, to and from the truck. One stands there like a slave driver during the last intermission, calling on the crew to get the curtain up so we don't run beyond midnight and have to pay overtime. The lighting man says, "I haven't focused the stars"; and I scream, "*Forget* the stars; start!" The minute the opera ends, all the sets and costumes and special lights must be put back on the truck to go off to the next city.

And after twenty-two years, I fear, fond as I am of many of the people in the tour cities, one does begin to grow weary of the social life. I arrive in Cleveland at one o'clock with a lunch on the plane, I work until five, and then change for a dinner with three hundred or four hundred people. At seven-thirty I excuse myself, because I am "taking the duty," I am to be the management man at the theater. But I cannot sit through *Carmen* in Cleveland, I am constitutionally unable to do it. So I hang around on the stage. At eleven-forty with blood and tears you get the curtain down, and then must go off to the Pavilion because there is a party.

In 1966 I extended the tour across the ocean, for a week in Paris. My friend Jean-Louis Barrault had taken over the management of the Odéon, one of the state-subsidized theaters, and I visited him there, and admired his lovely new surroundings. He said the Met should come to his theater, and I said it would really be impossible, the place was much too small, there was nothing in our repertory we could do except perhaps *Marriage of Figaro* and *Barber of Seville*. He said, "Fine! Bring them!"

There was a kind of logic to the idea, because both operas are to plays by Beaumarchais—and an invitation to Paris in the spring is irresistible to almost everyone. But we were playing Detroit on May 28, and the only possible schedule had us opening in Paris only three days later. We wanted to bring an all-American cast, and it must be admitted that we could not bring our very best. Nor were the two productions we offered among our most satisfactory. Our orchestra had to be reduced to thirty-six men to fit in the Odéon, which meant first political trouble within the orchestra and then performances on a scale much smaller than those we were used to giving. Roberta Peters, very tired, had a bad night in *Barber of Seville*, and the press flayed us. I suppose I did not make things any better by saying to a reporter that Miss Peters had had a bad night but the Paris Opéra had had a bad century.

Three days later, I wrote to the executive committee of the board:

I think it is wise to face up to the fact that the Paris visit was not a success. All sorts of reasons have been advanced—anti-American feelings, etc. etc. some of which may or may not be true. The fact remains that our first *Barber* performance was

[257]

not very good . . . It appears that the majority of the Paris public and press expected the Metropolitan to come with Leontyne Price, Birgit Nilsson, Franco Corelli, etc. etc. who are not easily cast in *Barber of Seville* or *Figaro*. We all knew right from the start that it would have been better for the Metropolitan to go abroad with *Aida* and *Turandot* or works of that category but we also knew that we probably would have had to wait another fifty years for such a visit to materialize.

. . . I did not have the strength to resist the temptation of a Paris visit. The responsibility for this is entirely mine—Mr. Bliss advised against the visit and proved right. Yet I feel no real harm has been done to the Metropolitan. We were royally received from important social quarters and there is no question that the majority of the audience enjoyed our performances. The press is approximately as hostile as the New York press so that is nothing new . . .

In Paris, incidentally, the party really did make up for something. It was given by the Rothschilds, in a style I did not believe existed any longer—liveried footmen, candlelit ballrooms, etc. for the entire company, with Mouton-Rothschild on every table. But the trip was a mistake nonetheless.

Among the decisions my successor and his board will have to make is whether the tour is worth what it costs. The economic loss may be less than it seems, because the Metropolitan has now contracted to give year-round employment to all its people, and recent experience does not indicate that six or seven additional weeks of capacity business can be expected in New York itself. Also, the tour was and perhaps still is important to the national position of the company. When and if a bill is introduced in Congress that would add significant federal subsidy to the Metropolitan's income, the senator from Ohio will be able to vote for it with a clearer conscience if the Metropolitan plays a week in Cleveland. Both the Metropolitan Opera Guild and the Metropolitan National Council have been able to function on a nationwide basis, partly because of the Texaco broadcasts of the Saturday matinees, but also partly because of the company tours; and between them the two organizations (both started originally by Eleanor Belmont) bring the Metropolitan half a million dollars a year.

# 23

The year after Miss Callas left us marked my tenth season at the Metropolitan, and perhaps the apex of my relationship with both the board and the public. Friends and board members supplied or raised half a million dollars to pay for six new productions—*Trovatore, Figaro, Gypsy Baron, Tristan, Fidelio,* and *Simon Boccanegra.* Among the debut artists of that 1959–60 season were Birgit Nilsson, Christa Ludwig, Giulietta Simionato, Elisabeth Söderström, Anna Moffo, and Jon Vickers. True, we lost Otto Klemperer, who had been signed to conduct *Tristan,* when he fell asleep with a lighted pipe in his mouth and awoke in a sheet of flame. *Gypsy Baron,* which I had hoped would be a second *Fledermaus* for us, proved not even a first *Gypsy Baron;* we were never able to revive it. But Peggy Webster gave us again for *Boccanegra* the sweep and high drama she had uncovered in *Don Carlo,* and in *Tristan* Birgit Nilsson scored one of the greatest triumphs the Metropolitan Opera had ever seen; the reception of her debut warranted a sizable front-page story and picture in the New York *Times.* In the words of Irving Kolodin, Miss Nilsson "proved herself . . . to be the greatest of rarities, a performer—like Flagstad before her and Caruso before *her*—to whom the size of the Metropolitan was not a hazard, but an advantage."

The size of Miss Nilsson's triumph placed me in a quandary ten days later, when I found myself without a Tristan to partner her third Isolde. Ramon Vinay had been scheduled, but he was having vocal difficulties; he had barely made it through the previous performance, and simply did not feel well enough to undertake this killing role after only four days' rest. All right, we had a cover: Karl Liebl, who had in fact sung Tristan ten days before on the occasion of Miss Nilsson's debut. But this was New York in December: Liebl had a cold. The Metropolitan being the company it is, we even had a *third* Tristan lined up, the young tenor Albert Da Costa. By now it was four o'clock of the day of the performance, and I was beginning to get quite worried. I called Da Costa, and my worst fears were realized —he, too, was sick.

Even if I could have imagined myself stepping in front of the curtain to announce a change of opera to that sold-out and over-stimulated house, and I couldn't imagine it, we no longer had time to put anything else on stage. I consulted with Miss Nilsson and then spoke with my three tenors again. None of them felt up to an entire *Tristan;* could each of them take an act? They agreed. When the house lights went down, before the music began, I came onto the stage, and was greeted by a great moan from all corners of the house—the general manager appears only to make the most important announcements, and everyone thought he knew that this announcement had to be: Miss Nilsson has canceled.

So I began by saying, "Ladies and gentlemen, Miss Nilsson is very well," which brought a sigh of relief from almost four thousand people. Then I went on: "However, we are less for-

tunate with our Tristan. The Metropolitan has three distinguished Tristans available, but all three are sick. In order not
to disappoint you, these gallant gentlemen, against their doctors'
orders, have agreed to do one act each." There was laughter in
the house. I added, "Fortunately, the work has only three acts,"
and there was a roar of laughter. Never has *Tristan und Isolde*
started so hilariously. But Miss Nilsson sang gloriously and to
this day I am grateful to my three tenors for saving a terrible
situation.

Then the good cheer went out of this season, with the most
terrible tragedy ever to strike at the Metropolitan Opera. It
happened in March, in Act II of our production of (appropriately) *La Forza del Destino,* with our all-star cast of Renata
Tebaldi, Richard Tucker, Cesare Siepi, and Leonard Warren,
who had only four nights before scored an immense success as
Boccanegra. I was standing in the wings. Tucker and Warren
had finished their duet, and Tucker had been carried offstage in
the litter appropriate to a badly wounded soldier. He got off
the litter and we stood whispering together while Warren worried about opening the "Urna fatale," then did open it and
launched into his paean to revenge. "Gioia," he sang, "oh,
gioia"—and then pitched forward like an oak felled by a woods-
man's ax. To anyone near the stage, it was obvious that something very serious had happened. Schippers stopped the
orchestra, and I ordered the curtain lowered while Tucker ran
to Warren's side.

Warren's wife was in a nearby box with the family priest
(born Jewish, Warren had converted to Catholicism and become extremely devout). They came running to the stage. I
had someone call Mario Sereni, our cover baritone for the evening, and went out to join the throng, pushing my way through
choristers who had surrounded the fallen man, many of them
kneeling and praying. Our house doctor, Dr. Adrian W. Zorg-

niotti, came rushing up from his seat, and began working to resuscitate a man who was in fact beyond help. I stepped before the curtain to assure the audience that he was being treated, and that the performance would resume when Sereni arrived. Twenty minutes later Dr. Zorgniotti, ashen, told me Warren was dead. His wife couldn't believe it; who could? Continuing the performance was, of course, unthinkable; I returned to the stage, in the fully lighted house, and asked the audience to rise "in memory of one of our greatest performers."

The theater leaves no time for mourning. I was on the telephone the next day, engaging Anselmo Colzani to fill in for Warren in many of Warren's performances toward the end of the season and on tour. But Warren's death was a terrible blow to the musical quality of our Italian wing: his was a unique voice of great beauty and power, perfectly placed for Verdi. Never an actor, he worked hard at everything he did, and invariably improved his dramatic performance from year to year. I honored him especially, perhaps, for the care he took of himself, not racing around to parties or to perform in far places, making sure he would be in the best possible condition for every performance at the Metropolitan. His death very visibly damaged the quality of our opening-night the next season, and his loss was felt for years throughout the schedule.

Early in the next season, 1960–61, we lost two other stalwarts of the house—Dimitri Mitropoulos and Jussi Bjoerling, both still active artists. But the year did bring us the sensational double debut of Leontyne Price and Franco Corelli, the first appearance at the Metropolitan of Gabriella Tucci, the sensation of Cecil Beaton's *Turandot* and the delight of the Merrill-O'Hearn *L'Elisir*, an excellent Alcestis from Eileen Farrell in a new production both designed and staged by Michael Manuel, one of our permanent staff, and a *Tannhäuser* from Georg Solti that finally made people stop talking about when George Szell might be coming back. Because every season seems to need a failure, this one supplied Flotow's *Martha* in a translation I need no longer defend now that I am no longer general manager, and a production very like the one that had succeeded for Ebert (who directed) in Berlin but was clearly not going to be a success in New York. We had Victoria de los Angeles and Richard Tucker, an almost perfect cast. The work was a particular favorite of Mrs. Belmont's, and the production was paid for by the Opera Guild; but in retrospect I have no excuse to offer; it was a mistake.

Meanwhile, however, more serious mistakes were waiting in the wings. I had planned the 1961–62 season to open with a borrowed production of Puccini's *Girl of the Golden West*, one of the few operas in the international repertory that had their world premiere at the Metropolitan; Leontyne Price would sing Minnie. The production was borrowed (from Chicago) rather than built fresh because the American opera houses that did their own large-scale productions (in effect, the Metropolitan, Chicago, and San Francisco) were seeking to find how they could work together to cut costs. But the fact that we had limited our losses on the opening-night production acquired a sinister connotation in many minds, especially the always suspicious minds of the New York critics, when the summer of 1961 found us in our first great labor crisis.

Probably the greatest surprise for me in my work in America was the role, the attitudes, and the importance of the labor unions. Early in my regime, when I was desperately trying to get this situation sorted out in my mind, I called on Reggie Allen for a list of the Metropolitan's union contracts, and got back fourteen names:

Theatrical Protective Union, Local #1
Associated Musicians of Greater New York, Local 802

59. With Cyril Ritchard at stage rehearsal of *La Perichole*

60. Renata Tebaldi, Franco Corelli, Rudolf Bing, Maria Callas backstage, Opening Night, 1968

61. *Die Meistersinger,*
Act II

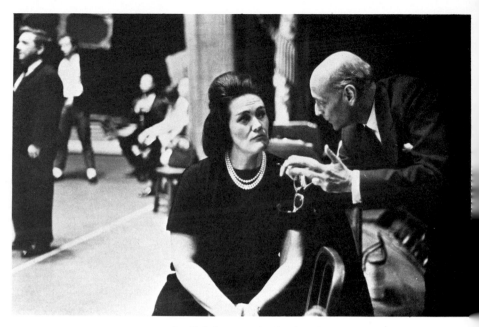

62. With Joan Sutherland

63. Rudolf Bing, Arthur Goldberg (hidden), Maria Callas, John V. Lindsay at opening of eighty-fourth season, 1968

American Guild of Musical Artists, Inc.

United Scenic Artists, Local 829

Theatrical Wardrobe Attendants Union, Local 764

Association of Theatrical Press Agents & Managers, Local 18032

Building Service Employees, Local 54

Building Service Employees, Local 32B

Amusement Clerks and Concessioners Employees' Union, Local 1115-C

International Union of Operating Engineers, Local 30

International Brotherhood of Firemen, Oilers and Maintenance Mechanics, Local 56

International Alliance of Bill Posters, Billers and Distributors of the U.S. and Canada, Local 2

Treasurers and Ticket Sellers Union, Local 751

Erie Transfer (an indirect contract with the Teamsters Union)

In those days, all these contracts expired at different times: we were eternally negotiating with somebody about something. Fortunately, perhaps, we had no labor-relations experts on our staff, so the negotiations were uncomplicated; and the unions, knowing the depth of the financial pit from which the Metropolitan had climbed in the years right after the war, were not disposed to make outrageous demands. The stagehands, for example, Theatrical Protective Union Local #1 (an affiliate of the International Alliance of Theatrical and Stage Employees), did not seriously seek to hold the Metropolitan Opera to the same terms as its standard form contract with the then profit-making Broadway theater. With vaudeville dead and nightclubs dying, and the market for live music eroding under the assault of the high-fidelity gramophone and FM radio, musicians and choristers were glad to have jobs, fearful of endangering the survival of opera as a separate institution. It is odd to think, fifteen years later, that in the 1950s some members of the Metropolitan Opera board and some members of the New York Philharmonic board were working on a scheme to merge the two orchestras and save money.

But even in those years there was always an air of menace, a threat to walk out. In 1953 it was the musicians; in 1954, the stagehands; in 1956, AGMA—complicated by charges against Bob Herman for acting as a management representative in negotiations although in his capacity as an occasional stage director he was a member of the union. Management could never do anything right. As I wrote to Lincoln Lauterstein, the Metropolitan's counsel, in 1954, "We cannot win at this game. If we prepare a season without an agreement we are attacked for acting irresponsibly. If we say we will not prepare a season without an agreement by a certain date, we are told we are exercising undue pressure theatening lockout or whatever."

With the passage of time, we were more and more victimized by a letter-of-the-law attitude. In the 1950s, if a performance went one minute after midnight, the unions would forget it rather than charge us for the full half hour of double time the contract called for once that witching moment had passed. But in 1965, when we were playing summer concert-operas at Lewisohn Stadium, the musicians held us to a half-hour overtime payment even though the concert had in fact ended on time, because the conductor was still on the podium and the men were taking another bow when the clock struck. My favorite example of this sort of demand came after our trip to Paris. We had taken with us an orchestra of only thirty-six men, because that was all the pit would hold at the Odéon. The members of the orchestra who did not go to Paris were, of course, paid for the week. But the timing of the trip was such that we gave a performance on a Sunday evening, paying double time to the thirty-six men in Paris. The orchestra committee then launched a grievance, because the men left home were not paid double time for not playing on that Sunday . . . In this instance, fortunately, the matter was not pressed to its conclusion, and the men settled for straight time for not playing.

I cannot explain why these antagonisms got out of control in 1961. Admittedly, the men had received only skimpy weekly raises during the 1950s (the average was only about 1 per cent a year), but we had steadily lengthened their season, which improved the income of the great majority, and there were increasing rehearsal payments, too. One of the problems was the desire of a unanimous conducting staff, all seven men, to be rid of a musician who had let Karl Böhm down badly in *Fidelio* and *Flying Dutchman*. Other conductors had handled this problem only by shifting solo passages away from this man and to other men in his section. Nevertheless, the union insisted on the reinstatement of the man, and elected him to the negotiating committee for the next year's contract. Though I had written as early as July 1960 to ask all our unions to get contract proposals in to us by October of that year, the musicians did not come in with their "demands" until April of 1961.

And the demands were ludicrously out of line with our resources. Base pay was to be increased from $170 a week to $268; rehearsal pay from $3.30 to $7.50 an hour. In sum, the demands would have more than doubled musicians' pay (which was running at an average of about $245 a week, including overtime and other extras). We offered various increases and a new pension plan, adding up to about 14 per cent over the life of a three-year contract. All the other unions in the house settled for something like those terms, but the musicians held out, and did not even reduce their demands (to $78 rather than $98 a week additional salary) until August, when the leaders of the other unions publicly requested them to do so.

By then we had already had to notify all our artists for the 1961–62 season that we were releasing them from their contracts because we couldn't be sure there was going to be a season. A week later, we formally announced cancellation of the 1961–62 season, and I went off for my long-delayed summer vacation. But political leaders intervened. At the request of Mayor Robert F. Wagner, members of my staff resumed meetings with the union on August 10, but made no progress. By August 17, I had heard from twenty-eight artists that they had either signed contracts with other houses for the coming season or were in process of negotiating them. The Metropolitan thereupon dropped out of the negotiations with the musicians on the grounds that no season of Metropolitan quality would be possible.

Meanwhile, Leontyne Price and Risë Stevens had appealed to President Kennedy to intervene. I could not see what President Kennedy could do to restore to our roster European artists who had already signed elsewhere, and (unwisely) said so. But the members of my board, who were of course all American citizens, took a different view of the powers of the presidency. Tony Bliss met with Secretary of Labor Arthur Goldberg in Denver, where Goldberg had gone to give a speech, and I flew back from Italy to Washington.

Under the heaviest kind of pressure, we agreed during the last week of August that we would try to reconstitute the season, and would accept binding arbitration of the disputes with the musicians. Secretary Goldberg said he would appoint someone the next day, but I said, "No—my agreement was for Goldberg to mediate personally." The President okayed this novel assignment for a Secretary of Labor. Goldberg said, "The President is confident that the Metropolitan will have one of its greatest seasons ever." I said to Goldberg, "Perhaps the President would like to run the Met and let me handle Berlin." A few days later I was invited to a reception at the White House, and the President caught sight of me and came over. "Would you still like to run Berlin?" he said . . .

My reason for requiring Goldberg's personal participation was my feeling that if some award were made well beyond our resources, the fact that it came from a Cabinet member would give us an irrefutable claim for government support. But Goldberg did not look on this arbitration as a political matter; he set to work to master the facts of the case. I was immensely impressed by his way of picking up fantastically intricate problems he had known nothing about, and his ability to ask questions that penetrated to the heart of the dispute. His award, when it came, was reasonably close to our offer—$10 a week instead of the $5 we had offered (or the $98 they had demanded) in the first year; a three-year contract; and a rise over the three years to $16 per diem (then the government's own travel figure) while on tour. Meanwhile, our season was neither so crippled as I had feared (though we did have to make significant cast changes in more than half the performances) nor so excellent as President Kennedy had proclaimed. Miss Price had her opening night, but to my surprise (and hers) Minnie turned out to be too heavy a role for her to sustain, and after a performance and a half she turned it over to Dorothy Kirsten. Our one new production of the season was Verdi's *Un Ballo in Maschera*, directed by Günther Rennert, then Intendant of Hamburg, later the boss of Munich.

One matter Goldberg had declined to decide: the affair of the dismissed musician. He turned it over to Theodore W. Kheel, New York's most acclaimed arbitrator, who ultimately concluded that under the contract the Metropolitan did have the authority to dismiss the man. Erich Leinsdorf and I both testified and were cross-examined, very unpleasantly. Böhm had been ready to testify (even though the union in its counterclaim had forecast an effort to embarrass him by arguing that he had once made a mistake at a notoriously tricky moment in *Meistersinger*), but fortunately his personal participation was not necessary. Cleva, to my horror (and, to give them their due, to the horror of the New York critics), was brought up on charges at Local 802 for having cast aspersions on the abilities of a fellow union member; but the matter was not pressed.

This was a watershed episode in the history of the Metropolitan. Though there had been a demand for arbitration of all dismissals during our 1958 negotiations, questions of the continued competence of members of the orchestra had been handled before 1961 on a professional basis. The conductors would meet and discuss deficiencies, if any, and their recommendations and requests would be passed on to the orchestra committee, then headed by a very responsible violist named John Di Janni. He would consult with his committee, who would accept some of the recommendations and make counterproposals with regard to the others. We invariably agreed to a request from a man's colleagues that he be given a second chance (the disputed musician of 1961 had already had his second chance). Now it became difficult to get the conductors to express their views publicly (they still had no hesitation about complaining privately to management), and the orchestra committee increasingly took an attitude of Them versus Us. The Metropolitan had to commit itself not to dismiss any member of the orchestra during the length of the contract, regardless of any deterioration in his performance.

I had found these negotiations vastly distasteful. If one has ten dollars and wants fifteen and asks for twenty, that's bargaining. But if one has ten dollars and wants fifteen and asks for two hundred that is, it seems to me, childishness. Psychologically, the negotiators for the unions seem to *need* a fight—I had the feeling that if you took their list of demands and granted

[ 270 ]

every one at the first session they would be unhappy. They have to be able to show their membership what a bloody fight they had. Once in a negotiation with the stagehands I leaned forward over the table and said, "I'm awfully sorry, I didn't get that. Would you mind screaming it again?" The only sensible aspect of the procedure was the famous side bar, where one could go in a break in the meetings, and say to a man, "Now, look here, what's this all about?" There is no question that my style and personality are not right for the American labor movement. They don't feel comfortable with me, and to tell the truth I don't feel comfortable with them.

But my disillusionment with the process was as nothing to the musicians' disillusionment with Goldberg's award. He had been general counsel to the CIO before joining the government, and the men had thought he was one of theirs. Much was made later of the fact that he had been my guest at opening night of the season. As a rebuke to the conductors for their role in the affair of the dismissed player, the men dropped the former custom of standing on the entrance of the conductor. They also went looking for a more practical revenge.

Three years later, when all our 1961 contracts expired, the other unions agreed to new five-year contracts, running from 1964 to 1969, and bridging the period when we would be entering our new house in Lincoln Center. The Metropolitan made great concessions to win a peaceful move, including a guarantee of year-round employment by the end of the contract term, which of course vastly increased everyone's income. But the musicians would not make a deal. They would benefit as much as everyone by the year-round guarantee, but they would give nothing in return. For two years, under the advice of counsel, they played without a contract. Then, just before the opening night of the new theater, when they had us trapped in a corner, they threatened strike.

The man who had advised this behavior was Herman Gray, an experienced labor lawyer and an intelligent man, but uncompromising in any contretemps with the Establishment. After we had agreed to a contract with the musicians that guaranteed every man a minimum of $17,000 a year by 1968–69 (and most of the orchestra would get more) he raised all sorts of new issues as part of contract "clarification." He protested when we could not release men from rehearsals for negotiating sessions to suit his convenience. When he demanded a negotiating session on a Sunday, and our lawyer begged off because he had personal obligations that Sunday, Gray's response was to say, "In their seats of power the Metropolitan management seems to forget that even the little man will take just so much and not more. Like the Bourbons of France, they never learn." That was the style. It was, of course, very satisfying to his clients in what were billed as negotiating sessions but were really opportunities for Gray to reveal his talents for vituperation. Once, I remember, I made a weary answer to one of these tirades, and Gray snapped, "Are you trying to show your contempt for the way I conduct a bargaining session?" All I could say was, "On the contrary, Mr. Gray, I am trying very hard to conceal it."

Once the musicians had done so much better than everyone else by employing Gray and Gray's tactics, AGMA also engaged Gray's office for their next negotiations; and the result, it now seems inevitably, was the disastrous strike of 1969. By then many of the unions with which we deal had acquired a militant leadership that incited the membership and was then afraid to disappoint the expectations so unwisely aroused.

Of course, not all right and justice are on one side in these matters. I could easily sympathize with artists and craftsmen who saw us paying huge sums for new productions, building an immense palace in Lincoln Center, increasing to astronomic heights the fees of the star singers we needed if we were to sell subscriptions and tickets at the box office—and meanwhile pleading poverty to the orchestra players, the chorus, the ballet, the stagehands, the craftsmen in the shops. Everyone in an opera house has reason to feel frustrated. The orchestra not only must take orders from conductors, but sits in a pit, out of sight; the ballet is always better than what an opera company asks it to do, because opera companies produce opera; the chorus are all more or less disappointed soloists; the stagehands and technical crew always feel that directors and designers have organized their work without considering what is most convenient and practical for them. Everyone has temperament—in America, even the sanitation men have temperament. And I am quite sure I am not always a sympathetic boss, though I must say I do not understand the popular notion that I am a tyrant, a notion which I do not believe has much credence inside the opera house however widely accepted it may be outside.

It must also be said that up to the present, the unions have been right in their judgment of how much traffic will bear. The 1969 contract was hopelessly expensive, not only in salaries but in conditions, which are money, too. We give seven performances a week, but the members of the orchestra by contract now play only five; if we ask for more, it's overtime. The same for the chorus, and in a more complicated way for the comprimarios. So we either have to hire more people, which is extremely costly, or (as my board has demanded) reduce our forces, which may turn out over the long run to be even more costly by destroying the quality of a huge house that simply does not sound right with a chorus of sixty voices and an orchestra of seventy players. So far, the Metropolitan has been able to raise ticket prices and solicit contributions to cover—almost—a budget that has run to more than $20 million a year. But our attendance at the higher prices since the 1969 strike has never reached the percentages we averaged in the years before, and in 1971–72 the board felt

[ 273 ]

it necessary to reduce prices in certain sections in hopes of luring back some of our missing audience. Some day an economic disaster will bring to mind the fact that management and unions in opera are on the same side. We are both trying to survive.

# 24

Our new productions in 1962–63 were variously received by the critics—*Die Meistersinger*, renewing the collaboration of Nathaniel Merrill and Robert O'Hearn, was enthusiastically praised (as indeed it should have been, with a second-act set that was at once the most expressive and the most realistic I had ever seen), and almost everyone liked the solution by Carl Ebert, Oliver Messel, and Karl Böhm for the difficult problem of staging a chamber opera like Strauss's *Ariadne auf Naxos* in a house as large as the Metropolitan. Our two "star" productions did much less well with the press, the critics liking neither Henry Butler's direction nor Rolf Gérard's sets for *La Sonnambula*, which we staged for the benefit of Miss Sutherland (what they really didn't like was the dramatic substance of the opera, which neither Butler nor Gérard could have done much about); and nobody inside or outside the theater liking the *Adriana Lecouvreur* we staged for Miss Tebaldi, even though we gave her the ideal Maurizio of Franco Corelli.

The reception she received in this role diminished Miss Tebaldi's confidence in herself (in truth she was not singing her best), and less than a month later she retired from opera for the rest of the season. In this instance the reviews, though cruel, were not without justification. But over and over again during my twenty-two years I found my work of running the world's greatest opera house almost unbearably complicated by nasty, ill-informed New York reviews written by critics whose competence to lead public taste seemed to me very slight.

Sometimes I thought that part of my problem with the critics was the result of my unusually good relations with reporters. The general manager even of an important opera house does not in the present perilous state of the world hold such an important job, and when I look at my press file I am amazed at the coverage I received all over the world and almost continuously. Reporters found me what is called good copy. I never declined comment, and I usually said naughty things or ordinary things in a naughty way. Over the years I had watched people who had an inborn gift to attract publicity. When Beecham *sneezed*, it made the newspapers. Max Reinhardt, on the other hand, would withdraw discreetly whenever reporters or photographers came to a theater where he was working, which made them wild to follow him. I followed Reinhardt's technique, making myself just difficult enough to inspire reporters to feel that I must have something interesting to say. In the union disputes, I think the Metropolitan received less than fair coverage; such incidents are covered by labor reporters whose instincts incline them to the side of the strikers. But in general, especially in the early years, I had a phenomenal press.

With the reviewers my relations were much less good. Some of the fault was mine. A general manager should take a mother-hen attitude toward the people who work in his theater and defend them against attack by whatever means he can find. During my first season, we offered a bargain-basement, in-

adequate production of *Cav* and *Pag,* which was the subject
not only of condemnation in the press but of a personal "Dear
Friend" letter from Bruno Walter, warning me that productions
of that quality were discreditable to my management. The productions could be defended, for the sake of argument, as modern and innovative, and I did so defend them in public, accusing
the critics of being old-fashioned in their approach. Not being
used to counterattack, the critics reacted to my defense even
more vigorously than I had reacted to their attack, and a pattern
for subsequent relations was set.

Psychologically, the position of a critic is very difficult. He
cannot *exist* until somebody does something, which is an unhappy, frustrating set of circumstances. Only rarely does anyone set out to be a critic as he might set out to be a painter or
a composer. In nine out of ten cases, becoming a critic is the
result of frustration, a failure to make a career as a violinist or
a pianist or a composer. Human nature being as beastly as it is,
a critic makes a name for himself with bad reviews—to make a
name with good reviews a critic has to be a giant with great
enthusiasm and sense of mission, and there are always very
few giants. The ordinary critic looks for the sort of nasty remark
that "makes news." I remember once in Chicago, years ago, reading a review of a recital by Artur Rubinstein, in which the
critic wrote that "a sixty-year-old pianist attacked a forty-year-old
Steinway." I don't consider that amusing, but apparently it
helps sell papers.

Opinion, of course, is just that: disagreements are to be expected. But often a wrong opinion is buttressed by unchecked
statements of fact. It is, for example, an article of faith among
New York reviewers that Met productions have not had sufficient rehearsals. In fact, compared with Scala, Vienna, Munich,
or Covent Garden, the Metropolitan rehearsal standard is high.
Critics never come to the house during the day, so they don't

see that every day of the week not only the main stage but all the large rehearsal rooms down in the third basement are crammed with activity from morning to late afternoon. And critics don't talk to world-famous artists, except on formal interview occasions, so they never hear, for example, of the experiences of Leontyne Price and Birgit Nilsson in Vienna and Milan, where they may arrive on the plane in the morning and be onstage in performance that night with colleagues they met just before the curtain went up. This sort of thing did happen at the Metropolitan before, but never in my time was a revival put on without at least two piano rehearsals onstage and one orchestral rehearsal onstage.

In recent years, our productions have averaged (some of course get more than others) about ten hours of orchestral rehearsal for each. The last *new* production of my administration, Verdi's *Otello*—not an unfamiliar work to the cast or the orchestra—had nine piano rehearsals onstage, three orchestral rehearsals onstage (after several orchestral rehearsals downstairs), two days of technical rehearsal, a piano dress, and a final full dress. Zeffirelli and Böhm get no more time than that anywhere in the world.

Our rehearsals aimed at the creation of a total production, which is a bigger gamble than the purely musical effort on which many other theaters concentrate, and the Metropolitan was organized for the most efficient possible use of the available time. Jean-Louis Barrault staged *Faust* at La Scala after producing this opera at the Metropolitan, and I asked him to compare the two experiences. "The orchestra and chorus are perfect," he wrote me from Milan. "Everything else is sacrificed to the *note*—it is a vocal trapeze . . . Organizationally (the unions): when a Mediterranean tries to apply the rules, it is terrible. As a Mediterranean, one waits for him, as a member of a union he leaves on the dot and one doesn't know any more where he is . . . All this gives one a great liking for La Scala, but you will not be astonished if I hold my heart for the Metropolitan and all who compose it . . ."

Admittedly, there are standards of rehearsal the Metropolitan does not try to meet. I went to a performance of *Otello* in East Berlin, and during the first act you held onto your seat—you were afraid the storm would blow you away. Felsenstein had taken the chorus to a wind tunnel, where they had learned exactly how you lean into a strong wind. I ran into him during the intermission, and he said, "Sorry you had to see *this* performance—some of my choristers tonight were bending only to wind strength 3, not to wind strength 4." He had just come back from Moscow where, he said, he had worked for eight months on a production of *Carmen*. The Metropolitan cannot do that, but I don't see why it should be done—I can't imagine how anyone can sustain interest in *Carmen* through eight months of rehearsing it. A professional director can get a beautiful performance in four weeks, especially at a modern house where you can have lighting onstage, soloists in a stage-size rehearsal room, and orchestra in yet another room, all at once.

But to the New York critics, who have never been to a working rehearsal in my time at the Metropolitan, these questions about "number of rehearsals" are just for figures they can put on a piece of paper. They don't know that Deiber will work with Corelli for twenty minutes on a single gesture of the left hand in *Werther*. Reviewing our triumphant new *Tristan* in fall 1971, the critic of the New York *Times* gave great praise to the designer, Günther Schneider-Siemssen, but did not even *mention* the director, August Everding. With all respect to a fine designer, anyone who knows the first thing about how an operatic performance is put together understands that a designer works from the conceptions of a director, and that except in the case of a Chagall *Magic Flute* (which is clearly *sui generis*) it makes no sense to speak of the "conceptions" of a designer.

Some New York critics—and this is precisely what a critic should *not* do—take up causes against, occasionally for, one singer or another. Take Franco Corelli, one of the outstanding talents of our time. Of course, he has some faults, but I for one think his Werther was an outstanding theatrical performance. He is the incarnation of opera—this fantastic-looking fellow who sings like that, a special timbre, a soft sound, without apparent effort. From the moment he stepped on the stage, he *was* the Romantic poet. One critic tore him to pieces time after time, complaining particularly about his French diction—when I know that the man doesn't speak a word of French himself. Similarly, Olin Downes, who was, however, a much more distinguished critic, once publicly complained about Risë Stevens' German, a language he did not speak at all and she spoke with the fluency of a native. Another critic (this one in Chicago) made fun of Fernando Corena's French, not knowing that Corena, despite the Italian name, was born and brought up in French-speaking Switzerland, and spoke French before he learned to speak Italian.

I have found in the New York critics no feeling for true distinction. I once heard a shocking *Magic Flute* conducted by Arturo Toscanini—but he was still Toscanini, one respected him. Jean-Louis Barrault appears to me a towering figure; even if he makes a mistake he should be treated with respect. But the reviews of his *Carmen* were attacks on his genius. Even if he had made a mistake—and I did not think he had, but others did—there is something to be said for the mistake of a genius as against a right answer from a pedestrian artist. But these small-minded men came back, over and over again, whenever there was a change of cast, to renew their attack not on what they regarded as a mistake but on Barrault personally.

There were some moments of unbelievable nastiness. In early 1971, one of the critics attacked me for having scheduled *Tannhäuser* for the opening night of the 1972–73 season, which would be the first night for my successor as general manager. Opening nights, these days, must be planned two years in advance—which the critic should have known. At the time that I signed the contracts for *Tannhäuser*, the Metropolitan's search for my successor seemed to have failed, and I thought that, much against my will, I would probably have to take yet another year as general manager; I was planning, in short, the opening night of my season, not my successor's. Moreover, opening night of 1972 presented some very special problems. We owed an opening night to James McCracken, who had been deprived of that recognition by the 1969 strike. Marilyn Horne had made one of the most exciting debuts the house had known in recent years, and was a natural choice for an opening night. Unfortunately, these two artists physically are throwbacks to the age of Melchior and Traubel, and it is by no means certain that modern audiences will accept them in roles where they are accustomed to figures like those of Corelli and Verrett. *Tannhäuser* has the advantage of being an opera played in flowing robes. And both McCracken and Miss Horne have expressed a desire to expand from the Italian repertory in which they have made their careers to Wagnerian roles.

Finally, all the Metropolitan union contracts expired in summer 1972, which argued strongly for an old rather than a new production at the start of the season. Directors are available to the Metropolitan only for brief periods; any delay associated with a new production may mean the loss of the man responsible for staging it. I would hope and expect that a new management will receive a season of grace from the unions, but there was no reason to expect that I would be given such favors if I added a year to my tenure. Everything considered, *Tannhäuser* seemed the best choice. It was not until I read it in print that

I could have imagined the notion that I had scheduled *Tann-häuser* for opening night because it is a dull opera and I wanted to make my successor look bad. Mr. Gentele's decision to go with a new *Carmen* using the same artists reflected a judgment different from mine. Now an inexpressibly sad fate has dictated that we will never know whether his decision was correct or not.

American critics rarely hear the work of the opera houses they hold up before the Metropolitan as shining examples of virtue. Of course great things are done elsewhere. I was once at La Scala for a performance of Meyerbeer's *Les Huguenots* with a cast one might hope to duplicate but could never surpass. In Vienna I heard a magnificent *Tosca* with Price and Corelli, Karajan conducting. (Karajan once said to me that every conductor should do *Tosca* twice a year "and get rid of his aggressions.") I had dinner afterward with Egon Hilbert, Intendant of the house, and complimented him on the performance. "Yes, yes," he said complacently. "That's the miracle of Vienna." We had known each other for decades. I said to him, "Night before last, I was in the Staatsoper in Vienna and heard a *Faust* from St. Pölten [a minor suburb of the city]. *That's* the miracle of Vienna."

Verdi once told a young composer not to read the critics, but to read the box office returns, which allow of no dispute. For eighteen of my twenty-two years we played to 97 per cent of capacity, a record that can be matched by no other opera house in history—and most of those years we played in a theater where 20 per cent of the seats had obstructed or restricted views of the stage. During that time, I used to suggest every so often to Francis Robinson that we charge the critics for their tickets, but his face would turn pale and I gave it up. I thought it might be particularly appropriate to charge them for tickets to the Bing Gala on my last night as general manager in New York—they probably would have been willing to pay to see me go—but I decided I would rather have a reputation for mellowing with the passage of time.

Most of the time, the critics made no difference. They loved our *Barber of Seville,* and we could never sell it; they hated our *Carmen,* and for years there was never an empty seat. The rumors they spread, tipped off by this soprano who thinks she should sing Elisabeth or Elsa though she shouldn't (and I know who she is), or by that baritone who thinks he should sing Don Giovanni though he can't (and I know who he is), did not seriously interfere with the serenity of a theater where responsibilities were fairly assigned. Some of my board members were upset by a bad press (none of them was ever particularly pleased by a good press), but I could live with that. I suppose it can be said that every public gets the critics it deserves. There is at least one instance, however, where the press cost us considerable money in legal fees by involving the Metropolitan in a totally unnecessary lawsuit.

On October 5, 1967, the Metropolitan Opera introduced a new conductor, a young man named Bruno Amaducci, who came to us well recommended from Vienna. His debut work was Verdi's *Falstaff,* a notoriously difficult piece to conduct, requiring precise control of ensembles in which as many as nine soloists may join, plus a delicate comic fugue for orchestra, soloists, and chorus at the end. Leonard Bernstein had given us an extraordinarily gay and touching *Falstaff* in 1963–64, and in following seasons Joseph Rosenstock had conducted some heavy-handed but wholly professional performances of the opera. Mr. Amaducci, however, was not up to the assignment. The moment the dress rehearsal came onto the stage, it was clear that we had a problem. Members of the chorus, orchestra players, and soloists complained.

The fault was mine: I had hired Mr. Amaducci without ever

[ 283 ]

hearing him conduct, something I do not believe I had ever done before at the Metropolitan. Most of his experience, which I had not known, was as a conductor of concerts rather than of opera. And for 1967–68, it was irremediable: one does not find conductors competent to handle *Falstaff* by picking up the telephone in mid-season. Unfortunately, the lead time on contracts for appearances in the opera had grown so preposterously long that on June 30, 1967—four months before his first appearance in the house—we had to decide whether or not we wished to take up Mr. Amaducci's option for additional conducting assignments in 1968–69. I had offered him our 1968–69 *Rigoletto* on a weekly service basis, twelve weeks at $700 each, and he had accepted. Now, having watched and heard Mr. Amaducci work with *Falstaff*, I was not prepared to see him return and do the same to *Rigoletto*. Obviously, I did not wish to disturb him while he still had a number of performances to conduct, and it was not until December 1967 that I informed him we would not be requiring his services the next season. We were contractually obligated to pay him, of course, whether we asked him to work for us or not, and I felt we should pay him the full price. Though he could doubtless make money elsewhere during the weeks for which we were releasing him, I sent him a check for $8,400.

Greatly to my surprise, he rejected the check, and wrote me that he would insist on conducting *Rigoletto* at the Metropolitan in 1968–69. It had not in fact been announced that he would receive this assignment, but a number of people did know he had been asked. If he did not perform at the Metropolitan in 1968–69, he wrote me, it would damage his reputation. I replied:

> . . . This is something which is very difficult to discuss because obviously very few artists will agree with negative views of the

Management, but it is the job of the Management to form its own decision and then act accordingly.

I think you are wildly exaggerating the importance and consequences of your not returning to the Metropolitan Opera. Nobody follows artists' careers that closely; you are not yet a world famous name whose every move is reported all over the world. I am terribly sorry that this matter disappoints you and upsets you so much; needless to say there is no kind of personal feeling involved; we all like you. It just did not work out the way we hoped it would and it is much less harmful to you to cut an association almost before it starts than to let it continue and then not renew it.

I am terribly sorry that I cannot meet your request [to conduct *Rigoletto*] and I hope very much that you will take this matter in good grace and continue your European career, which I hope will be successful and you certainly have my very best wishes, also for a Happy New Year.

Mr. Amaducci thereupon sued to compel us to permit him to conduct *Rigoletto* at the Metropolitan Opera, and also for a million dollars in damages. As his lawyers put it, "Defendant's unlawful, unwarranted and unilateral attempt to prevent plaintiff from performing as orchestra leader and conductor not only causes and caused plaintiff mental anguish, humiliation, grief and distress but results in and will and did result in great and irreparable harm and danger to his name, career and reputation as an orchestra conductor." To describe the joys of which we were depriving him, Mr. Amaducci in his deposition said that "Performing at the Metropolitan is something akin to reaching the Holy Land." He forgot that even the Holy Land cannot admit all who reach it, and employs a stern gatekeeper.

The Metropolitan won the lawsuit without much difficulty, but the episode seemed to me extremely unfortunate, especially for Mr. Amaducci, who could have let it be known (without contradiction from me) that he was not returning to the Metropolitan because we didn't offer him enough money or (the most usual reason given) because the artistic conditions at our theater were so inferior that he wouldn't be caught dead working for us again. The damage done to his reputation was the result of his lawsuit, not of any action by us. In a deeper sense, however, the real villain of the piece was the press, because the New York critics had indeed, as Mr. Amaducci claimed, given him "mostly good" reviews.

The New York *Times* reviewed two of his performances. After one, its critic wrote, "Mr. Amaducci, the new conductor, managed very well to keep the music buoyant and flexible." After the other, another critic (neither, unfortunately, the senior critic of the paper) wrote that "A seasoned cast . . . again did full justice to the work, as did Bruno Amaducci, who conducted." The critic for the New York *Post* wrote that "The new young conductor Bruno Amaducci led a bright, clear, well-modulated *Falstaff* and contributed significantly to the afternoon's success." The critic for *Variety* wrote that "Verdi's *Falstaff* proved the case for everything being properly together. The essential discipline came from a 33-year-old newcomer from Italy, Bruno Amaducci, on the stick, who elicited great delicacy and beauty from the Met orchestra and singers." One of the city's lesser critics, in a publication called *Back Stage*, paid tribute to "a new and most accomplished conductor, Bruno Amaducci, who in this reviewer's opinion will some day be ranked among the Toscaninis, Bruno Walters and Fausto Clevas." That was quite a triumvirate to link together, all by itself.

Now, there were not two schools of thought among the musicians with whom Mr. Amaducci worked. As I said in my statement to the court, "He simply did not measure up to the Metropolitan's artistic standards; not only in my view but also in the view of all my musical colleagues, and indeed the orchestra, there was no hope to expect him to rise to the desired stature." Yet some well-known members of the New York musical press, whose negative opinions are forever cited to demonstrate how inferior the Metropolitan is to all the other opera houses of the world, were so ill informed about the musical values a performance of *Falstaff* should have that they hailed his arrival as a significant acquisition for the company. The defense rests.

# 25

The need for a new opera house for the Metropolitan had been obvious for a generation before my arrival, and during the later 1920s, just before the Great Crash, a number of projects had been bruited about. Wallace K. Harrison, our architect, once showed me the drawings he had made for an opera house to occupy the area in Rockefeller Center where the little esplanade and ice-skating rink and small office buildings are, facing Fifth Avenue. During the 1930s and 1940s, of course, such plans had been put aside. But with the development of the first "urban renewal" programs in the years right after the war, the possibility of placing a new opera house within the context of some larger development—with government support in securing the land—became a major topic of conversation among members of the board. They were talking about it when I arrived.

It was during my first active season as general manager that the Metropolitan received a firm offer of land, from Robert Moses, then the co-ordinator of all government-sponsored building projects in New York. The site was on Columbus Circle, where the office building associated with the Coliseum, a convention center, now stands. The offer was of 80,000 square feet for $15 a square foot, or $1.2 million. C. D. Jackson of Time, Inc., was made chairman of a "New House Committee," and quickly raised a first pledge of $500,000 from John D. Rockefeller, Jr. On July 24, 1951, George Sloan and Lowell Wadmond as chairman and president of the board formally agreed, by letter, to submit the agreed-upon bid; Lewis Strauss, then chairman of the Metropolitan's executive committee, had secured Moses's assurance that this "letter of intent" would reserve the land for the opera.

During the following winter, pledges for the new house neared the million-dollar mark, and Mrs. Belmont and Colonel Hartfield had several meetings with Moses and his deputy to discuss, as a letter from Jackson put it, "engineering surveys, design, relationship of the Opera House to the Convention Hall, etc." Nevertheless, without warning, in March 1952, Commissioner Moses dumped the opera house project in a letter sent simultaneously to Wadmond and to the press. I never learned his real reason for leaving the Metropolitan at the altar; his published reasons were a demand from the federal government for more housing on the site and a reluctance of the city government to give up real estate tax revenues (which was ludicrous, because the land at Thirty-ninth Street and Broadway, which would have been added to the tax rolls when we moved, had much greater commercial real estate value than the land we would have occupied at Columbus Circle).

I had been much more an observer than a participant in all this maneuvering, but when the proposals for a new house had to be abandoned I began to press the board for substantial modernization of the only house we had. The second fund-raising drive of my management, in 1952–53, was dedicated in large part to improvements in the building, including some changes in seating arrangements (which were to pay for themselves by increasing the capacity of the house) and technical improvements to the stage area. Thanks to the imagination of Herman Krawitz and the ability of the technical chiefs I appointed in 1954, the succeeding years saw a steady improvement in the resources we could offer the directors and designers who came to work at the Metropolitan—but the house was at best a relic of an earlier age. General Sarnoff, whose voice always seemed to carry authority, told a board meeting in 1951 that the physical condition of the building was so bad it would have to be abandoned, as unsafe, whether we had a new home or not, within ten years.

What revived the project for a new opera house was the danger of demolition then threatening New York's other nineteenth-century musical monument, Carnegie Hall, which I walked past every day on my way to work. Commissioner Moses was now involved in another slum clearance project just to the north of Columbus Circle, in an area generally known as Lincoln Square, the name of the place where Broadway and Columbus Avenue met. He called Colonel Hartfield, the member of the board with whom he felt most comfortable, and offered the Metropolitan a site as part of the renewal of this ghastly slum. Max Abramovitz, Wallace Harrison's partner in architecture, went to look at the area with Hartfield and Chuck Spofford. Some years later Abramovitz recalled one of the two of them saying, "What a hell of a neighborhood." Still, Abramovitz added, "Here was all that land, for virtually nothing." Spofford and Irving Olds, another Wall Street lawyer active on the Metropolitan board, began to look around for pledges to start work near Lincoln Square, but it was slow going. Then Harrison, who had been approached by the Philharmonic to design a replacement for Carnegie Hall, suggested a joint venture by the two musical organizations.

[ 290 ]

In the spring of 1955, Spofford and Arthur Houghton, chairman of the Philharmonic, approached John D. Rockefeller III for help; and that fall, under Rockefeller's sponsorship, an Exploratory Committee for a Musical Arts Center was established. As part of these explorations, I prepared a first analysis of what we would need in a new theater, some of it very rough ("there should be a special large room for orchestra reading rehearsals"), some of it quite specific ("a kind of green room for the reporters where they can leave their hats and coats as they are usually too stingy to check them"). I also raised a small but farsighted objection to the plan as a whole:

> In conclusion, and probably much too late, I feel it my duty to venture a little dissenting voice on the basic idea of combining a Philharmonic Auditorium and an opera house within the same block. Naturally, I don't pretend to be a traffic expert and I am confident that the authorities concerned will study this problem thoroughly. However, I think it may be wise to reflect upon the fact that, to my knowledge, in no city in the world are the opera house . . . and the large concert hall . . . on the same block. Added to the fact that, to my knowledge, nowhere in the world are traffic problems as serious as in New York, this suggestion may give one pause to think . . .

The influence of this dissent was nil. A public announcement of the existence of the Exploratory Committee was made in December 1955, and in June 1956 Lincoln Center was incorporated.

The project needed a "feasibility study," which was assigned to a Philadelphia engineering firm called Day and Zimmermann, who had never worked on an opera house. They sent men to look at the Metropolitan and interview people; I remember that they suggested to Herbert Graf that I worked for him, because he was a "director"—the only kind of "director" they knew about was a board member. They turned in a report claiming that we could perform for $263,000 in a new house the maintenance services that cost us $700,000 in 1956 in the old house, and that we could keep it open all summer with something like *Rosalinda*, a Broadway show of a few years back which they apparently did not know was nothing but a version of *Fledermaus*. But because we already knew pretty well what we wanted, their estimate of the costs of a new Metropolitan came to almost 50 per cent of what the building finally did cost, though the other theaters built at the Center eventually cost at least *four times* the prices suggested by these expert consultants. They also did us one immense favor, insisting in their report that the Metropolitan keep as endowment the money from the sale or lease of our Thirty-ninth Street real estate. In early 1957, on the understanding that we would not be made to contribute to the costs of our building any part of our possible nest egg, the Metropolitan formally accepted "constituent" status in the new project.

That summer, Krawitz and I visited Dr. Walther Unruh, the most highly regarded technical expert in the German theater (where many new buildings were going up to replace wartime losses), and arranged for him to serve as a consultant during the planning of the new house. Then we had an oddly inconclusive session with Harrison, a charming, cultured gentleman who seemed to want us to make design suggestions. We assured him that we wanted his architectural ideas, not our own. Presumably, design work was to start immediately, but it didn't. In December 1957 I wrote to Tony Bliss:

> This is just a note of worry. It is now nearly three months that we are all back since the summer and with the exception of one or two irrelevant questions, I haven't heard a murmur from the Harrison office on the new house. In particular, whenever one sees a design or a model of the exterior or interior, Mr. Harrison goes out of his way to emphasize that he has no

idea yet what the house will look like either outside or inside and that the present designs and models are merely rough indications, not really representing any kind of final idea . . .

I gather that, all going well, the Philharmonic plans will have to be finalized by this summer and you are no doubt aware that the outside of the Philharmonic building, which is to be planned and erected so much earlier than ours, will completely determine the style of our own building . . .

I realize that I am not an expert on these matters, nor is it my immediate business to interfere with this sort of planning. Nevertheless, I am sure you will agree that I am entitled to feel myself deeply concerned with it . . .

As must be obvious, I knew as little about architecture and building as the architects and engineers knew about opera. We had been told that we would be moving into our new house by 1961, and I had believed it. But there was money to be raised, occupants to be relocated from the rotting structures on the land, lawsuits to be fought off before any work could begin; and the job for the architects, designers, and engineers was much bigger than I had realized. And at every step there were policy questions that took considerable thought and even more time.

First there was the question of how large the house should be. One faction on the board said there must be 5,000 seats, and I fought them tooth and nail both for artistic reasons and because of my experience. So large a house would drastically limit our repertory. Even in the 3,800-seat Metropolitan we built *Così Fan Tutte* is not right; and I am not sure the house is good for *Figaro*. We had determined not to have amplification —and you can't always find singers with the lung power to fill a 5,000-seat house. It was by no means guaranteed that we could sell so many seats on a regular basis, and nothing is worse advertising for an opera house than large numbers of empty seats at many performances.

Then there was an argument about whether the new Metropolitan should be a "popular" house with only tiers of seats above the orchestra level, or whether it should retain the boxes and their anterooms for the richest patrons. Again I fought strongly, for the boxes. They are part of the frame for opera. The old Residenztheater in Munich is still the ideal house for the masterpieces of the eighteenth and early nineteenth centuries, because of the perfection of its auditorium frame. We had to be much bigger than that, of course, but we could and should keep some of the flavor.

Not long after my memo to Bliss, Harrison did begin to show us more detailed models of what was on his mind, complete with figures about seating capacity, sight lines, cubage of building, and costs. There were regular meetings of people from the architect's office, Krawitz, Dr. Unruh (flying in from Germany for as much as a month at a time), sometimes myself. Harrison's office became the home of a virtually life-size model of an auditorium, into which we would all peer, pretending to learn something.

Looking back from an office in a completed opera house that cost more than $50 million, it is hard to recapture the thrill of horror everyone felt when the construction company first told us that the plans Harrison was proposing would cost as much as $29 million. We were pressed to cut in all directions, and I fought back. The United States, I argued, simply could not *afford* to build a new opera house that looked old-fashioned and cheap next to the new theaters of Europe and Russia.

I was particularly unhappy about all proposals to reduce our backstage area. Herbert Graf had commented at a preliminary meeting that in a properly designed opera house the area behind the proscenium should be four times as great as the area in front of it. I wrote to Bliss: "I do hope we will not fall into the frequent mistake of theater building: that space and glamor are lavished on the front of the house and all savings are expected to come from the working area of the house without which, after all, the front of the house would never be full." Krawitz was asked to take $400,000 off the stage equipment and stage lighting budget, and in co-operation with our master mechanic Lou Edson did eliminate $125,000. Then he came to the electrical equipment:

> . . . We cut out considerable amounts [Krawitz wrote] but the net result of all our work increased the electrical equipment budget by $123,000. This came about because the electric switchboard requested by the electrical engineers without consulting us was actually inferior to the board we presently have. The money required to give us the correct switchboard plus other items overlooked by the electrical engineers make it appear as if we are increasing our requirements for lighting equipment. This is not so. What has happened is that our specifications are being budgeted for the first time . . . You may hear comments that we did not cooperate and that is why I am writing this memo . . .

As the meetings went on, technical considerations became increasingly dominant. There was a decision made, for example, that the sight lines from the balcony seats could cut off eight feet in front of the asbestos curtain, which meant that patrons in those seats would be unable to see the conductor, and I insisted on a change—the sight of the conductor at work is part of the experience of attending the opera. Seats in the back of the orchestra section, below the overhang of the boxes, would permit the occupants to see only thirteen feet up from the stage floor, clearly not enough to give them any sense of the sets and drops; the orchestra could not go back that far. All these decisions significantly affected both over-all design and construction decisions.

There were acoustical worries, constant acoustical worries.

Krawitz, Unruh, and Erich Leinsdorf met with Leo Beranek of Bolt, Beranek & Newman, the acoustical consultants for Philharmonic Hall:

> In theory we discussed certain projects which had proven to be failures, giving as examples, the M.I.T. Auditorium, the Royal Festival Hall, and the new Mann Auditorium in Tel Aviv. While we knew in advance that this firm acted as consultants for the M.I.T. Auditorium, it was only after we had criticised the three auditoria that we learned they were also acoustical consultants on the other two . . .

Later I would be given a preliminary tour of Philharmonic Hall, and I would notice that the wood of the stage was almost like concrete; it was so hard it was almost painful to walk on. I asked why this should be, and was told the wood had been treated with special fire-resistant chemicals. I said, "But won't that affect the resonance of the instruments that stand on the floor?" And the acoustical consultant who was taking me around said, "You may have a point there." I thought to myself, maybe I should become an acoustical expert; it seemed like an easier life than being an opera manager. Ultimately, the Metropolitan and Harrison chose Wilhelm Jordon from Denmark and Professor Cyril Harris of Columbia University, whose advice, thank God, proved correct.

Then, as a special item, there was the organ problem. Some of the more advanced thinkers at Lincoln Center and in our organization wanted an electronic installation rather than an organ. Krawitz and I made a trip to the electronic studio of the German Radio in Cologne, which I understand [I wrote in a memo] is the most up to date electronic sound studio in the world.

The leading technicians, musicians and administrators of the organization were extremely helpful and tried to impress

Mr. Krawitz and myself with the fantastic sounds that various of these new and amazing inventions can produce. I will admit that the imitation of the sound of an approaching and disappearing railroad train was rather stunning, but I could not possibly think of an opera in our repertory where this could be useful. I kept asking for the sound of pure bells (e.g., *Tosca* 3rd Act) or church organ (e.g., *Meistersinger* 1st Act). They seemed rather to resent my insistence on these sounds and said that it was not the purpose of the new electronic equipment to "imitate sounds that could be better produced by the original instruments" . . . in short, my own inclination and recommendation would be for a pipe organ . . .

To the credit of the men who ran the Lincoln Center board, it must be said that we ultimately got everything we could make a good case for, even though the costs soared and they—not we—had to raise the money. We got nothing just by asking, but we got everything we could prove we needed.

Toward the end of 1958, a great policy dispute over the future of Lincoln Center was triggered by a proposal to move the New York City Center, including its opera company, into what had been projected up to then as "the dance theater." I was furiously opposed.

My first reaction [I wrote Bliss] is one of dismay . . .
So far I was under the impression that Lincoln Center aimed at the highest cultural achievements and the constituents that up to now had been considered had belonged to the highest class in their field . . . The City Center Opera has no place in that group.

There is a further danger. The eyes of the world are now on Lincoln Center . . . The rest of the world and indeed the less knowledgeable parts of the United States will find it difficult to distinguish between two opera companies within the Lincoln Center . . . It would be to our grave disadvantage if the unique position of the Metropolitan was suddenly confused with a very much lesser organisation . . .

I understood from the earliest days of the Lincoln Center planning that the basic concept was that no other opera company should be permitted at Lincoln Center without the Metropolitan's approval. The question of the City Center was even then discussed. Does it seem fair that a gun should now be pointed at the Metropolitan's head just because political developments may put some money at the disposal of Lincoln Center for the building of a house which in fact is not wanted? . . .

What had happened was that everything had proved more expensive than planned, and the Lincoln Center board was sensibly afraid to raise the fund-raising goal before anything had been built. Governor Nelson Rockefeller had then agreed to make a major New York State contribution in the form of what had been discussed as the dance theater. Direct tax-supported contribution to Lincoln Center was most easily justified by support for a low-priced, popular house. Meanwhile, the City Center, which had been supporting Balanchine's New York City Ballet, was unwilling to see the company detached to be a separate entity under the wing of Lincoln Center. Mayor Robert F. Wagner lined up behind the City Center, and so did the Rockefeller family, and we were forced to accept something I considered very damaging.

I thought it was simply wrong to have two opera companies operating on different systems on the same square. It would upset the box office—people could see *Traviata* for $15 at the Met or $6 only one and a half minutes away. And later people would say they had seen a shocking *Traviata* "at Lincoln Center." The official proposal shown to us said merely that "Lincoln Center recognizes the Metropolitan Opera as its primary constitutent in the field of opera." The Lincoln Center board looked for "agreements as to repertoire and scheduling . . . between the two companies." Where these agreements did not spontaneously occur, "Lincoln Center will reserve the right to arbitrate or mediate or, if necessary, to bring about final decision." In other words, we would lose control of our own house. Fortunately, this empire building by Lincoln Center was resisted by the City Center as well as by ourselves, for they, too, had something to lose. Otherwise, as I wrote in a bitter memo, our board would probably have been "pusillanimous" enough to go along. As the time for opening Lincoln Center neared, both the City Center and ourselves had to fight off efforts by the growing Lincoln Center bureaucracy to take control of our houses and book outside attractions into them regardless of our needs and prospects.

Indeed, for a long time the question of the function of Lincoln Center as an entity was a matter of dispute. Naturally, William Schuman, who had resigned as president of the Juilliard School (the city's leading music school) to become president of Lincoln Center, wished to have as much influence as he could achieve. Equally naturally, all the "constituents" wanted to control their own work, and their own theater. The Lincoln Center bureaucracy made great plans to use our theater for the Hamburg Opera, the Rome Opera (both these companies did visit, for summer seasons), for the Vienna Staatsoper (which demanded too much money) and the Piccola Scala (which seemed silly for our big house), for other events that would be sponsored by the Center itself. Once an aspect of this running dispute broke into the newspapers. The Repertory Theater, though formed for Lincoln Center, had begun its life outside because completion of its building had been delayed, and it had not done well. Someone gave Schuman the idea that the man to pull this enterprise together was Herman Krawitz, and Schuman and the chairman of the Repertory Theater board approached Krawitz.

All this was *sub rosa*: only the producer of the Repertory Theater knew what was going on. And it was 1964, two years before the Metropolitan was to move into its new opera house, which Krawitz and Krawitz alone really understood, having been the only man in on every single step of the planning. I issued a statement saying that Krawitz had a contract with us and I would not release him from it, adding that Lincoln Center was "apparently deteriorating to a free-for-all jungle where constituents can raid each other at will." That night I had to go to Philadelphia, to hear some singer who was performing there, and at about midnight, shortly after I got to my room at the Bellevue-Stratford, Francis Robinson was on the telephone with some piece of news about something that had happened at the Metropolitan. "By the way," I said, "is there anything in the morning papers about the Krawitz affair?" He said, "Oh, yes . . ." It was on the front pages.

It now seems clear to me that I was wrong in fighting the entry of the City Opera to Lincoln Center. There have been no particular difficulties. They have helped us and we have helped them by lending singers, and many of our most valuable artists—like Judith Raskin, Shirley Verrett, Placido Domingo, Sherrill Milnes, Donald Gramm—have been "graduates" of the City Opera. Productions there have considerably improved (though I hope I am permitted my continuing opinion that they are simply not in the same league as Metropolitan productions), and the company's general manager Julius Rudel has become a major figure in the musical life of America. Apart from the works we both need to sell tickets—like *Bohème, Carmen, Traviata,* and *Rigoletto*—we have been able to achieve loose understandings about repertory. There was a brief fight a while back about Donizetti's three queens, which was a project Montserrat Caballé very much wanted to undertake for us; but we finally accepted the fact that Beverly Sills of the City Opera, having been born in Brooklyn, was entitled to priority in the portrayal of British royalty.

As the policy questions receded, I turned over more and more of the negotiations about technical details to Krawitz and his consultants. They planned the magnificent shops, great airy spaces with high ceilings and no pillars, co-ordinated to feed all necessary scenery, costumes, equipment, and supplies to the stage with maximum efficiency; they planned the side stages and the rear stage that can be slid into place fully set, putting an end to all those delays that had plagued operagoers in the old house, all the noises of stagehands at work that had broken the mood whenever sets had to be changed between scenes; they specified the large and small rooms and soundproofing and floors for dancing needed to rehearse everything properly. One interesting change late in the design process mingled the sexes of the dressing rooms for the first time. At the old Metropolitan, and in every European opera house I know, the dressing rooms for men and women are on opposite sides of the stage. But in the new Metropolitan, soloists of both sexes use dressing rooms on the same corridor, giving us the atmosphere of an adult enterprise rather than a school for adolescents.

I had one more great struggle with the architects, over the question of windows that could be opened. I insisted that European artists could not live in a conditioned-air atmosphere all the time, even though all the modern ways of controlling the humidity were employed. Indeed, I could not live that way myself; I demanded for the general manager's office a window that could open. The south façade of the building is made by literally scores of vertical marble strips jutting out from the structure, with narrow glass panels between them and horizontal steel bands across the glass at each floor level. To give me a window that would open required the addition of one small steel band halfway up one of what are six narrow windows in my not-very-large office. The architects insisted that this one little strip of steel, which you cannot notice even after you are told about it, would utterly destroy the aesthetic conception of the building. I fought it all the way to the board, and finally won.

My most important contribution to the looks of the building was probably my wife's lifelong friendship with Mrs. Marc Chagall. The front façade of the opera house was to be all glass behind high arches, giving a view of the grand staircase in the center of the public area, but also leaving two very large blank walls at either side. I proposed Chagall paintings of scenes from opera to cover these walls (they are not murals: they are on canvas and in theory could be removed), and having received approval for this proposal went to Chagall with a package suggestion of the two walls plus scenery and costumes for a new production of Mozart's *The Magic Flute*. As a result, the costs to the Metropolitan and to Lincoln Center were very much less than they might otherwise have been. Chagall says, incidentally, that the red figure playing the guitar on the wall to the left is a portrait of me.

The Chagalls spent considerable time in New York while he worked on both these projects, and they lived at the Essex House, down the hall from our apartment. Once my wife came to their rooms for tea, and found Chagall sitting at an easel and sketching a vase of flowers standing on a table before the window. Nina said, "That's pretty." Chagall said, "You like it? I give it to you!" Nina never told me about it, and one day, opening a drawer, I came on this square of canvas. I took it out to be framed, and when I returned to the art gallery where I had ordered the frame the proprietor came out to meet me. Would I, he asked, take $15,000 for the little sketch? . . . I thought to myself, what an amazing thing it was, that a man could sit in a hotel room and in a few minutes, with his wrist and fingers, paint something for which a businessman would later offer such a fortune. I thanked the proprietor of the gallery, and took the painting back to hang on our wall.

As the actual construction of the new house began (for a long time there was just an excavation which unfortunately tapped an underground stream, creating a large body of water known as Lake Bing), we began thinking of our new productions more and more as resources to be exploited in the new theater. In 1963–64 we had two giant productions—the Merrill-O'Hearn *Aida*, with African choreography (surely legitimate in the Egyptian setting) from Katherine Dunham; and Franco Zeffirelli's splendidly Tudor *Falstaff*. Solti conducted the first; Bernstein, the second. That spring saw the opening of the New York World's Fair, and our first May season in New York, two weeks to give Fair visitors a chance to hear opera at the Metropolitan. Fortunately, the weather was cool. With *Falstaff*, *Macbeth*, and *Otello* in the season's repertory, we were able to offer our own operatic tribute to the four hundredth anniversary of the birth of Shakespeare. This was the year Fritz Reiner was supposed to return to the Metropolitan, having retired from the Chicago Symphony. But he took sick during the rehearsals for *Götterdämmerung*, and tragically died.

The next season was to have opened with Joan Sutherland's *Norma*, but she decided rather late in the game that she was not yet ready for the part, and we opened instead with a new *Lucia*, which we certainly needed. Merrill and O'Hearn worked together again on a *Samson et Dalila* that introduced to the Metropolitan a first-rate French conductor, Georges Prêtre, who could have been a mainstay of the house for many years if only he had not decided that it was somehow discreditable to him as a Frenchman to conduct French music. (That seems not to make sense, and it doesn't; for several seasons, respecting his talent, I indulged Prêtre in Italian and German operas up to and including *Tristan und Isolde,* but despite his preferences his talents did lie exclusively in the French repertory and I finally had to decide that it was better not to have Prêtre at all than to have him conducting music for which he had so little affinity.) Birgit Nilsson sang a magnificent Salome for us, helped by the attentive direction of Günther Rennert, the carefully tailored choreography of Alicia Markova, and the always effective conducting of Karl Böhm; Irving Kolodin reported that her ovation "persisted through twenty-six curtain calls."

But for many the 1964–65 season was made meaningful by the debut of Elisabeth Schwarzkopf as the Marschallin in *Der Rosenkavalier.* She was not the first of the artists from whom I withdrew what had originally been a political veto—Gottlob Frick had been in the house a few years before—but she was surely the most important to that time. By 1964, those who had become old enough to vote in the last year of the war were turning forty; the time had come to forget it. Herself a very beautiful woman beginning to show the marks of approaching age, she was a perfect Marschallin.

We opened our last season on Thirty-ninth Street with a new production of the work that had opened the house eighty-three years before—*Faust,* with Barrault directing in settings devised by Jacques Dupont, choreography by Flemming Flindt of the Royal Danish Ballet, and Georges Prêtre (not yet having forsworn things French) conducting. Our superb cast included one artist who had made his debut with me—Cesare Siepi as Méphistophélès—plus Nicolai Gedda as Faust and Gabriella Tucci as Marguerite. During this season there were an astonishing number of major debuts—Mirella Freni and Gianni Raimondi as the lovers in *La Bohème,* Montserrat Caballé, Sherrill Milnes, and Nicolai Ghiaurov in *Faust,* Felicia Weathers, Grace Bumbry, Reri Grist, and Zubin Mehta. Miss Freni's debut brought the greatest tribute in the history of extraordinary statements by Zinka Milanov, who went running back to Francis Robinson's office to say, "She's so wonderful, this girl, she sounds like a young me."

But our thoughts were concentrated more and more on the new house, which was almost all ready in the spring. Harrison's partner Max Abramovitz had been convinced that part of the problem of Philharmonic Hall had been the impossibility of running full acoustical tests with a performance and an audience before the final "tuning" of the auditorium. Because we had a series of afternoon student performances (this year the opera was *Girl of the Golden West*), we had a ready-made occasion for a test without publicity, but I decided that rather than have rumors sweep through the city I would permit the press to attend. There was almost universal pleasure with the sound of the auditorium, especially the sound of the voices from the stage. The triumphant nature of the occasion was somewhat marred when the audience left and we found how many of our student guests had slashed the plush seats with their little knives; but that's New York.

At the end of that same week—on Saturday, April 16—we rang down the curtain on the last singing at the Metropolitan Opera House, in a grand Gala Farewell featuring appearances by the great stars of the old times at the house and arias and ensemble pieces from the great stars of the current company. There was a committee in existence to "save the Met," and enabling legislation was passed by the state government, but really the house was beyond saving. It was even further beyond saving at the end of the Bolshoi Ballet season that followed the Gala, because the audience took for souvenirs virtually everything that could be wrenched loose; that's New York, too. Know-

ing that something like this was likely to occur, we had already
moved to Lincoln Center everything we might wish to have on
display—the pictures and autograph letters and the like—in the
new house.

# 26

That first year at Lincoln Center was one disaster after another. Even for me, enjoying crises and tight corners as I do, it came to be a little much. Krawitz, Herman, Gutman, and I met in permanent emergency sessions, with new and difficult and often painful decisions to make every day. For our orchestra and chorus and ballet and stagehands, there were ten- and twelve-hour days. People would be called to work at ten in the morning, but when they got to the house something would have gone wrong, the director would have to change something in the staging, and serious work couldn't start until four in the afternoon. Everyone was dead tired all the time, especially from the waiting. Of course, people were paid overtime, but we drove them to a degree of exhaustion that cannot be compensated just with payment.

The fault was mine: I had overplanned the season. We were to have nine new productions, which probably can never be done, four of them in the first week alone, which *certainly* can never be done. I had not realized what a temptation all that lavish equipment would be to our designers—all of them felt they had to use this fabulous machinery. And then the machinery didn't work.

For our opening night, we had commissioned an opera from Samuel Barber, whose *Vanessa* we had all admired. He chose as his subject Shakespeare's *Antony and Cleopatra,* which I thought unwise—not one of the strongest plays. And he asked Franco Zeffirelli, who had directed Shakespeare in England as well as directing and designing operas and movies, to make the libretto for him *and* stage the opera. Zeffirelli was—we all were—somewhat doubtful about the music, and overproduced the opera. One scene involved the Sphinx and the revolving stage. When the sets and the chorus got on this stage, it proved insufficiently strong to hold their weight, and it broke down in a way that was irreparable for our first season. Sets had to be rebuilt to compensate, new staging had to be improvised for four new productions in the first week.

We had planned to have the New York premiere of Strauss's *Die Frau ohne Schatten* at the end of that week, but we could not do it: I announced a postponement. Karl Böhm, who was to conduct it, was dreadfully disappointed, and kept asking me why it had to be *his* opera that was postponed. He cheered up two weeks later, when this Merrill-O'Hearn production turned out to be the triumph of our first season. The machinery Merrill and O'Hearn finally used—including the basement stage, which could be lifted up into position (the original stage rising above it into the flies)—did work perfectly; and by permitting the public to watch this feat of magic, Merrill and O'Hearn restored to opera the quality of spectacle which is where it all started. *Die Frau* became for the first time anywhere an authentic popular hit. We also—I hasten to add—had wonderful performances from Leonie Rysanek as the Empress, James King as the Emperor, Walter Berry and Christa Ludwig as Barak and the Dyer's Wife.

Another of our new productions was unlucky in a more final way. I had been delighted and moved by Wieland Wagner's *Lohengrin* at the Hamburg Opera, and I had asked him to stage this work for our first year in the new house. But his drawings when they arrived were different from what he had done in Hamburg, austere, heavy, almost motionless. We had immense trouble with the chorus standing motionless for an hour—they were fainting like flies. Perhaps I could have convinced Wieland Wagner to make some not very large changes that could have restored the more romantic beauty of the production I had hoped he would do, but before he could come to New York to work with us on it, he died; and the assistant who took over was not, of course, empowered to change anything in what seemed a kind of memorial tribute to the man.

Later in the season we had another world premiere (Marvin David Levy's *Mourning Becomes Electra*), and there was Chagall's unique and overpowering (perhaps *too* overpowering) *Magic Flute*. He did some of the work on the paint frame himself, preferring to stand in one place and run the frame up and down rather than, like the usual scenic artist, working across. Fortunately, we had a Russian head painter and they got on fine. We also presented a new *Gioconda* and an enormous *Traviata* with very elaborate and expensive sets by Cecil Beaton.

Toward the end of the season there was a splendid *Peter Grimes*, Colin Davis conducting brilliantly, Jon Vickers the unforgettable Grimes. As Vickers would not have worked with Solti (and vice versa: they had fought about something), I did not regret the forced change of conductor. Any occasion that brought Vickers to our stage was reason for rejoicing. The other big hit of the first season in the new house, however, was the second Strauss opera, offering Birgit Nilsson's first Elektra in

America. I missed the first performance; as I wrote in a note I sent Miss Nilsson together with opening-night flowers, "This is the first Nilsson premiere that I am missing, but the last three months I am afraid have at last caught up with me and I am not quite well today and will make use of the weekend staying in bed. Of course I will be at the next performances and good luck tonight!" I received a kind of bouquet from Miss Nilsson in reply:

> Thank you so much for the lovely roses you sent me yesterday.
>
> I am sorry to hear that you are not well. We missed you very much yesterday. You know, you have spoiled us by almost always being at the performances and always at the premieres.
>
> There are some opera houses in Europe where one after a month or so is taken by surprise when one finds out that there is still a director around, occasionally.
>
> Thank you for spoiling us. Take care and please get well soon.

There is an Austrian saying that things work themselves out, and I was Austrian, but it isn't so. The massive overtime and the cost overruns on the new productions (which were not just tens but *hundreds* of thousands of dollars over budget) raised serious problems. And on top of all the desperate worries associated with the real Metropolitan Opera in its new house, I had to devote scarce time and energy and money to a recently formed touring company of young artists called the Metropolitan Opera National Company, which I was supposed to supervise by remote control.

The National Company was an expression of the typical American weakness for doing something—anything—for education and the young. Tony Bliss believed in the idea and pushed it on the board, but the guardian angel of the company was Mrs. DeWitt Wallace of *Reader's Digest*, a major contributor to the

Metropolitan. Mrs. Wallace had grown up somewhere in the hinterland, and she felt her childhood had been impoverished by the absence of opera. The way she liked to put it was, "If only I could have heard *Rigoletto* when I was a girl!" After a while, I began to feel that all she cared about was getting a *Rigoletto* out into the country—even a rotten *Rigoletto* would be better than no *Rigoletto* at all.

I was never pleased with the idea of a young touring company that bore the name of the Metropolitan Opera. That name was part of what we paid our leading soloists—it brought them television dates and recording contracts and invitations to endorse products for advertisers. Our lawyers were forever chasing down people who used the name when they didn't have the right to do so. Now the name was to be used for a group of unknown singers touring in productions designed to be hung in whatever auditorium space might be available in small cities around the country. But the board wanted it, and in 1964 the company was set up to plan a first tour for 1965–66.

To run the touring company, I hired a diumvirate of managers—Risë Stevens and Michael Manuel. Miss Stevens had retired from singing, but she was still, of course, one of the biggest names in opera. She would be invaluable in going around and talking up interest at the women's committees that would sponsor the company in the different cities. Moreover, she had a deep interest in young artists and in helping them toward careers: she could and would inspire singers. Manuel had been among our most practical stage people, an intelligent young man who knew about sets and costumes and rehearsal schedules as well as about the aesthetics of opera. They hired a company of attractive young singers, some of whom later came to the Metropolitan, and they made excellent arrangements at the modern Clews Hall in Indianapolis to give them a fine theater for rehearsing the productions and presenting the premieres.

But there was a conceptual problem. Because the company was to tour the hinterlands, they could not hope to draw customers with the kind of modern or experimental or just non-standard opera in which they would have appeared to best advantage. But when they presented *Traviata* and *Butterfly*, as they did in their first season, they were too subject to comparison with the performances of the parent company—which were, after all, available on the radio every Saturday. The extent to which Miss Stevens and Manuel felt they needed such identification was demonstrated by their insistence that I give their conductor an assignment at the Metropolitan the year before the tour began, so he could carry our grand name.

In their first season, Miss Stevens and Manuel kept their expenses within 3 per cent of their budget ($2.74 million spent as against $2.66 million budgeted), which was excellent. But their receipts, unfortunately, were 11 per cent below budget ($1.82 million taken in as against a budgeted $2.05 million). The gross loss of $917,000 was too high to be covered even when Miss Stevens raised some extra contributions, and the company in its first season showed a cash loss of $228,000, which the Metropolitan had to absorb.

In its second season—which unfortunately coincided with our debut at Lincoln Center—the company got into much worse trouble. Its receipts dropped to $1.52 million and the contributions made to it dropped to $70,000—and the cash loss was more than $1.1 million. And, speaking personally, I thought the performances were poor, even after making allowance for the youth and inexperience of the artists. To me, the National Company —for which I was ultimately responsible—was a very large last straw. Even though Mrs. Wallace offered to underwrite another season with a $1 million gift, I demanded the abandonment of the project, split my board, and won.

Before these traumatic events, the National Company had

64. Left to right: Zinka Milanov, Rudolf Bing, Mr. and Mrs. Richard Tucker, Mr. and Mrs. Robert Merrill on the occasion of the Tuckers' twenty-fifth wedding anniversary

65. Save the Met demonstration during the strike, September 1969

66. Zeffirelli's
production of
*Cavalleria Rusticana*
at the New Met

67. With Leonard Bernstein and Luigi Alva during rehearsal for *Falstaff*

68. Jess Thomas, Rudolf Bing (back to camera), Leontyne Price, Thomas Schippers, Ezio Flagello, Rosalind Elias, backstage, Opening Night at the New Met, 1966

69. Franco Corelli as Calaf and Birgit Nilsson as Turandot in
*Turandot*, Act II, Scene 2

70. *Der Rosenkavalier,*
Act II, with
Reri Grist (left)
as Sophie and Christa
Ludwig (center) as
Octavian

Louis Mélançon

71. Celebrating with Golda Meir and John V. Lindsay, 1970

72. Sir Rudolf and Goeran Gentele, in foreground. Robert Herman is at far right. Opening night of the eighty-seventh season, 1971

been the remote excuse for some other very unpleasant moments. Among those who had come to our first night at Lincoln Center was the Earl of Harewood, an old friend of mine from Glyndebourne days, who had been one of my successors at the Edinburgh Festival and had then served as controller of opera planning at Covent Garden. As a cousin of the Queen, he was much in demand socially in New York. Among those to whom I introduced him was Tony Bliss, who was extremely and rightly impressed with him. Bliss had learned more about the workings of the Metropolitan than any other president of the board I have ever known or heard about, and had played a major and constructive role for ten years. But he and I had been having a serious dispute about the extent to which the Metropolitan Opera could present ballet evenings. I felt we were unlikely to offer better ballet than the New York City Ballet or the American Ballet Theatre, and would thus be unable to sell tickets at anything like Metropolitan Opera prices, even if we did somehow put together a plausible ballet season. The Metropolitan subscription audience was not a ballet audience. Bliss was insistent that I was missing a major opportunity. Now along came the Earl of Harewood, who had worked at Covent Garden, home of the Royal Ballet as well as the Royal Opera.

Bliss brought Harewood to New York to travel for a while with the National Company, and make recommendations about ways to improve its performance. The Bliss Foundation made a grant to pay for Harewood's travel. When Harewood did reappear in New York, he came to the opera four and five times a week as Bliss's guest. Instantly the news got around. Everyone in New York knew that the Metropolitan was floundering in deep water in its new home. Many people knew that Tony and I had been arguing about the National Company and the role of ballet. They read the handwriting on the wall: the Metropolitan would soon have a new general manager.

I thought all this was somewhat premature, and I asked for a meeting of the executive committee. I said, "We all know that even the happiest marriages can fall apart," and I looked around the room—everyone in it except for Wadmond and myself had been divorced at least once. "Mr. Bliss and I have had a happy marriage for ten years, but now it is quite apparent that Mr. Bliss wants a new general manager, and it seems he has found one. Therefore, I am asking you to accept my resignation."

There was some unhappiness around the table. Mr. Bliss said he did not think the board should accept my resignation, and that he should resign. Then nobody resigned, and we continued as we had been. Except that the strains of this desperate season became too much for Bliss, and soon, quite apart from the Harewood problem, he did resign as president. George Moore, one of the leading men at the First National City Bank, who had been chairman of our finance committee, succeeded him. Later my happy personal relations with Bliss were restored, and he was a friend to my management on the board, and remained a friend to me to this day.

Though Moore and I have had a number of disagreements since, I must admit that in those first months he was magnificent—he appeared in the Metropolitan's hour of need as Churchill had appeared to save England. Grasping the nettle, he increased the Metropolitan's box office prices at mid-season; and having proved that the customers were willing to bear their share (everyone in New York wanted to get into the new opera house that first season: we sold out virtually every night, even at the highest prices), he was able to go and with help from Peggy Douglas raise by far the largest contributed fund opera anywhere has ever known—more than $7 million. In theory, this money was for our losses in the first year at Lincoln Center; in fact, it also covered the very heavy losses (almost $1 million a year) we had suffered in the two last seasons in the old house. The board in those years had slacked off on its fund-raising efforts partly to help Lincoln Center complete its capital campaign and partly because the fact that we were about to become the owners of prime commercial real estate at Thirty-ninth Street had made it too easy for the company to borrow money to pay its bills.

For me, Moore as leader of the board became uncomfortably similar to George Sloan in the same capacity two decades before. Every year, there was a battle with Sloan to get authorization for new productions; now there were similar battles with Moore. In fact, it became impossible to use in the Moore regime the tactic of taking the contributions of the Opera Guild and the National Council as subsidies for new productions, because Moore argued (quite correctly) that we would receive this money anyway and therefore should put it in the general fund. Under Moore, too, much time and attention had to be given to assorted schemes for adding to the income of the company, many of them very similar to the treasure hunts on which we were forever setting off during my earliest years.

There were in the old days three categories of profit-making efforts—recordings, television, and touring. When I arrived, I found a contract with Columbia Records that guaranteed the Metropolitan $20,000 a year in royalties from what were projected as four full-length opera recordings a year. But in fact Columbia never made four recordings a year, and the Metropolitan's earned royalties never reached the $20,000 guarantee (which was paid, of course, nonetheless). When the time came to start renegotiating this contract, in 1950, I attempted to set up what I described as a "triple entente," by which RCA Victor and Columbia would join with us in a series of Metropolitan Opera recordings, from which everyone would profit.

While expressing interest in such an arrangement, Victor

proceeded to sign up to exclusive contracts a number of the artists who sold tickets for us and records for whoever owned their services, and we wound up with a new and somewhat unsatisfactory Columbia contract which permitted the record company to deduct from our future earnings the royalties we had not earned in the preceding years. With the exception of Richard Tucker and Eleanor Steber, Columbia signed none of our most important artists. Many of the Metropolitan recordings had to appear with what we called "charity casts" (the casts the management schedules for a performance for which the house has been bought in advance as a benefit). Our net earnings from Columbia dropped to about $11,000 in 1952 and reached only $21,000 in 1953, and after a second contract with that company we let relations lapse.

In the mid-1950s we went another route, contracting with the Book-of-the-Month Club for a mail-order series of opera recordings—the Metropolitan Opera in your home, by subscription only. Reginald Allen's analysis predicted a net to the company of $50,000 per recording, but very little profit was realized. As part of this contract, we recorded our second operetta hit, Offenbach's *La Perichole,* which turned up in the stores under the RCA Victor label: there was some small print I hadn't noticed. Ultimately, with union contracts making the cost of recording prohibitive in the United States, we simply licensed RCA Victor to use our name on recordings made in Europe. This labeling was worth little to us or to them, and long before George Moore's day all hope of income from recordings had been abandoned. In 1966, however, we did make $60,000 from a special project in which RCA distributed swatches of the gold curtain with a souvenir album of the old house.

Television was another but not dissimilar story. The opening night of the opera had been televised before my time, and

*Don Carlo* was also televised, but without sponsorship. In 1951 I established a television department within the Metropolitan Opera and engaged the William Morris Agency to be our representatives in such matters. "In view of the great importance that we believe TV is able to assume for the future of opera in the United States," I told my first end-of-season press conference, "it was felt that the Metropolitan Opera should be in on the ground floor and should indeed as time passes take the lead in the development of this new art: TV opera." That fall John Gutman priced out three studio productions for the Dumont network—Mozart's *Abduction* for $35,000, Ravel's *L'Heure Espagnole* for $32,000, and *Barber of Seville* for $34,000. Dumont bought none of them. Another prospect for this period was the CBS color-television system, which had been approved by the Federal Communications Commission, but before we could get much beyond the talking stage, CBS decided not to proceed with the development of this service.

In 1952–53 we explored foundation-subsidized television and closed-circuit theater television. The first turned out to be more profitable than the second. The Ford Foundation was then picking up the bills for a program called "Omnibus," and we adapted *La Bohème* and *Fledermaus* for abridged presentation in a studio. There were arguments with the unions about what we would have to pay them (especially the scenic artists and the stagehands), and arguments with the foundation about what they would have to pay us. In the end, they gave us $130,322, and we spent only $96,000, and the bookkeepers buried the embarrassingly large profit in our then-confusing accounts. In theater television, we became co-venturers with a company called Theatre Network TV, and our first presentation was the Guthrie *Carmen* with Risë Stevens, offered in some twenty-two cities across the country. Financially, this did a little better than break even, but technically it was a disaster: it was necessarily a black-and-white picture and nobody thought it was satisfactory, even though we had to perform the opera by floodlight in the opera house.

William Morris made a deal with Ed Sullivan for us, involving opera evenings just before and just after our opening night. "I'll do you a series of scenes of Vice, Horror, and Ecstasy," I told Sullivan, but he wasn't interested. Less than a month before the programs were to go on the air, Sullivan came to call on John Gutman for the first time. "What are you going to do on the shows?" Gutman asked, believing somebody in the Sullivan operation had been making plans. "I don't know," Sullivan said. "You tell me . . ." The result was a delay of some years in the execution of the contract.

We were still involved with TNT, and planned our opening night in 1954 for nationwide theater television, as a potpourri of the first act of *La Bohème,* the second act of *Barber,* and the first two acts of *Aida.* I wrote to Roberto Bauer, asking him to mollify del Monaco, who had been promised the honor of opening night and now found himself forced to share it with Tucker. Highlights rather than a complete work made sense, I argued, for "the large audiences in the provinces, most of whom have never in their lives heard of opera." John Gutman hated the results, but I thought they were promising, and I urged my associates in speaking to the press to take the "basic line" that "provided the unions will on further occasions be as helpful and co-operative as they were this time this could be developed into an important source of revenue for the Metropolitan." But the unions were not helpful, the economics of the situation proved less attractive than I had hoped, and we never tried theater television again. Twice we were able to sell television rights to occasions at Lincoln Center: opening night netted us $50,000, and my farewell Gala brought $65,000.

The major venture (and major failure) was the tour assembled for the second year of *Fledermaus* to exploit the extraordinary success of the production in my debut year. While we were first talking about it, I was approached by Sol Hurok with the proposal that he would book this second company on tour, siphoning off in the process a considerable fraction of our anticipated profits. When I said I thought we could take care of this problem ourselves, having recently staffed up to book our own spring tour (a task he had performed in previous years), Hurok decided to assemble a *Fledermaus* company of his own and to offer it around the country in competition with ours. A number of the singers he engaged had been associated with the Metropolitan in past years, and local managers in several places identified them as Metropolitan Opera artists, thereby further confusing the issue. After the immense publicity given to our production, in any event, the name *Fledermaus* carried for many people a clear connotation of the name Metropolitan. We were, in other words, touring in competition with ourselves.

And 1951–52 was the heyday of McCarthyism. Jack Gilford, who had been so able a comedian for us in New York, was one of the few regulars from the original company we could release for the tour, and we were delighted to have him. But somehow his name had gotten into one of the little red books that were then the Bible for American anti-Communists, and almost everywhere we went some local American Legion post was engaged in propagandizing against our production, accusing Gilford and the Metropolitan and me and probably Johann Strauss of God-knows-what. Reginald Allen apparently once told Quaintance Eaton that the *Fledermaus* tour "was not the failure everyone thought it—We didn't lose our shirts. We merely pulled the string after twenty-two instead of thirty-one weeks." But I'm afraid we really did lose our shirts. Columbia Records, which could hope to benefit from the tour by selling more copies of its recording of the operetta, had put up $70,000 for production expenses, to be repaid out of the profits of the tour. Not a penny was repaid to Columbia, and by the time we got everything untangled the loss to the Metropolitan Opera, over and above the Columbia subsidy, was $108,000. We did not try ever again to make money by touring second companies.

These were the ventures of the Sloan years, when I was under constant budget pressure—at one point in 1952 the board even, insultingly, questioned whether the Metropolitan should pay for my annual spring trip to Europe. I wrote to Wadmond,

Some directors are of the opinion, as I happen to be a European myself, that the Association is expected to pay for my personal pleasure and holiday trips and that these visits, in fact, are not much more than my private visits to Europe.

I have since looked a little more closely into the situation and find, which no doubt everyone on the Board knows, that Mr. Gatti-Casazza went to Europe every single year of his long tenure as General Manager . . . When . . . Mr. Johnson took over in 1935 it was too late for him then to go to Europe that particular year, but he did go in 1936, 1937 and 1938. Obviously, he could not be expected to go in the summer of 1939 when world war was very nearly upon us. Naturally, he did not go during the war . . . Equally naturally, he did not go in 1946 or 1947 because it would obviously have been impossible to start importing former enemy singers as quickly as that . . . Mr. Johnson did go to Europe in 1948 and his representative, Mr. St. Leger, went in 1949.

It is quite clear that a European visit is an absolutely essential tool of the General Manager of the Metropolitan Opera . . . I don't think I am unreasonable if I say that I am not prepared to engage singers I have not heard myself . . .

and I went on in that vein for three more pages. I marvel today at my docility under attack.

Halfway through my first season, the Metropolitan board

launched a $750,000 fund-raising campaign; by the end of my second season, the money was almost all gone. The 1951–52 budget of $3.5 million was overspent by $172,000, which was in percentage terms the most seriously erroneous budget I offered before the first season in Lincoln Center, and our deficit was $361,000. I wrote to Reggie Allen: "I am as mystified as you are. There is no possible excuse why Orchestra, Chorus and Ballet salaries should be so far out, in fact should be out at all . . ." Later it turned out that the estimates given to me for budget purposes had omitted some items of expense and counted one income item twice. Fortunately, the next year one expense item was counted twice, so that our estimated deficit of $220,000 turned out to be only $160,000.

It was not until the remarkably able William Hadley came with George Moore in 1967 that I ever received a really clear picture of how the money flowed at the Metropolitan. We had had accountants before, but Hadley was our first real director of finance. Of course, this doesn't come for nothing—while I was put under maximum pressure to cut my artistic budget every year, the expenses of the accounting department quadrupled.

In summer 1952 I wrote Allen from the Dolomites:

Now, frankly, between you and me, I don't think the Met can be run with a deficit of much less than round about 300,000—unless, again, we have no new productions. All considered this compares not at all unfavorably with La Scala, Vienna or Berlin. It is the old story: either we are one of the world's leading opera houses or we are not. I am not at all unmindful of the fearful problem of how to raise the money, but this cannot be MY problem; I am very much afraid this terribly knotty question will have to be "had out" after my return and with my contract expiring it may not be easy. You and Max [Rudolf] may be able to hint the difficulties when you see Mrs. B[elmont] in Maine. Please try to dispel the notion that

I am "stubborn"—I am not and you and Max can testify how I with you and Max worry about finance but I am responsible for the artistic standard of the House, which IS the reputation, international reputation, by which it lives . . .

That December, angrily, Sloan put through a $1.5 million fund-raising campaign, partly to pay for modernizing some parts of the house, partly for what he considered my extravagances in running it. The decision to proceed with the campaign was taken concurrently with the decision to give me a new three-year contract. Even so, though I had told Spofford when I agreed to come that the Met absolutely needed five new productions a year for some years to regain its artistic quality, I had been held to four productions in 1950–51 and 51–52 and cut back to only three in 1952–53—and in early 1953 I was told that I could have none at all for 1953–54. When I got the board to overrule its chairman and approve new productions for the coming season, I established the situation that made the middle ten years of my tenure so much easier than the first or last six.

Nevertheless, Sloan did not give up easily. In the spring of 1953 he made a trip to Vienna, and returned with advice for the Metropolitan Opera community:

. . . We of the Metropolitan have much to learn—we, the Directors and Management—we the artists and stagehands—we the opera-going public of New York City, and we the radio listeners throughout the United States and Canada.

The public must not expect or demand too much in these difficult times in the way of splendor or grandeur in scenery and costumes so long as it enjoys glorious voices on the stage supported by one of the finest opera orchestras in the world.

The singers, members of the orchestra, chorus and ballet, must play their part even to the point of making sacrifices . . . they must acquire a better understanding of the overall financial difficulties and do their part . . .

The stagehands must come to understand that they too are an important part of the whole and that this whole cannot exist if they make excessive demands . . .

As Management and as Directors we must dedicate ourselves anew to this great task of preserving the Metropolitan for our community and our nation and it is imperative that we do so in the most economical manner without impairing artistic standards . . .

Note especially the idea that the public "must not expect or demand," as though purveyors of entertainment can give orders to the public. That fundamental failure to comprehend the nature of the theater is what I was dealing with then, and in my last years had to deal with again.

Meanwhile, on the other side, I was confronted with furious complaints from Eugene Berman about my "parsimoniousness," and with anger from Peter Brook and Rolf Gérard at my insistence, for example, that they pay from their own small fees the costs of having a technical assistant fly from London to the south of France to bring them models of the sets for *Faust* and hear their criticisms. The sort of cheese-paring we did can be measured, perhaps, by my request to Cyril Ritchard to permit some of the choristers in the first act of the Berman-designed *Barber of Seville* to be dressed as beggars rather than as strolling musicians, "because we could use some of the innumerable beggars' costumes from Berman's *Forza del Destino*" and save on costume costs.

The eventual *modus vivendi*, arrived at under the leadership of Tony Bliss, was that the Metropolitan operation would be expected to balance its books on a basis that the costs of new productions would not be included in the debit ledger (for new productions were, after all, capital investments)—but routine contributions from board members, subscribers, and friends would be counted with box office and rental receipts when mak-

[ 323 ]

ing up the credit ledger. New productions would have to be financed by the contributions of the Guild and the National Council (an outside-New York group of large contributors formed by Mrs. Belmont in 1953), and by any individuals or corporations we could find who were willing to make gifts for this purpose.

The first such gift for a production, of course, had been Nin Ryan's family's for my debut *Don Carlo*. The next came in 1955–56, when Martha Baird Rockefeller, who had been a concert pianist before she married John D. Rockefeller, Jr., paid for a production of *The Magic Flute*. Thereafter, I believe Mrs. Rockefeller gave us at least one new production every year, and two productions in many seasons. It was a comfortable relationship. I would call on her and say, "You know, my dream has been to complete the cycle of the Verdi Shakespeare operas. We don't have a *Falstaff*. I have Bernstein and Zeffirelli, so-and-so to sing—can you help us?" And she would say, "Of course."

When Mrs. Rockefeller died in 1971, she left the Metropolitan a bequest of $5 million. It was said in the New York *Times* that this legacy marked her approval of the appointment of Mr. Gentele as my successor, but with all respect to all concerned the will establishing this gift had been drawn long before Mrs. Rockefeller ever heard his name. She and I got on very well, I believe. I cherish a copy of a letter Mrs. Rockefeller once wrote to Mrs. Belmont on the subject of the productions her gifts had financed, in which she said that they gave "evidence (if more were needed, which it is not) of Mr. Bing's rare perception, judgment and leadership in one of the most complicated positions in the world of music."

There were many other individual donors—Mrs. DeWitt Wallace, Mrs. Albert Lasker, Francis Goelet, John Newberry of Detroit, Mrs. Izaak Walton Killam of Montreal. Every so often we got a new production because someone had a special, unexpected interest—like Cornelius Starr, a New York insurance executive who was appalled by the fact that cherry blossoms and chrysanthemums were presented side by side in our old *Madame Butterfly*, and commissioned a real Japanese *Butterfly* from which such horticultural solecisms would vanish. In 1963–64, in what may turn out to have been a major breakthrough, American Export/Isbrandtsen Lines put up $110,000 for a new production of *Aida*; and a few years later Eastern Airlines put up half a million dollars for the *Ring* cycle Günther Schneider-Siemssen would design for Herbert von Karajan.

Every so often there was a gift we could not take. McNair Ilgenfritz, a box holder at the opera and amateur composer, left the Metropolitan $75,000 on condition that we produce one of his one-act operas. I had what still seems to me the ingenious idea of doing it in a studio for television, which would have been cheap, and would very likely have been salable because the story was big in the press and a large public would have been curious. But my legal advisers didn't like the idea at all, and we let the $75,000 go.

We continued, of course, to explore the possibilities for added income. New productions became Guild benefits at higher prices, and there were frequent galas to benefit the house. In 1964 we made a deal with National General, a new Hollywood film-producing company, to make a movie of our production of *Turandot* with Nilsson, Price, and Corelli, each of whom was ultimately paid $5,000 for her or his courtesy in granting an option for a film National General finally decided not to make. Many of these ideas were just foolish. Moore came back from his house in Spain in 1968 with a neighbor who is a film director, both of them very excited about making a movie of *La Bohème* set in the Paris student revolt. I said, "Where are there two bars of revolutionary music in *La Bohème*? What music are they going to throw rocks by? You can't add music to a Puccini opera, not with the Metropolitan name on it while I am general manager of the Metropolitan."

In 1968 NHK, the Japanese television network, taped a live performance of *Barber of Seville,* at a small profit to the house, though the hopes of selling the tape throughout the world were soon disappointed. There were also outside sources of income that few people, for some reason, ever mentioned—most notably, the Texaco-sponsored Saturday afternoon broadcasts, which members of the board seemed to regard as natural and inevitable. A poster based on one of the Chagall murals brought in $60,000; and the Metropolitan may receive as much as $100,000 as its share of the proceeds of an art book based on the Chagall *Magic Flute.*

But with the accession of George Moore and the return of the bankers to a dominant position on the Metropolitan board, we are once again concentrating on mass-communications gimmickry that should somehow solve all our problems. Krawitz put endless hours into negotiating with all the unions so that we could offer Metropolitan productions for theater television once again—at a hoped-for profit to the company, if all went well, of $25,000 for each of two performances. There has been much talk and much negotiating about cable television, TV cassettes, and other miraculous devices. I hope I can be pardoned for not believing in it.

Together with the prayerful invocation of such outside revenues there came a renewal of ignorant attacks on me and my associates for our alleged wastefulness. I was always being asked why we trim our costumes with real fur, when of course we *didn't* trim our costumes with real fur, or why the chorus ladies wore real diamonds, when of course there wasn't a costume in the house where the jewelry was anything but glass or plastic. The greatest singers of the world don't fit easily into blue jeans. It takes a great effort to clothe Montserrat Caballé well, and that effort must always be expensive. Also, a high order of sturdiness is necessary for any costume that is going to have to be packed up in trunks right after each use on the Metropolitan spring tour. In truth, the best quality is the cheapest way for the Metropolitan to produce opera over the long run: the price of Eugene Berman's *Rigoletto* costumes scandalized my board in 1951, but we were still using those costumes, and they still looked good after well over one hundred wearings, in 1972. Ultimately, as I kept telling the board, if the Metropolitan Opera wishes to put on City Opera productions it will have to charge City Opera rather than Metropolitan Opera prices.

Moore could not believe there is a basic unbridgeable difference between a theater and a bank or a rug factory, because the human element is 100,000 per cent more at an opera house. He sent around poor fellows who had never been on a stage before to analyze every motion everybody made on our stage. They were there for weeks, at a cost of thousands of dollars, following the men around—the heads of my departments wanted to quit—and finally they had little to recommend.

Planning the 1972–73 season which Mr. Gentele has inherited, I was told again, for the first time in almost twenty years, that there could be no new productions. We had *Siegfried* already built, left over from the year of the big strike, when Karajan canceled, so that didn't count. And when Mr. Gentele signed on he was permitted, as a mark of grace, a single new production for his opening night. Since then there has been talk about any number of new productions to be given under his management, but very little talk about where the money is coming from. My last year as general manager was disfigured by incessant and severe pressure to take as much as $1 million off the artistic budget, and every time I said this simply could not be done I was screamed at. Moore like Sloan before him underestimated our obligation to the patron paying high prices to sit in the Metropolitan Opera, presumably in hopes of witnessing a great performance, not an economical one.

My concern for the future of the Metropolitan is that succeeding managements, being so new here, may not have the strength to stand up against the truly unceasing clamor of the bankers. It has been hard enough for me recently, and I had twenty-two years of experience at it. I have in my time added up a budget for a planned season and found there were too many performances by top-priced artists, too many big productions needing extra stagehands and orchestra and chorus; and in the interests of the survival of the house I have changed some of the names—"cooked with water a little bit," as we said in the planning sessions. But in general, as a guiding principle, I believed and insisted that quality will find sponsors, that by making Metropolitan productions as good as they can be the general manager ultimately secures rather than damages the future of the house.

I put much of this in a letter to Lowell Wadmond on March 24, 1952; and for the benefit of my successor, his board, and the public I think large parts of that letter still bear reprinting:

> I find myself greatly worried and am anxious for your advice. I cannot overlook the fact that important members of the Board, including our Chairman, are deeply concerned about certain aspects of my management; in fairness to myself perhaps I might confine the statement to say "about one aspect of my management"—finance.
>
> I am acutely aware of the Metropolitan's financial situation and I don't think that any of the directors can out-do me in worry and concern about this situation. Indeed, I think it would not be wrong if I said that I am spending about sixty to seventy per cent of my time dealing with administrative and financial matters instead of spending that amount of time on artistic problems.
>
> I have the feeling that there is a basic difference in outlook

and if you will permit me I would like to try in this letter to analyze the situation, at least to clear my own mind.

An opera organization can be run on an expensive level or on a cheap level. I am trying to run the Metropolitan Opera, deliberately and with conviction, on the expensive level. However, on either level operations can be conducted extravagantly or economically. I also believe that I am conducting our affairs on their expensive level in an economic manner. I also believe, however, that important members of the Board consider the fact that our operations are on an expensive level already as extravagant. That, I think, is the basic point of difference. Therefore, however important an addition to the budget of $30,000 or so may be, this would not solve the basic question of approach to the whole problem of the level on which the Metropolitan Opera's management should be conducted.

The question of whether an operation like ours is run extravagantly or economically is answered by the facts of whether people are overpaid, whether there are too many people in various departments, whether time or materials are wasted, etc. etc. I submit that my management can stand up very well to any such inquiry . . .

One of the main points at issue between some members of the Board and myself is the question of new productions and the large expense involved in such new productions. Naturally, it is the way of least resistance to say "let us cut new productions" and thereby of course save all the money involved which, indeed, may balance our budget . . . The Metropolitan Opera has had great conductors before my time, it has had great singers before my time, and in spite of all that it had fallen to a level where it ceased to be a theatre of great artistic interest . . .

The enormous success accorded to our new productions and the almost exaggerated interest suddenly shown in the Metropolitan Opera, both nationally and internationally, speak pretty clearly that changes were overdue and are welcomed even though individuals may disapprove of individual measures, which is only natural . . . [Yet] I still have the impression that some members of the Board seem to think that the new productions are more or less a private fancy of mine and that in particular I wanted these vehicles to show off my own ability for what it may be worth. These members of the Board do not seem to recognize that I do not look upon these productions as my special toys but as the basic artistic necessity to revitalize the Metropolitan and to make it what it once was and what it should be—the world's leading opera house. I hope I may feel that the beginning of my efforts in that respect have at least shown that I am on the right way.

Now, Mr. Sloan very rightly has taken up my statement at a recent committee meeting that I don't think that $50,000 per production is an adequate figure . . . The whole difference arises from—if I may be forgiven for saying it—what is in my view a wrong approach to the budget. It is unrealistic to say "here are $150,000, and now go ahead and make three productions." The only realistic way is to ask what three new productions will cost and then provide the funds accordingly. I am greatly distressed that in this year's budget the $200,000 figure originally provided for new productions will appear considerably overspent; but again it is not a question of having spent recklessly, carelessly or extravagantly. If you only had the time I could prove to you in innumerable cases where and how we have cut expenses and saved money but—and this brings me to the first part of my letter—we are of course operating on an expensive level and this is the basic question. I have come here under the impression that I was supposed to manage the world's leading opera house in the world's capital within the world's most important country. This is not only a privilege but it is a great responsibility with many obligations. These obligations as I see them, and I admit this frankly, are in the first place artistic. The Metropolitan Opera will be judged by future critics on its artistic merits and not on deficits or profits.

. . . I have very deep and, I hope you will believe me, sincere convictions about the running of artistic organizations, and I have assumed my present job with enthusiasm and a deep feeling for my responsibilities. I now find myself in a conflict between what apparently the Board expects of me and what I feel is in the best artistic interests of the House. This is a serious situation which I cannot take lightly and I wonder whether you can let me have your friendly views and advice.

Today the figures seem ludicrously small. I had to abandon a *Boris Godunov* for which Mrs. Wallace had given me $300,000 because the costs were going to be closer to $500,000. Yet the principle remains the same: it is still a scandal that the greatest opera house in the richest country in the world cannot mount a production of *Boris Godunov* to the proper artistic standards. The press has leaked the fact that my successor plans to mount Berlioz' *The Trojans,* next to which *Boris Godunov* is a chamber opera. I hope those who must take over from him in the current emergency will be able to carry out those plans.

# 27

In the middle of the worst crisis of the fall of 1966, when I was not certain we would have the money to meet the next week's payroll, I had to keep in the back of my mind the eternal negotiations we had undertaken to secure the services of Herbert von Karajan at the Metropolitan Opera, an arrangement that could explode in all directions at any moment.

I had first heard Karajan's work when Walter Legge, the English recording company executive who is Elisabeth Schwarzkopf's husband, brought him to London for his Philharmonia Orchestra, and of course I understood from the start that Karajan was a conductor of extraordinary quality. In the 1950s, however, I had arrogated to myself at the Metropolitan the authority to decide who had been and who had not been too touched with the Nazi brush to work in New York. Flagstad I knew had done nothing wrong; Furtwängler had been cleared, for me, by Yehudi Menuhin, whose judgment I profoundly trusted. Miss Schwarzkopf and Karajan had been described to me as having done more than was necessary.

But of course both had been very young in the Hitler days, and, as noted above, with the passage of time these scars healed even with the New York public. Karajan did very well without the Metropolitan, becoming undoubtedly the leading musical figure of Europe. In the later 1950s he became head of both the Vienna Staatsope and the Salzburg Festival (a position offered to me before it was offered to him, though he did not know that), and then he was also conductor of the Berlin Philharmonic and of the Orchestre de Paris and a regular conductor at La Scala and God knows what else. As boss of the Vienna Opera, he undertook to stage and especially to plan the lighting for many of the performances he conducted. He developed a theory that lighting was the visual correspondence to the music, and essential to the interpretation of opera, a theory which I must admit I could never take very seriously. Once after one of his most murky performances in Vienna—I believe it was a *Tristan*—he told me that he had had eight full-length lighting rehearsals for it. I said, "I could have got it that dark with one."

After I had decided to engage Miss Schwarzkopf I began making serious efforts to engage Karajan, who in the meantime had set off a major explosion in the musical world of Austria and left his posts there. Of course, he would not come to New York for any ordinary production, and I had to worry about the reaction of others in a repertory house if I gave him the kind of extraordinary treatment he would certainly demand— not to mention my constant concern about costs. Ideally, one wished him as a conductor, not as a director and lighting designer, which meant asking him to work with a director of sufficient strength to intrigue him artistically and balance him in personality. My first attempt was, I thought, very imaginative. Karajan had one major rival for the laurel of world's sexiest conductor: Leonard Bernstein. Bernstein had just given us a triumphant *Falstaff*, but had declared he would not return to conduct it the next season. Given the rivalry inherent in the somewhat parallel situations of the two men, I thought it might be possible to intrigue Karajan with the chance of taking over Zeffirelli's *Falstaff* and doing it even better. I asked my agent in northern Europe, Alfred Diez, to sound Karajan out delicately on the question. To my horror and annoyance, Diez wrote him a letter—which, as I told Diez, I could easily have done myself—and the answer to the letter was of course negative.

Negotiations were now opened, in a sense. I offered Karajan a *La Bohème* in the new house, again with Zeffirelli directing and designing, and failing that a *Trovatore*. Both proposals were refused, but Karajan was clearly interested in doing something at the new Metropolitan Opera House. Wagner was of course a possibility, though it might mean taking him on as director and lighting man, which I had hoped to avoid. In March 1965 I wrote cautiously, "I would not suggest one of the *Ring* operas unless you would be willing to commit yourself to do the whole *Ring* over a period of three or four years . . ."

As it happened, Karajan was planning what he considered his definitive statement of the *Ring*. It was a multi-piece jigsaw puzzle, involving recording sessions with the Berlin Philharmonic, where he could rehearse the artists at the expense of Deutsche Grammophon; four annual first performances with the casts of the recordings at his own Easter Festival in Salzburg; perhaps some film or television sessions; and then repetitions by the same casts at the Grand Théâtre in Geneva, where my former colleague Herbert Graf had become general manager. Then something, I never knew what, went wrong in Geneva— perhaps there wasn't enough money, perhaps Karajan was disappointed with the Orchestre de la Suisse Romande, which plays in the pit at that house. One day in Paris I received a call to my hotel room from Karajan. His Geneva plans had fallen through; would I be interested in his *Ring?* I said I would be interested in anything that brought him to the Met.

The *Ring* operas were among the few works that had been restaged in the last years of the Johnson regime, in rather unfortunate settings that assumed the Rhine had to look at least a little like the Hudson. I had done only two complete *Ring* cycles in my years at the Metropolitan, partly because I was unhappy with the productions, partly because it was so difficult to assemble a satisfactory cast—and so costly when the cast was gathered. The work on the four operas of the *Ring* was at least the equivalent of the work on six other operas, and I expected at least six or seven performances a season of any work we revived (more of almost anything newly produced). But one cannot do more than three *Ring* cycles, plus perhaps two or three extra *Walküres* and *Götterdämmerungs*—at most, eighteen performances, as against thirty-five to forty performances at least for an equivalent amount of work on other operas in the repertory. In general, the artists engaged for the *Ring* will not be available for other operas in an Italian-oriented house like the Metropolitan, and the *Ring* being the extremely arduous labor that it is they cannot be asked to sing too many *Ring* performances in too brief a time. Considering the weakness of our settings and the severe shortage of singers of true Wagnerian strength, the game did not seem worth playing. But in the new house, with Karajan doing it, the *Ring* could be the crown of our repertory.

Of course, we would have to make major concessions. Though all the expenses would be ours (we could scarcely expect our unions to let us import Karajan's Salzburg sets, which would not fit anyway, the proscenium in Salzburg being forty feet wider than the one at the Met), these productions would have to be Karajan's productions, not Metropolitan productions. Historically, I had always said that I controlled casting at the Metropolitan Opera, but in fact, for conductors like Monteux, Ansermet, and Böhm, I had taken advice. Now I had to go a step further, and give Karajan veto power. We were particularly eager to have him use American singers for his Valkyries, to save us travel expense and to maintain a degree of Metropolitan Opera presence, and Karajan agreed to come to New York in November 1965 to complete contract negotiations for the four years of building the cycle (starting in 1967) and to audition Metropolitan artists. There was one stipulation from me: Birgit Nilsson was the world's greatest Brünnhilde and a great heroine to the New York operatic public. Any new *Ring* cycle we did would have to feature Miss Nilsson. Karajan agreed, although he knew that she was in process of recording the *Ring* with Solti and would not be available for his recordings.

Unfortunately, in making these plans we had rather forgotten about Miss Nilsson's own preferences and priorities. The fact is that she and Karajan do not like each other: the chemistry is wrong. In December 1965, while we were basking in the sun of a rather successful Karajan visit and a signed contract, a letter arrived from Miss Nilsson to Bob Herman:

. . . Finally, let me say a word about the great maestro, who gave me the honor of his visit here in my hotel, last week. The way I understand it, there are three things taking place, which make up together his big project: performances at Salzburg, at the Met, and recordings. As you know, I have recorded *Walküre* (Brünnhilde) last month, and so I cannot do it again at the moment. I have therefore suggested to sing Sieglinde on the record, and Brünnhilde at the Met and in Salzburg. However, this idea fell on negative ground with him—he hardly seemed to believe that I could sing the part at all.

There are two reasons that make me believe you will have to count on another Brünnhilde:

1) He is not willing to accept me to be part of the recording,

[ 336 ]

which is my condition if I am to participate in the other two parts of his project.

2) Before he spoke to me in Vienna, he has asked other singers to sing Brünnhilde, which shows that he is not really keen to have me.

I am sure you understand, that I only like to take part in projects, for which I am really wanted and appreciated.

I replied frantically:

I have just seen your letter to Bob dated December the eleventh from Vienna. *Please* do not penalize me and the Metropolitan for any possible annoyance you may feel about Herr von Karajan.

I made it my absolutely first condition from the very first moment this project was discussed that you should be our "Brünnhilde" and Karajan has not for one moment disputed that decision. On the contrary, he has happily and without question accepted and endorsed it. Naturally, he wanted you also to record as "Brünnhilde" and it is not his fault that you are not available for his recordings. It is for that reason that he listened to other "Brünnhildes" as he, obviously, must have another "Brünnhilde" for his recordings and, indeed, we must have another "Brünnhilde" to cover your performances.

I hope you will not make your recording "Sieglinde" a condition of doing "Brünnhilde" in Salzburg and at the Metropolitan because it is only fair and reasonable that he should have the "Sieglinde" who will sing in Salzburg and at the Metropolitan also record "Sieglinde."

As I said at the beginning, if you make this a condition which he simply is unable to accept, you are just penalizing me and the Metropolitan, and I hope and trust that this is not your intention. I am telling you here and now that if you refuse to do our "Brünnhilde" in the Karajan project, I will call off the whole project, and I really don't think this is what you can want.

[ 337 ]

Would you do me a great favor as a special Christmas present and send me a cable by return, assuring me that you will make yourself available for the Salzburg and New York "Brünnhildes" without recording the "Sieglinde" . . .

Please don't make me assure you even more than I have already how much you are wanted to do these "Brünnhildes," not only by me and all of us here and, indeed, the whole of New York, but also by Karajan. I really beg of you not to ruin this project by declining the "Brünnhilde" invitation, because ruined it will be: I am not going to do the new *Ring* without Birgit Nilsson . . .

This drew not a cable but another letter:

Many thanks for your letter concerning the new *Ring*. I must confess that I am surprised to hear that you would be willing to give up such a big project as a new *Ring* production, simply because I would not be in it. This is a little strange, since you made your arrangements with Mr. von Karajan before asking if I was available.

Mr. von Karajan had cabled me to Buenos Aires at the end of August, to ask me for his Salzburg project. I answered, as you know, that I would be interested under certain conditions. From the end of August to the end of November I heard nothing from him. In this period he was—I am told—looking for other Brünnhildes. This is of course his right to do—but if I really am so important to this project as you tell me, would it then not be normal to first clear conditions with Brünnhilde No. 1 before looking for a cover . . .

In the end Miss Nilsson did agree to sing the Brünnhildes at the Metropolitan, but not at Salzburg. This left Karajan with a problem, which he attempted to solve by demanding that we maintain two complete casts for the *Ring* operas, alternating them in performance. Dealing with Karajan was extremely difficult, because there were so many different intermediaries who had to be used for different purposes. Signor Mattoni was his personal manager, with him almost always; Herr Doktor Steffan was his business manager with whom one had to clear contracts; Monsieur Glotz in Paris was his artistic manager; and Mr. Wilford in New York handled his affairs in America. At one time or another one would hear from all of them, often with overlapping messages. The demand for a second cast seemed to me impossible: I wrote to Glotz,

> I fully understand the maestro's views, but I am afraid he must realize that he is coming to a large repertory house which geographically is completely isolated, and therefore *must* have and rely on understudies. The only exception for this rule can be made if we have equal or almost equally good casts for all parts.
>
> I cannot with the best will in the world agree that we have anything approaching equal quality in the case of "Brünnhilde" and of "Siegmund" . . . In the last resort, even with such an outstanding, prominent and famous conductor as Karajan, I will and must be responsible for what goes on in this house; as you know, I have gone along with quite a few of the maestro's casting suggestions which do not in the least agree with my own conceptions or ideas, which, indeed, I find very dangerous—but I have accepted that . . . I think that Nilsson and Vickers are recognized here, probably as the most outstanding representatives of their respective parts at this time, and, as I said, I think it would be irresponsible on my part to have them unnecessarily replaced by artists, however distinguished, but inferior in these particular parts . . .

Further correspondence with Glotz followed, but this was clearly a matter on which I would have to speak with Karajan, and I said so. On a spring Saturday in 1966 when I was on tour with the company a cable from Glotz arrived in New York:

KARAJAN WILL WAIT YOUR TELEPHONE CALL TOMORROW SATURDAY MAY 14TH BETWEEN 10 AND 11 AM EUROPEAN TIME AT HOTEL LA PACE MONTECATINI ITALY

The next day another cable arrived from Glotz:

MR BING HAS URGENTLY ASKED SALZBURG FESTSPIELHAUS
AND ME POSSIBILITY OF PERSONAL COMMUNICATION WITH
KARAJAN STOP AS I INFORMED MR BING BY CABLE YESTER-
DAY LARGELY ON TIME MR VON KARAJAN WAS READY TO
ACCEPT THIS TELEPHONE CALL THIS MORNING STOP INSTEAD
OF IT MR VON KARAJAN RECEIVED TODAY AT SEVEN PM
EUROPEAN TIME THIS TELEGRAM QUOTE REGRET BING ON
TOUR WITH COMPANY PLEASE ADVISE WHERE TELEPHONE
OR LETTER MAY REACH YOU NEXT WEEK METOPERA UN-
QUOTE STOP MAY I ADD STATEMENT THAT WE KNOW SINCE
LAST WEEK THAT MR BING IS ON TOUR AND WE KNOW
EQUALLY WELL THAT AMERICA DISPOSES OF A HIGHLY EF-
FICIENT TELEPHONE SERVICE STOP MR VON KARAJANS FIXED
CABLE ADDRESS FOR NEXT WEEK WILL BE TEATRO ALLA
SCALA MILAN ITALY

That was a little much. I wrote Karajan a letter:

I am very much troubled. I cannot continue to deal exclusively with your representatives who in my view are not making
things easier. I am not used to being asked to make telephone
calls at five in the morning, quite apart from the fact that the
telegram with that rather silly suggestion arrived five hours later
than the stipulated time—regardless of the fact that I happened not to be in New York.

What is much more important and much more disturbing is
that in my letter of April twenty-seventh I have asked what I
consider not only important but totally legitimate questions
. . . The way this whole problem has been handled, or rather
not been handled, does not give me confidence in the future.

It is for that reason that, at this late hour, I must ask you,
completely clearly and frankly, whether you feel it is wise for
us to go through with this plan. I am more and more convinced
that you are unused and unwilling to adapt yourself to the
conditions that, unfortunately, must prevail at a large repertory

theatre and that cannot give you the supreme artistic control which you enjoyed in Vienna, in Salzburg, and certainly with all your orchestras and other associations, but which you cannot, to the same degree, exercise at the Metropolitan Opera . . .

It is an unhappy situation, and the final decision in the circumstances must be yours . . . No copies of this letter have been sent to anyone else . . .

When this letter produced no answer, I sent a telegram asking whether he wanted to announce the cancellation of the *Ring* project or wished me to do so. That produced a telegram in reply, to the effect that he had indeed cabled me at his earliest opportunity, not having been at La Scala as Glotz thought, and had sent a letter of full reply to the hotel where I would be staying in Paris at the end of May (this being the year of our appearance at the Odéon). The letter said that he still preferred two separate casts, and believed

that you fare better with this solution. First and foremost, the competition which exists between two casts is always raising them to a higher artistic level. Secondly, the feeling of safety in having two casts adds much to the tranquillity of the whole enterprise. This is, on another level, the reason why I prefer a twin-engine airplane. And although you refer in your letter to the Metropolitan Opera as a repertory theatre, you will doubtless agree with me when I tell you that when and wherever I conduct, my approach to my work is based on a standard of a festival *en permanence*.

Now, as you do not share my view on this fact, have it your way . . .

This was a most useful and interesting letter, proving (what we had not known for sure) that Karajan really did want to do his *Ring* in New York, and really was prepared to compromise when absolutely necessary. There were still moments of trouble about casting—after asking us to offer Thomas Stewart the first

Wotan, he then personally offered it to Walter Berry in Vienna, which caused no end of correspondence and telephoning right in the middle of our crisis weeks in fall 1966—but the really major casting problems were now solved.

The production problems, however, still lay ahead of us. In February 1967 Günther Schneider-Siemssen, who was to design the *Ring* for Karajan in both Salzburg and New York, came to the Metropolitan with final drawings which horrified my technical staff. I cabled Karajan:

AFTER SLEEPLESS NIGHTS AND MANY DISCUSSIONS WITH MY COLLEAGUES MUST DISCLOSE TO YOU MOST SERIOUS CONCERN ABOUT DIMENSIONS AND WORKABILITY RING DESIGN STOP ENORMOUSLY IMPRESSED BY BEAUTIFUL CONCEPTION BUT FEAR THAT MAGNITUDE OF PRODUCTION NOT MANAGEABLE FOR REPERTORY HOUSE WITH LATE AFTERNOON STAGE REHEARSALS EVERY DAY AND MATINEE PERFORMANCES SATURDAY STOP PARTICULARLY AS RING PROGRESSES AM TERRIFIED OF CONSEQUENCES FAR BEYOND MERE EXPENSE STOP SCHNEIDER SIEMSSEN WHO WAS MOST HELPFUL WILL EXPLAIN TO YOU IN GREATER DETAIL BUT I FEAR WE SIMPLY MUST ASK NOT JUST FOR SIMPLIFICATIONS BUT FOR DRASTIC ALTERATION OF BASIC CONCEPT WHICH WILL MAKE THESE PRODUCTIONS FIT INTO COMPLICATED REPERTORY PLEASE ADVISE REGARDS

This called again for Karajan's personal intervention. After talking the problems over with Schneider-Siemssen, he yielded to our need for a less monumental tree in the first act of *Walküre* but refused to compromise on the basic structure for Acts II and III. Karajan wrote reassuringly that "we found out that after the manufacturing process is done the whole thing is not complicated, is well manageable and quite simple to operate." But on the lighting difficulties he would neither reassure me nor yield an inch:

. . . It is the visual part of the interpretation of the music and needs precision . . . After thirty years of concentration and experience with the *Ring* and after three years of preparatory work with Schneider-Siemssen this artistic conception presents my innermost thoughts on the work itself. For the first time I will present to American audiences my idea of producing and directing an opera, and I think that they are entitled to see the opera as it was originally conceived and agreed upon. In all fairness I therefore have to state that I am unable to change this production which must be done as it was . . . conceived . . .

Now it was my turn to yield, in fear and trembling. The extra expense that could be involved in extra lighting crews and extra time for them, extra stagehands, extra storage and trucking could well run to many tens of thousands of dollars in each year that we produced the *Ring*. Bob Herman, Rudy Kuntner, our technical chief, and David Reppa, our construction chief, went to Salzburg for Karajan's *Walküre*, and to my great relief came back enthusiastic about the performance and sanguine about our chances of mounting it without wrecking everything else in our season. Kuntner thought we could achieve with our largest lamps (5 kw. at 110 volts) the effects Karajan had achieved in Salzburg with his largest lamps (10 kw. at 220 volts). Karajan suggested an experiment—"One of the six projectors which must be on the lighting bridge should be set up in the Metropolitan so that it strikes the most distant playing surface indicated in the lighting plan. There the intensity should be measured with a light meter and I can then say exactly on the basis of the comparison of measurements in our house, if the values are equal." They were not equal, and the Metropolitan spent some thousands of dollars to equip our projectors with 10-kw. lamps, which are not manufactured in the United States . . . What was especially annoying about the expenditure was that the new lamps were to be used not to give us additional radiance but to make more complex the effect derived from shining a light through an almost opaque slide. Nevertheless, Rudy Kuntner later told me that there *was* a difference of effect: Karajan knew what he was doing.

To make sure we would not have a blowup in the fall, we suggested to Karajan that Schneider-Siemssen and Klaus Lehnhoff, Karajan's assistant, come to New York in August to supervise the setting up of the basic lighting apparatus, and that he himself make a flying visit to be sure everything was ready for the intensive work he would wish to do when he came to prepare the performance. He agreed, suggesting in addition that we engage an associate of his from Salzburg to work in the lighting booth, which we refused to do unless he was willing to pay the man, which he wasn't. Then the Friday and Saturday arranged for his visit in August turned out to be days when he wanted to make recordings at his home studio in St. Moritz, and those were the only days we could offer—the next week we had to begin work, by contract with others, on our new production of Gounod's *Roméo et Juliette*. Karajan suggested that we postpone his premiere, which was of course impossible.

Again there was much transatlantic cabling and letter writing, and again there was a compromise: we did without his presence in August and arranged four extra lighting rehearsals, at considerable overtime expense, for his time in New York. A minor storm blew up in September, when we discovered almost by accident that Schneider-Siemssen had not done the costumes himself: Karajan had contracted their design out to George Wakhevitch, who would have to be given credit on all the bills we were about to print, and would also have to receive a fee—from us.

But eventually, in October, Karajan did arrive, and set to work with an intensity that can be imagined only by those who have in fact watched this great conductor in rehearsal, the talent and artistry, industry and professionalism that come together in one artistic unit. The level of tension rose in the house the moment it was known he had entered the door, but the results were good. Everyone worked his best because he was working for Karajan, and it was known that Karajan paid attention to everything.

There were a few unanticipated side effects. Because Karajan raised the level of the pit higher than any other conductor had ever had it (the press, noticing something but not knowing what, thought he had brought a higher than usual podium!), all the other conductors began to feel it was a point of honor for them to raise the pit, too. At one difficult moment I rather wished I had agreed to let him bring his man to the lighting booth. Lighting instructions cannot go from the designer to the men under American union procedures: they must pass through Kuntner. But that is all to the good, because Kuntner keeps a meticulous book from which (with counterpoint from the stage manager's book) any production can be re-created after its inventor has departed. With Karajan the system was complicated, because at several rehearsals he was conducting the orchestra and studying the lighting at the same time. Then he operated by passing his instructions to Lehnhoff, who crouched beside him at the podium and relayed them to Kuntner, who would in turn tell the men. "More light on Wotan!" Karajan said to Lehnhoff. "More light on Wotan!" Lehnhoff said into the telephone to Kuntner. "More light on Wotan!" Kuntner said into the mike to the man in the booth, whose mike, unfortunately, was live into the house. "Who," he wanted to know, "is Wotan?" I was in the hall; I fled.

Everyone came to respect Karajan very highly. He was magical with the orchestra, and extremely helpful to the singers, giving them every cue. He has phenomenal technical ability and can follow singers almost uniquely well when he wants to, which he usually does. There is never a fight during a performance; it just cannot happen with Karajan. He is also now a respectable stage technician. Kuntner had started with the normal craftsman's scorn for the dilettante, going off to Salzburg with a chip on his shoulder. I expected trouble; there could be trouble between Kuntner and directors much less demanding than Karajan. The normal course of events was that the director or designer came to me and complained, and I called Kuntner in and said, "Rudy, I'm sure it's silly, but try it." Karajan handled Kuntner perfectly, and he became a partner—not just a collaborator—in all Karajan's electrical effects.

Nevertheless, the house was always under a shadow while Karajan was there, because there was always fear mixed with the respect. I never established personal contact with him. He is very shy and I am very shy, and none of the usual procedures can be used. You offer him a cigarette, he says he doesn't smoke. You offer him a drink, he doesn't drink. Let's have lunch; he never has lunch. When he returned the next fall to add *Das Rheingold* to his *Die Walküre* and the first-act rehearsal for *Die Walküre* did not come up to his expectations, he did not come in to me to discuss his problem but called his manager. I got a letter from Ron Wilford: "Maestro von Karajan has just telephoned me concerning the dress rehearsal for the first part of *Walküre* at the Metropolitan today. He asked me to write you in his behalf and to inform you that the standard of today's rehearsal was not acceptable to him." It is hard to develop any great feelings of warmth when collaborative work is done on that basis.

*Die Walküre* had been a somewhat smaller conception of the work than we were used to in New York (*Das Rheingold* was, I thought, better scaled), and Miss Nilsson had felt her warrior Brünnhilde somewhat out of place. She was also annoyed at the fact that in Karajan's staging she had to sing the *Todesver-kündigung* scene from a perch about fifty feet back from the proscenium. After the 1968–69 *Walküre* she made a wry comment or two about the hardships of working with a humorless man like Karajan, and something got into the papers. Karajan wrote me to protest my failure to rebuke Miss Nilsson, and to demand that she publicly acknowledge her complete satisfaction with his musical and artistic direction. Trying to duck out from between them, I made the great mistake of noting in a letter to him that, after all, their disputes predated their time together at the Metropolitan. I then heard from Wilford: "The Maestro says that this statement is simply not true—in his fifteen years of collaboration with Miss Nilsson he had not had any disagreement." But if the lady "does not wish to express her regrets for the statements attributed to her by the press, it means that she considers herself as being outside the team of artists involved with Maestro von Karajan's artistic world."

It is hard to know what would have happened to the rest of the *Ring* project if there had been no strike. Karajan wanted to postpone the *Götterdämmerung*, and thus the completion of the *Ring* cycle, because no one tenor could handle two cycles of the two Siegfrieds in the time scale of Salzburg, and only one currently active tenor (Jess Thomas) was both qualified for and willing to take the assignment. When the 1969 strike reached into the period in which Karajan was to do the three Wagner operas, he assured me that he was remaining available, which was a human touch, but then the strike ended and he wasn't available. He also inquired—a very human touch, for which I am grateful—about the possibility of his participating in the Bing Gala which rang down the curtain on my administration of the Metropolitan. Obviously, he should return to the house, and perhaps someday he will.

The dispute between Karajan and Miss Nilsson greatly reduced the time Miss Nilsson allocated for the Metropolitan in the 1971–72 season in which the *Ring* was to be completed. From an originally planned eighteen or twenty performances, she cut us down to eight. But those eight, with the *Ring* cycle postponed, gave us the glorious new *Tristan und Isolde* that won over even the press during my final season, so perhaps everything worked out for the best.

Karajan was unquestionably the outstanding artistic phenomenon of my latter years at the Metropolitan. Leonard Bernstein, for all the excellence and grace of his *Falstaff,* made much less impact: his interests were entirely musical. The season of the strike, he very generously bailed out Franco Zeffirelli and myself by conducting *Cavalleria Rusticana* when Thomas Schippers was held to commitments elsewhere at the only time this new production could be mounted. Despite his background and reputation, Bernstein was curiously untheatrical. He wanted us to do *Cav* after *Pag,* to give him the final curtain, which would have been extremely difficult to explain to Richard Tucker (who would have been deprived of *his* final curtain along with conductor Fausto Cleva). But one look at that immense flight of cathedral steps on the stage for *Cavalleria* should have told Bernstein that this set could not possibly be built on a side stage and moved, or put up during the intermission between the two operas—it takes sixty minutes. When Karajan disappeared from the *Ring* project, I thought I might offer it to Bernstein, but several of the more important singers were reluctant to undertake this project with a conductor who had never been in the pit for a Wagner opera in his life. He probably would not have taken it, anyway: these productions necessarily present Karajan's vision. It will be interesting to see the extent to which Rafael Kubelik can make this *Ring* his own when he conducts it in 1974–75.

Without downgrading in the slightest the importance of such new singers as Montserrat Caballé, Mirella Freni, Martina Arroyo, Placido Domingo, Sherrill Milnes, Nicolai Ghiaurov, and Ruggero Raimondi, it seems fair to say that the most important debuts of my later years were those of conductors. In addition to Karajan and Bernstein, there were Zubin Mehta, Colin Davis, Alain Lombard, and two very young Americans, Christopher Keene and James Levine, who revitalized the *Luisa Miller* which was probably the most successful of all my efforts to restore neglected Verdi operas to the Metropolitan repertory.

Except for Karajan and perhaps Davis, all these conductors suffered to greater or less degree from lack of experience, and this problem is likely to grow worse. I went to Toronto to hear Zubin Mehta conduct *Tosca* before I engaged him, and he was *funny*—but he was clearly very talented, and the risk was worth taking. Except for *Tosca*, every opera he conducted at the Metropolitan was one he learned for the first time for that purpose. By contrast, Karajan worked two years at Ulm and two years at Aachen, conducting everything at a German repertory house; and then he was Karajan; he knew. Today talent is found too soon, and sent off to conduct difficult operas at international festivals. Instead, these boys should go two years to Magdeburg and two years to Stuttgart, and then they would be great conductors. America pays much attention to the training of singers—perhaps too much: the Metropolitan Opera Auditions have become a bore of little productivity for the company. Someone had better start paying attention to the training of conductors.

# 28

There is no doubt in my mind—none at all—that it is time for me to leave the Metropolitan Opera. When Moore and Wadmond came to me in the fall of 1970 to say that their search for my successor seemed to be stymied and to ask whether I would stay another year, I had no hesitation in telling them that it would be a bad idea for them and for me. After twenty-two years I am no longer so fascinated by the work of the general manager of the Metropolitan. The crises are predictable, and resolving them becomes more a chore and less a source of satisfaction with the passage of time. My last season's achievements were much less my own than those of twenty years before: much of the most interesting work I did in the 1950s was done in the last five years of my regime by Bob Herman and Herman Krawitz and the highly competent staff of assistants to them, a cadre that did not even exist at the Metropolitan Opera as I found it. And one no longer deals in quite the same way with the most interesting artists; now they all have corporations, and almost

[350]

the first question that is asked about any contract is its tax consequences.

I used to be at the house virtually every night, to visit artists in their dressing rooms before a performance and wish them luck, and to greet them after the first curtain calls and congratulate them; often I would stay until the very end. By my last season I was in the house for perhaps three performances a week, when there was a major novelty or an artist who expected special service, and I almost always left after an act or two. Because I was no longer always there we had established a "duty roster" of management people who were guaranteed to be available in the building as I had been years before.

Of course, if there was any thought that there might be trouble, I would go to the performance, up to the very last days. Schippers opened some cuts in *Die Meistersinger* in 1971–72, and took an expansive approach to the work, which left us in great danger of running beyond midnight even though we raised the curtain at seven-fifteen. I went backstage with a stopwatch, I told Schippers to forget about accepting applause and bowing to the audience when he first climbed the podium, I hustled the curtain calls, I made sure that the curtain rose again after the shortest possible legal intermission. The house saved more than $1,000 a night in overtime that would have been charged if the performance ran a minute beyond midnight, at the cost of several ulcers in the company.

From start to finish, I planned my working day so that I could go home between the afternoon's work and the performance, to relax with Nina and the dog; and Nina and I almost always ate alone in the apartment. We accepted very few dinner invitations and gave few dinners; our entertaining was done at the general manager's box in the opera house. It was a rather special kind of entertaining. I almost never invited to the box an active singer or conductor, and I rarely asked board members or contributors. Instead, I filled the box on most evenings with members of the diplomatic and consular communities, especially from the United Nations. As a great international house, I felt we had international obligations, and also that opera-loving diplomats, because their work kept them on the move, were unlikely to get to attend performances at our usually sold-out theater unless we invited them.

The mayor of the city also had access to the box whenever he wanted to entertain distinguished visitors. Mayor Lindsay used this service much more often than his predecessors; among the guests he brought I remember Emperor Haile Selassie, the King of Morocco, and Mme. Golda Meir. In my office, to which we would retire during an intermission when such eminent guests were in the party (among the design features of the new house is a door giving easy access from the corridor by the general manager's office to the corridor behind the boxes in the auditorium), Mayor Lindsay caught sight of a little model of a Sphinx, which Franco Zeffirelli gave me after *Antony and Cleopatra*. "Rudi," the mayor said in mock horror, when Mrs. Meir was seated, "isn't that thing Egyptian?" I said, "Yes, but it's from before the Six-Day War." When my knighthood was announced in the press, I received literally hundreds of letters from diplomats now retired or on assignment away from New York, congratulating me and remembering their evenings as guests of the general manager at the Metropolitan.

I did not live in New York, really; I lived at the opera house. Sunday, when the house was dark, I usually stayed in bed. When we did see people socially, my wife and I sought relaxation, which meant people not connected with opera or opera boards, but old friends from England and Europe. I doubt that I went to half a dozen films during the twenty-two years, and those were in the summer weeks when Nina stayed in the

Dolomites but I had to return to start work on the coming season—or to battle with the unions.

I was mugged once, in Central Park at about five o'clock of a cold Sunday afternoon. I was taking Pip for his medicinal walk when a voice behind me said, "What's the time?" I spun around because the voice was so close to my ear, and I saw a man with a knife—a large knife. He said, "Give me your money and your watch." I didn't like to give up the watch—it was a British Army watch, worth perhaps $25, which was a souvenir of my days as a fire warden during the war. I told the newspapers this, and the next day was severely rebuked at the opera house by Zinka Milanov. "The general manager of the Metropolitan Opera," she said sternly, "does not carry a watch worth only twenty-five dollars."

Another moment when I lived like every New Yorker was the power blackout of 1965, when the Metropolitan went dark like everything else. We were still in the old building. I sent everyone home, of course, but in those days we had under our wing a little private ballet school, which made a small profit for the house and contributed trained supers to productions. Many of the students were children, and I didn't see how I could send them home in the dark. With flashlights and candles I herded them all into Sherry's, the second-floor restaurant with windows onto Broadway, where the children could at least see the lights of the cars and it wouldn't seem so scary. We called the parents, who came and picked up their children. Finally, I satisfied myself that the house was empty and clear, and went out to a car that had been called for me, which took me to the Essex House. The lobby was packed; nobody who had a room above the fifth or sixth floor was walking up. I certainly wasn't walking up thirty-six flights. The manager of the hotel, not a blonde, slipped the key to a second-floor room into my hand, and I had a night's sleep.

[ 353 ]

At the house my relations were, I believe, correct with everyone and pleasant with almost everyone. Inevitably, I made enemies. It goes to the ego nerve of an artist to be told, "No, you can't do this part," and that artist does not leave the room as a friend. But though it is fashionable to say that morale was low at the Metropolitan, I never knew what that phrase was supposed to mean. Whatever meaning it did have, those who said it could not prove it, and I could not disprove it. I thought that the Metropolitan was basically a happy house, because everyone had the fundamental security of knowing what he was supposed to be doing every day. I had no social contact with the company, which meant that people could be sure there was no favoritism. Of course one likes some artists more than others—there are vibes going out all over the house all the time—but I never let these things influence me consciously. People were not lied to or played against each other. Promises were kept, and there was no politics.

I found most singers hard-working and reliable, but of course theirs is a strange situation in life. If they are mediocre artists they are living with a tragedy: it is much worse to be a mediocre artist than to be a mediocre post-office clerk. If they are great artists, they wake up one day to find themselves catapulted into enormous fame and riches. They have cover pictures in *Time* and *Newsweek*, their telephone never stops, they race from Vienna to Covent Garden to Milan to the Metropolitan, they have dinner at the White House, their income rises to $500,000 a year or even more. And for most, this apotheosis follows immediately upon almost total obscurity. Not everybody can take it. I said in a television interview that what made these people so prominent was a throat disease. That was tactless, but it is perfectly true: many singers are regarded as great artists simply because their vocal cords are not the same as yours and mine. But what this means is that their livelihood depends on two little threads in the throat: of course they're nervous. When they go onstage, they are fighting for their lives all the time.

When I moved into Edward Johnson's office, I retained his secretary, Reva Freidberg, who remained as my secretary for ten years before marriage took her to a home instead of an office. Even so, she continued to work for me part-time, handling the invitations to the general manager's box from her telephone and typewriter at home. (This was very nearly a full-time job: I had fifteen hundred guests a season in my box.) Her successor was a Greek girl appropriately named Hope, with a sunny temperament; and she, too, was married. Then I was blessed with the ideal secretary in every way, Dorothy Doubleday, who was very efficient and very pretty—which helps: it's so much more pleasant to see a pretty face in the anteroom when you come to work. Inevitably, after four years at the Metropolitan, she too was married.

My next secretary brought to my office a love story worthy of opera. Herself a religious girl, she was in love with a Catholic priest who was in love with her—an interesting man, who is also a talented painter. Such stories are less shocking today, I am told, than they were then; at the time, both of them were extremely troubled. I used the Italian connections an opera manager acquires to get him released from his vows so they could marry in the Church, and they moved to California, where he teaches at a university.

Mary Smith, my secretary in the last years, had been a receptionist in the outer office. She is the only one of my girls who has also been a performer: I went to hear her in an amateur Gilbert and Sullivan production. Like Dorothy Doubleday, she is a pretty, cheerful person; when I came to the office grumpy, it gave me a good start to the day to see her. Also in that same anteroom, working mostly for John Gutman, was Florence Guarino, who was at the Metropolitan—obviously as a kind of child-secretary, for she cannot be that old—before I came. She will continue in the same office as Mr. Kubelik's secretary, giving the house an important continuity.

Indeed, I left to Mr. Gentele and Schuyler Chapin everywhere in the house a staff Mr. Gentele recently described to me as "very well brought up." The men who seem to me the very best, my immediate assistants Bob Herman and Herman Krawitz, are unfortunately leaving, as is my long-standing colleague and friend John Gutman. But Francis Robinson will continue his suave and knowledgeable supervision of our public and press relations, and the assistants to Herman and Krawitz remain—excellent young men like Paul Jaretzki, who has helped plan so many seasons, Peter Diggins, Michael Bronson, and Charles Riecker. In the stage departments, I leave the superbly competent Rudy Kuntner, Dick Hauser, David Reppa, and Joe Volpe. Only the musical administration could be questioned, Max Rudolf being long gone and his successor George Schick having left to be president of the Manhattan School of Music; and Mr. Gentele had more than taken care of that weakness for himself by engaging a musical director, a post I frankly avoided because it seemed to me to divide a responsibility that I thought should be the general manager's alone.

The Metropolitan as I leave it is a going concern, despite all the pleas of desperate poverty from the board. No doubt my last season was financially disappointing. The country seems to be broke, the management of the Lincoln Center garage has been such that our patrons can't find a place to park their cars, and many New Yorkers have become afraid to go out at night—all of which meant lower sales at the box office the past season. At a time when each 1 per cent off at the box office means $100,000 of lost revenue over the year, a drop of 5 per cent is of course very serious to the economy of the house. But the economy will turn up, the garage situation can be managed if anyone at Lincoln Center cares enough to manage it, and protection can be improved; and the house does now have the resources to absorb a time of troubles.

I cannot help resenting somewhat the way my business management was put in a bad light in the last years. When I came to the Metropolitan, there were essentially no assets. Now there are sixty productions in good shape (which do not appear anywhere on the books), profit-making real estate where the old house stood (which yields $600,000 a year as a rental, but is carried on the books as an asset of only $1.8 million); three warehouses that we own, not rent; more than $1 million worth of paintings and sculpture in the new theater; and an endowment fund of $6 million, much of it created by not taking into current income gifts that could have been used to eliminate the deficits of my last years. Mrs. Rockefeller, for example, gave us $500,000 to help finance the trip we hoped to take to the World's Fair in Osaka in 1970. When this journey fell through, I asked her if we could keep the money for other purposes, and she said we could—but it was only after the strongest sort of remonstrance that I was able to get even half of this gift allocated to current income. The Ford Foundation grant of $2.5 million was given to meet our extra expenses in the new house, and matched by another $2.5 million of contributions. About half this total was spent over the three or four years ending in 1968, and then Moore sat on the remaining $2.5 million—not a penny of it was made available to my management until half a million was detached in 1971–72 at the insistence of the auditors. With the funds available, our budget could be balanced—if not in the black. I understand and sympathize with the need to arouse donors and appear poor to the unions—and I gratefully acknowledge that the solvency of my regime was made possible by the brilliant fund-raising work of Peggy Douglas's Development Fund—but the result of all the agitation has been an unfair stigma on my administration. Mrs. Douglas, a wonderful person and a phenomenal fund raiser, was the first to admit, generously, that it was the quality of our product which enabled her to meet her goals. People don't contribute four or five million dollars a year for something they don't like.

As every retiring manager must, I leave to my successor the unpleasant task of telling certain well-loved artists that it is better to depart when the public says "Already?" than to wait until the public says "At last!" I also leave a time bomb I am grateful did not go off in my time, which is the question of the relations between European artists and the American Internal Revenue Service. Nearly all the Europeans at the house had their tax returns prepared for years by an accountant who is now in prison for violating tax laws. Truly remarkable deductions were taken under his advice—wives became managers, poodles became secretaries. Artists would come to the Metropolitan for ten weeks, make $100,000, and show a loss on their tax returns. I was told that Miss Nilsson once said she had deducted me as a dependent on her tax return, and I believe it. In theory, the Metropolitan deducts 30 per cent of the income of foreigners to cover tax liabilities, but in fact these days the Metropolitan pays the entire fee to a foreign corporation which supplies the artist's services. This situation will have to be regularized somehow, but the people who write the new rules must know that opera singers get special tax advantages everywhere else in the world, and if the government insists that they must pay in full in America the Metropolitan will be unable to engage the singers and conductors its public expects and deserves. The house will suffer enough in the next few years from the impact of currency devaluation without imposing the trauma of real taxation.

Though I remain a British subject, unaffectedly proud of having been knighted, I expect to stay in New York: after twenty-

[358]

three years, the Essex House is home, and we could not hope to adjust to new chambermaids elsewhere. I suppose I am seventy, because I was born in 1902, but I will certainly continue to work—first, it now appears, as a "Distinguished Professor" at Brooklyn College in City University. I will surely have days when I will miss the productive hysteria of our theater, which has been my life for so long; but for a while at least lecturing will be theater enough for me. The farewell ceremonies have been warm and will produce happy memories: when I stepped onto the stage on opening night in 1971 (to announce for Placido Domingo that he wasn't feeling well but would sing anyway), I was first astonished and then touched by the standing ovation the audience was good enough to give me. I was moved, too, by the gesture of the Metropolitan Opera Guild in presenting me with a rare letter in Verdi's hand, about *Don Carlo*, and by the generosity of everyone in the company in the occasion of my Gala.

I have had—it is a thing one does not think of until it is gone—a great deal of just fun running the Metropolitan Opera House. I remember the *Fledermaus* on the last night of the season in 1955, when Reggie Allen and John Gutman and Francis Robinson and I came out on stage with brooms, and Reva Freidberg dressed in a *Pelléas* beggar's costume came out with a big cleaning cloth, to show the audience the diligent crew cleaning up after the second-act party. But I remember also a moment in the summer of 1971 when a routine memo from Paul Jaretzki reached me at our summer retreat in the Dolomites, and I read it with mounting anxiety. The subject was the June post-season at Lincoln Center in 1973. This artist was unavailable for that day, that one had already agreed to do something at Covent Garden, the other one . . . I was appalled by the problems presented, by all the new plans that would have to be made, by the intrusion on my summer vacation. And then

I realized—the season in question was *1973*. The memo had come to me for my information only, not for my decision. A palpable weight dropped from my mind: I was no longer responsible.

When I wrote this last page, and when this book was first made ready for the printer, there were four words following the previous paragraph, "Over to Mr. Gentele." The senseless tragedy of Goeran Gentele's death inevitably creates uncertainty about how the opera will be managed in the years immediately ahead, who will pick up all the responsibilities I have gladly laid down. About Mr. Gentele himself, I can say little: he held himself apart from me as I, in similar circumstances, had held myself apart from Edward Johnson. But he was at all times a gentleman and men of whom that can be said are always missed. I offer what little condolence I can to his widow and daughter, and to his close colleagues in Sweden and New York. The show, of course, goes on without him as without me; we are all part of opera's history.